D1570171

Biosocial Bases
of
Criminal Behavior

Biosocial Bases
of
Criminal Behavior

EDITED BY

Sarnoff A. Mednick UNIVERSITY OF SOUTHERN CALIFORNIA

Karl O. Christiansen UNIVERSITY OF COPENHAGEN

ADMINISTRATIVE EDITOR *Jane Passant*

WITH A FOREWORD BY *Marvin E. Wolfgang*
UNIVERSITY OF PENNSYLVANIA

GARDNER PRESS, INC., New York
Distributed by HALSTED PRESS
Division of John Wiley & Sons, Inc.
NEW YORK   TORONTO   LONDON   SYDNEY

Copyright © 1977 by Gardner Press, Inc.

GARDNER PRESS, INC.
19 Union Square West
New York, New York 10003

Distributed solely by the HALSTED PRESS
Division of John Wiley & Sons, Inc., New York

Library of Congress Cataloging in Publication Data
    Includes index.
    1. Criminal anthropology—Addresses, essays, lectures.
    2. Devian behavior—Addresses, essays, lectures.
    3. Juvenile delinquency—Addresses, essays, lectures.
    I. Mednick, Sarnoff A.   II. Christiansen, Karl O.
    HV6115.S65   364.2   76-20560
    ISBN 0 470-15185-4

Printed in the United States of America

Foreword

by Marvin E. Wolfgang

In recent years there has been a revival of interest in genetic, physiological, endocrinological factors associated with various kinds of human behavior. Part of the reason is that new, more sophisticated and technologically fascinating research tools are now available for measuring the relationship between these factors and behavior. Because crime is contained within analysis of deviant behavior, and because statistically significant differences in biologically related problems are found to be associated with records of criminality, the studies contained in this volume require special attention.

This is not a cyclical return to biosociality, not a revival of Lombroso, Hooten, Schlapp and Smith or Sheldon. The studies reported here are new and exciting, buttressed by control groups and experimental analyses. Psychopathy, schizophrenia, adoption and twin studies acquire, by their accumulation, a thrust that is unmistakably of importance to the social research community.

Moreover, the reliability and validity of the Danish recordkeeping system are almost beyond criticism. The criminal registry office in Denmark is probably the most thorough, comprehensive and accurate in the Western world. The editors of this volume are among the most respected students of social psychology and sociological criminology.

The late Karl Otto Christiansen had the attribute of integrity of research shared by few of his colleagues. Sarnoff Mednick is known to students on both sides of the Atlantic as an erudite scholar of psychology and criminology.

The studies reported here are, if not unique, most uncommon. There is no research I know of in any other country to match them. Both positivistic and the "new" or radical criminology, as well as the concerns in socialist countries will find these researches relevant. The research is apolitical and based on the best canons of science. Sociological criminology welcomes these multi- and interdisciplinary researches that embrace our understanding of criminality and criminals.

Finally, it should be said that no nefarious genetic or biological interpretations should be made from the studies reported here. These are genuinely scientific designs and analyses that should be incorporated into the domain of erudite scholarship. The authors employ proper caution and care in presenting their findings that may challenge some previous positions but should be added to the normally cumulative writing of science that seeks to define, describe and analyze major variables in the biographies and behaviors of persons who have been known to deviate from statistical and legal-moral norms.

Dedication

On May 22, 1976, soon after this book was completed, Karl Otto Christiansen died of a heart attack in Minneapolis. He was at the University of Minnesota lecturing in criminology.

Karl Otto was one of the world's truly distinguished criminologists. He helped shape policy and direction for almost every important international, European, and Scandinavian decision-making organization in the field of criminology. He was *the* senior Scandinavian criminologist; he was the first to introduce sociological thinking into Scandinavian criminology.

It is a tragedy that he did not live to see the completion of his massive and definitive study of criminality among Danish twins. His report on this work forms Chapters 4 and 5. The project is continuing in accordance with his plans.

He was a beloved man. His quick, quiet sense of humor required alertness and perceptiveness for full appreciation. He placed human welfare, honesty and objectivity above all else. When conservative elements of the Danish Government cited rampant criminality as grounds for closing down a Copenhagen community of independent souls (Christiania), Karl Otto, using police statistics, publically reported that criminality was actually lower in Christiania than in the remainder of Copenhagen. He drily attributed a recent crime increase in Christiania to the bad influence of the surrounding community. His debunking statement helped Christiania to survive (at least to date).

This book is dedicated to his memory.

S. A. M.
June 28, 1976
Copenhagen

Preface

Experiential and biological factors have competed for the attention of investigators involved in what Hirschi and Rudisill have called "The Great American Search" for the "Causes of Crime." Early in the second decade of this century environmentalism began to displace the dominant nineteenth century genetic and biological explanations of the behavior of man. Criminology was not exempt from this new influence. Charles Goring's research in 1913 dramatically rejected Lombroso's "atavistic physical type" theory of crime. Goring's work coincided with and contributed to a wave of environmentalism; it has since been Exhibit A in the case against biology. Social organization, social influence, and social experience became, and are currently, the dominant explanations of the causes of crime. Any theory with biological implications was rapidly associated with the almost poetically evil name of Lombroso and regarded with suspicion.

The criminal justice systems of the Western world have until recently been organized with reference to the nineteenth century biological theories. The social-causation theorists' criticisms have caused society to reform criminal justice systems. These changes have been made both on the basis of elementary human kindness and in the belief that they would reduce levels of criminality and recidivism. Criminality and recidivism have not been reduced. It is likely that this "failure" will tend to produce a shift of emphasis of researchers in this field away from reliance on pure social causation. But it has been shown that the old biological theories do not have the explanatory power to replace current social theories.

This book recommends a consideration of the interaction of biological and social forces in producing criminality. Casual perusal of this volume may alarm social causation theorists because of our rather firm findings of the importance of genetic and physiological factors in crime. On the other hand, the geneticists may be disturbed by the fact that these findings are so dependent on social variables for the salience of their expression. For example:

1. Genetic factors are linked with the origins of crime; closer inspection of the data reveals, however, that the power of the genetic factors in explaining crime is rather weak in the lower classes and relatively great in the middle classes.

2. A good deal of the work in this volume discusses autonomic nervous system variables. These variables have been shown to explain important amounts of variance in crime. Here again, analyses of the manner in which family and social class interact with physiology sharpen the explanatory power of both.

As in the case of genetic factors, physiological variables have good explanatory power in the middle classes, but little in the lower classes. The relative failure of genetic and physiological variables in these classes suggests that economic and social deprivation are more critical in explaining crime in the lower classes. The middle-class criminal seems to be more genetically and physiologically predisposed.

It is curious that in order to see the action of social forces with more precision we must first account for the variance attributable to genetic and physiological factors. In order to better understand the operation of biological factors we must first control social variables. We hope this volume can serve to illustrate this method of analysis of sociobiological interplay.

Sarnoff A. Mednick
June 29, 1976
Copenhagen, Denmark

Acknowledgments

A variety of Danish institutions and agencies have, until now, good naturedly cooperated with what must have been an irritating number of questions, requests for information, and other extraordinary inquiries from the Institut. The responses they have provided have formed most of the data for the research described in this volume.

Professor Erik Strömgren, Dr. Annelise Dupont, and fru E. Torp have been extremely helpful in providing the cooperation of the Demographic Institute of Risskov. The Ministry of Justice has been very helpful in encouraging our work. Mr. G. Ekelund of the *Rigsregistratur* has facilitated access to the National Police Register. The *Folkeregister* has been instrumental in locating our populations. The Ministry of Religion has been of great help for the "chromosome" study (Chapter 10) in permitting us to establish our population on the basis of their church birth registers. Mr. Harry Hansen of the Rigshospitalet church birth register was particularly helpful in this connection. Professor Mogens Hauge of the Danish Twin Register has worked closely with Karl Otto in planning and executing the twin study. I should like to thank him for his continuing support and assistance since Karl Otto's death.

I know that Ruth Christiansen was heavily involved working with Karl Otto on his part of this volume; he would have wished to thank her for her help. I thank her for her continued and valued friendship.

My wife, Birgitte, has influenced the design and interpretation of these research projects. Her advice has been especially important in the formation of conclusions from these findings.

Fini Schulsinger has been a wise advisor and coworker on the psychiatric and social aspects of criminal behavior. His cooperation has been critical to the progress of this work.

Annalise Kongstad has been Karl Otto's chief assistant for the twin study. Her independent and highly responsible efforts have been instrumental in producing the results reported in Chapter 5.

Jane Passant, our administrative editor, did everything from helping to select the title to organizing the index. In the midst of typing and retyping chapters, she translated Chapter 4 from the original Danish. She organized and conducted correspondence with authors and publishers. She helped with determination of the style of the presentations. She has earned the gratitude of the two editors and all the coauthors.

Lis Kirkegaard-Sørensen and Barry Hutchings, who have been with the Institut many years, were early supporters of our interest in asocial behavior.

To the other fellow authors of the book I wish to extend a special "thank you" on behalf of myself and Karl O. Christiansen.

Sarnoff A. Mednick
Copenhagen
September 1, 1976

Acknowledgments of Research Support

Most of the research reported in this volume has been supported by grants from the Center for Studies of Crime and Delinquency. The interest, encouragement, and wise research suggestions of Dr. Saleem Shah were critical to the involvement of Mednick in research on the origins of asocial behavior. Dr. Shah first suggested that electrophysiological measures be made of the XYY subjects (see Chapter 11). The grants that have supported Mednick's activities in this area are MH 19225, 24872, and 25311. These grants are responsible for the work in Chapters 1, 2, 7, 9, 11, 13, 14, 15, 16, 17, 18, and 19. Christiansen's work on the twin population is also currently being supported by MH 25311. The pilot work on the twin population was supported by the Danish Research Council for Social Sciences and the Institute of Criminal Science, University of Copenhagen.

Two of the projects described have been supported by the World Health Organization, Geneva (Chapter 1, Mauritius Project and Chapter 6, Psychopathy Project).

The adoption studies were all made possible by contracts between the United States Public Health Service and the Psykologisk Institut, which produced the original adoption files. These were compiled by Kety, Rosenthal, Wender, and Schulsinger (1968) for their studies of the genetics of schizophrenia. Goodwin (Chapter 8), Schulsinger (Chapter 6), and Hutchings and Mednick (Chapter 7) wish to gratefully acknowledge their permission to use these files.

Goodwin's work in alcoholism (Chapter 8) was supported, in part, by U.S.P.H.S. Grant DA4RG008, National Institute of Mental Health Grant AA00256 and a Research Scientist Development Award AA47325 from the National Institute of Alcohol Abuse and Alcoholism.

Siddle's work on psychophysiology and delinquency was supported by a grant from the British Medical Research Council to Professor T. C. N. Gibbens, and was performed under the auspices of the Department of Forensic Psychiatry, Institute of Psychiatry, University of London.

The work on the chromosome anomalies (Chapter 10 and 11) is supported by the Center for Studies of Crime and Delinquency U.S.P.H.S. (Grants MH 23975, 21989, and 24872.)

The Danish Medical Research Council supported the work on the effect of criminal families (Chapter 2).

Contributors

Eskild Bakkestrøm, *Research Associate, Psykologisk Institut, Kommunehospitalet, Copenhagen*

Brian Bell, *Research Associate, Psykologisk Institut, Kommunehospitalet, Copenhagen*

Gösta Carlsson, *Professor, Brottsförebyggande Rådet, Stockholm*

Karl O. Christiansen, *Professor, Kriminalistisk Institut, University of Copenhagen*

Roger H. Foggitt, *Professor, Gloucestershire Community Training Centre, Gloucestershire*

Donald R. Goodenough, *Professor, Educational Testing Service, Princeton*

Donald Goodwin, *Professor,* University of Kansas, Kansas City.

Irving Gottesman, *Professor, University of Minnesota, Minneapolis*

Kurt Hirschhorn, *Professor, Mount Sinai School of Medicine, New York*

Barry Hutchings, *Associate Professor, Institut for Klinisk Psykologi, University of Copenhagen and Psykologisk Institut, Kommunehospitalet, Copenhagen*

Lis Kirkegaard-Sørensen, *Research Assistant, Psykologisk Institut, Kommunehospitalet, Copenhagen and Neurosehospitalet Montebello, Helsingor*

Joachim Knop, *Research Assistant, Psykologisk Institut, Kommunehospitalet, Copenhagen*

Janice Loeb, *Research Assistant, Psykologisk Institut, Kommunehospitalet, Copenhagen*

Claes Lundsteen, *Clinical Assistant, Rigshospitalet, Copenhagen*

Sarnoff A. Mednick, *Psykologisk Institut, Kommunehospitalet, Copenhagen and* University of Southern California, Los Angeles

A. R. Nicol, *Professor, University of Newcastle-upon-Tyne,*
     Newcastle-upon-Tyne

David R. Owen, *Associate Professor, Brooklyn College, New York*

John Philip, *Professor, Rigshospitalet, Copenhagen*

Fini Schulsinger, *Professor, Psykologisk Institut, Kommunehospitalet,*
     Copenhagen

Joseph Sergeant, *Research Assistant, Psykologisk Institut,*
     Kommunehospitalet, Copenhagen

David Siddle, *Professor, University of Southampton, Southampton*

Martha Stocking, *Research Associate, Educational Testing Service, Princeton*

Jan Volavka, *Professor, Missouri Institute of Psychiatry, St. Louis*

Herman A. Witkin, *Professor, Educational Testing Service, Princeton*

Contents

Part II—GENETIC FACTORS IN ASOCIAL BEHAVIOR

Twin Research

Adoptee Research

Alcoholism

XYY Chromosome Research

Chapter 1

A biosocial theory of the learning of law-abiding behavior

Sarnoff A. Mednick

Students of civilization have attempted to understand the origins of antisocial behavior by study of those who defy or ignore society's sanctions. This chapter takes a slightly different tack; it attempts to examine the bases of obedience to society's sanctions. It assumes that law-abiding behavior must be learned and that this learning requires certain environmental conditions and individual abilities. Lack of any of these conditions or abilities would hinder socialization learning and might, conceivably, be partly responsible for some forms of antisocial activities.

How do people learn to be law-abiding? This chapter describes socialization learning in terms of the interaction of early family training and individual physiological characteristics. If there are lacks in either of these spheres the learning of law-abidance will be incomplete, retarded and/or unsuccessful.

Most offenders are convicted of having perpetrated only one, two or three relatively minor offenses. These offenders are doubtless instigated by socio-economic and situational forces. There is, however, a small group of offenders (perhaps only 1% of the male population) which may be characterized as extremely recidivistic. In a Copenhagen birth cohort of over 30,000 men described in Chapter 10 we found that this minute fraction of the male population accounts for *more than half of the offenses committed by the entire cohort.* Similar results have been reported for the city of Philadelphia by Wolfgang, Figlio, and Sellin (1972). It is especially this small active group of recidivists that are hypothesized to have had their socialization learning influenced by deviant physiological charac- teristics. In emphasizing biosocial interactions the approach also seeks to help in the explanation of those cases of antisocial behavior which seem to have no apparent social cause as well as those cases in which an individual seems extraordinarily resistant or invulnerable to powerful criminogenic social forces (criminal family, extreme poverty, broken home background, etc. . . . See Chapter 2 for an example of this method of study).

Hidden crime.

Before going further with this exposition, perhaps I should make clear that I define a criminal as an individual who is registered as having been convicted of a violation of the penal code. In no case will this mean that our studies have utilized a prison population. All the individuals studied were functioning in society. We are concerned about the possi- bility that hidden crime may be governed by a different set of laws of nature from registered crime. We are, however, encouraged to continue working with registered crime by relatively strong evidence that the hidden criminal is the less serious, less recidivistic criminal (Christie, Andenaes and Skerbaekk, 1965).

LAW-ABIDANCE LEARNING IN CHILDREN

Children almost certainly do not come into the world with a set of inborn behaviors which unfold into civilized behavior. An objective con- sideration might in fact suggest that the behavior of young children is dominated by rather uncivilized immediate needs and passions. Becom- ing civilized consists in part of learning to inhibit or rechannel some of these passions.

Hare (1970b), Trasler (1972), and others have discussed the possibil- ity that the psychopath and criminal have some defect in avoidance learning that interferes with their ability to learn to inhibit asocial re- sponses. Much of this has been inspired by the 1957 study by Lykken indicating the difficulties psychopaths have in learning to avoid an elec- tric shock. These results have found some empirical support. Hare has suggested that the empirically observed and reobserved autonomic hyporeactivity of the psychopath and criminal may be, partially, the basis of this poor avoidance learning. To better understand this, let us consider the avoidance learning situation. In particular, let us follow Trasler (1972), and consider how the law-abiding citizen might learn his admirable self-control. When one considers the modern urban center in terms of the temptations and, in fact, incitements it offers to a variety of forms of asocial behavior, one is impressed with the restraint and forebearance of the 80–90% of the population, who apparently manage to avoid committing repetitive or heinous crimes. Reading of books such as *The Lord of the Flies* and observation of intersibling familial warfare suggests that there actually *are* some strong instincts and passions that society must channel and inhibit to maintain even the poor semblance of civilization we see around us. The type of learning involved in this civilizing process has been termed passive avoidance; the individual avoids punishment or fear by *not* doing something for which he has been punished before.

Let us consider the way children learn to inhibit aggressive impulses. Frequently, when child *A* is aggressive to child *B*, child *A* is punished by his mother. After a sufficient quantity or quality of punishment, just the thought of the aggression should be enough to produce a bit of anticipatory fear in child *A*. If this fear response is large enough, the raised arm will drop, and the aggressive response will be successfully inhibited.

What happens in this child after he has successfully inhibited such an asocial response is critical for his learning of civilized behavior. Let us consider the situation again in detail.

1. Child *A* contemplates aggressive action.
2. Because of previous punishment he suffers fear.
3. He inhibits the aggressive response.
What happens to his fear?
4. It will begin to dissipate, to be reduced.

We know that fear reduction is the most powerful, naturally occurring reinforcement psychologists have discovered. Thus the reduction of fear (which immediately follows the inhibition of the aggression) can act as a reinforcement for this *inhibition* and will result in the learning of the inhibition of aggression. The fear-reduction-reinforcement pattern increases the probability that the inhibition of the aggression will occur in the future. After many such experiences, the normal child will learn to inhibit aggressive impulses. Each time such an impulse arises and is inhibited, the inhibition will be strengthened by reinforcement. What does a child need in order to learn effectively to be civilized (in the context of this approach)?

1. A censuring agent (typically the family) *AND*
2. An adequate fear response *AND*
3. The ability to learn the fear response in anticipation of an asocial act *AND*
4. Fast dissipation of fear to quickly reinforce the inhibitory response.

Now I wish to concentrate on point 4. The speed and size of reinforcement determines its effectiveness. An effective reinforcement is one that is delivered *immediately* after the relevant response. In terms of this discussion, the faster the reduction of fear, the faster the delivery of the reinforcement. The fear response is, to a large extent, controlled by the autonomic nervous system (ANS). We can estimate the activity of the ANS by means of peripheral indicants such as heart rate, blood pressure, and skin conductance. The measure of most relevance will peripherally reflect the rate or speed at which the ANS recovers from periods of imbalance.

If child *A* has an ANS that characteristically recovers very quickly from fear, then he will receive a quick and large reinforcement and learn inhibition quickly. If he has an ANS that recovers very slowly, he will receive a slow, small reinforcement and learn to inhibit the aggression very slowly, if at all. This orientation would predict that (holding constant critical extraindividual variables such as social status, crime training, and poverty level) those who commit asocial acts would be characterized by slow autonomic recovery. The slower the recovery, the more serious and repetitive the asocial behavior predicted. Note that although we have concentrated on electrodermal recovery (EDRec), the theory also requires another ANS characteristic, hyporeactiveness, as a predisposition for delinquency. The combination of hyporesponsiveness and slow EDRec should give the maximum ANS predisposition to delinquency.

TESTS OF THE THEORY

To test this notion we first turned to a longitudinal study of some 13 years duration (Mednick and Schulsinger, 1968). We have been following 311 individuals whom we intensively examined in 1962. This examination included psychophysiology. Since 1962, 36 have had serious disagreements with the law (convictions for violation of the penal code). We checked and noted that, indeed, their EDRec was considerably slower than that of controls. Those nine who have been clinically diagnosed psychopathic have even slower recovery.

Siddle et al. (1973) examined the electrodermal responsiveness of 67 inmates of an English borstal. On the basis of 10 criteria, these inmates were divided into high, medium, and low asociality. Venables suggested to Siddle et al. that they also measure EDRec in their sample. Speed and rate of EDRec varied inversely as a function of asociality. EDRec on a single trial was surprisingly effective in differentiating the three groups. (See Chapter 13.)

Bader-Bartfai and Schalling (1974) reanalysed skin conductance data from a previous investigation of criminals, finding that criminals who tended to be more "delinquent" on a personality measure tended to have slower EDRec.

In view of the relationships that have been reported between psychophysiological variables and asocial behavior, and in view of our interest in better understanding the apparent genetic predisposition to asocial behavior, we next turned to a study of the heritability of psychophysiological behavior. We (Bell, Mednick, Gottesman, and Sergeant) invited pairs of male 12-year-old twins into our laboratory. Interestingly enough, EDRec to orienting stimuli proved to have significant heritability (consistently higher for left hand than for right; see Chapter 14). This finding would suggest that part of the heritability of asocial behavior might be attributed to the heritability of EDRec. Thus a slow EDRec might be a characteristic a criminal father could pass to a biological son, which (given the proper environmental circumstances) could increase the probability of the child failing to learn adequately to inhibit asocial responses. Thus we would predict that criminal fathers would have children with slow EDRec. In Table 1 we present data on the electrodermal behavior of children with criminal and noncriminal fathers. As can be seen, the prediction regarding EDRec is not disconfirmed. It is interesting that the pattern of responsiveness of these children closely resembles that which we might anticipate seeing in their criminal fathers (Hare, 1970b). Results of other studies in our laboratory have replicated these findings.

Hare (1975b) has recently tested this ANS-recovery theory on a sample of maximum-security prisoners. More-psychopathic prisoners show significantly slower EDRec than serious, but less psychopathic, maximum-security prisoners. In one figure Hare plots the EDRec of the prisoners along with that of male college students. The prisoner and student curves are worlds apart! Hinton (personal communication, 1975) also finds the EDRec of more asocial prisoners (in an English maximum-security prison) to be slower. In an ongoing study we are finding that criminals reared in a noncriminal milieu have slow EDRec. Children reared in a criminogenic milieu who resist criminality evidence fast EDRec (see Chapter 2).

Table 1

**Skin Conductance Behavior During Orienting Response Testing in Children
with Criminal and Noncriminal Fathers**

Skin Conductance Function (Right hand)	MEAN SCORE		F	df	p
	Noncriminal Father	Criminal Father			
Basal level skin conductance	2.51	2.33	.09	1,193	n.s.
Amplitude (in micromhos)	.031	.016	.03	1,193	n.s.
Number of responses	2.79	1.55	8.51	1,187	.01
Response onset latency (in seconds)	2.11	2.18	.07	1,97	n.s.
Latency to response peak (in seconds)	2.05	2.38	5.32	1,95	.05
Average half recovery time (in seconds)	3.75	5.43	4.26	1,90	.05
Minimum half recovery time	2.26	4.33	8.80	1,90	.01

Note: During Orienting Response testing, the child was presented 14 times with a
tone of 1000 cps.

In a rather compelling study, Wadsworth (1976) traced all the males
registered for delinquency from a sample of the 13,687 births which
occurred in England, Wales and Scotland between March 3 and 9 in 1946
(Douglas et al., 1958). They had had their pulse taken in 1957 just before
a school medical examination (deemed to be a mildly threatening event).
This pre-examination pulse rate predicted whether or not a boy would
achieve a record of serious delinquency by the age of 21 years. These
results must be given special consideration in view of the representativeness of the population.

Here is what we have said so far:

1. There is a theory of social learning of law-abiding behavior that
has as a unique and key element, the specification of specific autonomic
nervous system factors as useful aptitudes for effectively learning to
inhibit asocial behavior.

2. Some empirical tests were described that could have disconfirmed
this hypothesis. No grounds were found for rejection of the hypothesis
in experiments conducted in Denmark, Sweden, England and Canada
under a rather large variety of situational conditions and criterion group
definitions.

Please note that my emphasis of these physiological factors in this chapter should only be understood as an attempt to call attention to this type of approach. The percent of text devoted to the physiological variables does not relate to their perceived importance in the total field of criminology.

MAURITIUS PROJECT

To obtain a meaningful answer to the question of the relevance of these ANS variables for the etiology of asocial behavior, one useful research design would involve testing 100% of a reasonably large population of children, following them, and determining the relative probability of antisocial behavior among those who are physiologically predisposed. In terms of our theoretical orientation, such predisposed children would be those who are among the slowest in autonomic recovery and the weakest in autonomic response. In Mauritius, a group of investigators (Schulsinger, Mednick, Venables, Raman, Sutton-Smith, and Bell, 1975) have tested the entire population of 3 year olds in two well-defined areas (Vacoas and Quatre Bornes). From smallpox vaccination records, all the 1800 three year olds in the two areas were located and invited in for testing. The tests included:

1. Psychophysiology (heart rate, bilateral skin conductance, and skin potential).
2. EEG—(not the entire population).
3. Birth data (not the entire population).
4. Cognitive development.
5. Medical examination.
6. Laboratory observation ratings.

These children are now in school, and we are developing a system for the collection of behavior ratings. This work is being organized by Cyril Dalais. At this point we know that the children with slow EDRec are those who did not cry in the laboratory, were less concerned and frightened about the testing, and were less anxious.

With respect to the understanding of the etiology of antisocial behavior, the critical question is whether (as in the 1976 Wadsworth study) the autonomic variables will predict which of the 1800 children in this cohort will evidence serious antisocial behavior. We are planning to follow these children to attempt to answer this question. The answer will have some importance in planning of prevention of delinquency (see Mednick and Lanoil, 1977). Also of importance to such attempts at prevention is the determination of what other outcomes are observed from the children with autonomic deviance. Perhaps weakness in learning socially conforming modes of living is accompanied by some increase in potential for creativity or originality. We must ascertain all possible outcomes before we take any action in this sensitive area. Clearly it is a desirable goal to reduce the frequency of delinquency. Before doing this, however, we must be clear, via longitudinal study, about any additional unwanted effects intervention may have. (See Chapter 3 for further discussion of problems in primary prevention of delinquency.)

Chapter 2

An example of biosocial interaction research:

The interplay of socioenvironmental and individual factors in the etiology of criminal behavior

Sarnoff A. Mednick

Lis Kirkegaard-Sorensen

Barry Hutchings

Joachim Knop

Raben Rosenberg

Fini Schulsinger

There are areas in cities where very large proportions of male adolescents and adults become criminals (Hurvitz and Christiansen, 1971). The social and economic circumstances in these ghettoes are doubtless responsible for this alarming degree of criminality. However, in spite of the fact that almost all of the children in these ghettoes are exposed to these social and economic circumstances, they do not *all* become criminal. Some, often many, are rather law-abiding. Perhaps though they live in the ghetto, they do not have the same specific social, economic, or family circumstances as those who become delinquent. It is also possible that they have certain personal characteristics that protect them from delinquency.

In the same manner it may also be asked why criminal-free families, in orderly, middle-class neighborhoods with relatively reduced frequencies of delinquency, still produce some serious criminals. Perhaps, in these cases some personal characteristics of the individual "protect" him from law-abidingness.

This chapter is a first report of a project asking what personal charac-teristics or experiences protect from or induce to delinquency in the face of apparently opposing environmental forces. The project builds on the fact that children, raised in families with parental criminality, them-selves have an increased risk of evidencing criminality (Hurvitz and Christiansen, 1968).

Our major questions are: What distinguishes the law-abiding indi-vidual raised in a criminal family? What distinguishes the criminal raised in a relatively crime-free family milieu? In this chapter we examine intel-ligence and peripheral indicants of autonomic functioning as personal characteristics.

Autonomic functioning.   In the preceding chapter, Mednick (1976) has presented a theoretical account of the possible role of autonomic ner-vous system (ANS) factors in the learning of law-abidingness. It is suggested that from punishment experiences children learn to fear their asocial impulses. When the anticipatory fear is great enough, these im-pulses are inhibited. This inhibition is followed by a reduction in the anticipatory fear, which reinforces the inhibition response. The faster the postinhibition fear reduction, the greater the reinforcement effect and the better the learning of inhibition of asocial impulses. The speed of the postinhibition fear reduction is hypothesized to be a function of the speed of recovery of the ANS from imbalance. Faster ANS recovery should yield faster fear reduction and greater reinforcement and faster learning of the inhibition of asocial responses. Slow ANS recovery should be associated with poor learning of asocial responses. In the context of this study it would be expected that fast ANS recovery would be a personal characteristic that would protect from criminogenic influ-ences. Slow ANS recovery would tend to predispose to asocial behavior, even in the absence of criminogenic pressures.

Aspects of ANS functioning including recovery can be estimated by recording of peripheral indicants such as heart rate, skin conductance and potential, and blood pressure. These estimates are used in this study to test the theoretical statements related to recovery and other aspects of ANS functioning (see Mednick, Chapter 1; Siddle, Chapter 12).

Intelligence.   Empirical reports on the tested intelligence of criminals has most frequently found them relatively low in intelligence (Blank, 1958; Frost and Frost, 1962). There are, however, contradictory results in which criminals have not scored lower in intelligence than controls (Fields, 1960). As is so often the case in this type of research, careful examination of the studies suggests strongly that the contradictory findings are often due to reports from a variety of rather arbitrarily selected samples. Most studies draw on prison populations, little effort has been made to secure representative samples.

Such an effort was made in this project. We ascertained the registered criminality of a total birth cohort of males and their parents. We then examined criminal and noncriminal sons. The four groups of sons underwent an intensive examination; part of this examination consisted of electrodermal measures and subtests of the Wechsler Adult Intelligence Scale (WAIS). The distribution of these intelligence test scores and electrodermal reactivity across these four groups is the subject of this chapter.

We hypothesized that in a criminogenic environment, high intelligence, and fast electrodermal recovery (EDRec) would tend to protect a child against criminality. High intelligence may tend to result in rewards to the child for intellectual performance in the school system. This may provide generalized rewards for the child's conformance and law-abiding behavior. These rewards may tend to be less in those with lower intelligence levels. In an analogous manner, in noncriminogenic environments, low intelligence would tend to result in relatively meager rewards for learning of school conformance and law-abidingness.

Thus, we predicted that noncriminal sons from criminal families would have relatively high intelligence and fast EDRec, whereas criminal sons from noncriminal families would evidence relatively low intelligence and show slow EDRec.

METHOD

Determination of criminality

For purposes of this study, a criminal is defined as an individual with an official record of a conviction for an offense against the Danish penal code. This leaves out a large number of individuals who commit crimes that do not result in convictions and individuals who are not caught by the police. However, studies have indicated that those committing "hidden crimes" tend to have a less severe degree of criminality. They commit fewer and less-serious offenses (Christie, Andenaes and Skerbaekk, 1965). In Denmark there are two official sources of information on criminality, the National Police Register (*Rigsregistratur*) and the Penal Register (*Strafferegister*). The National Police Register (NPR) contains a national record of certain police contacts with Danish residents. The Penal Register (PR) is a register of court actions resulting in convictions, including precise information on the laws violated and the punishments exacted.

Details of subject selection. Our aim was to identify a birth cohort and from this cohort to select individuals with and without criminal records who had families with and without criminal records. We began with 1944 consecutive male live births, January 1, 1936 to September 30, 1938 at Rigshospitalet in Copenhagen, Denmark. We then sought to determine the identity of the father, mother, and son. To properly identify an individual for purposes of checks in the criminality registers, we needed both their names and birth dates. This proved to be impossible in the case of 544 of the fathers. In many of these 544 cases paternity was also uncertain. These cases were dropped from the population, leaving 1400 cases. Some efforts made to determine the effect of dropping these 544 cases from our population, are described below. For the 1400 remaining families we then checked in the NPR for registration for criminality. There exist three possibilities in the NPR with respect to registration of an individual:

1. *He is not listed at all.*
2. *He is listed only for minor offenses.* These include traffic offenses, disorderly conduct, and the like. At worst, they are punished with a small fine.
3. *He is listed for more serious transgressions.*

For criminal fathers selected for this study we required a court conviction for a violation of the criminal code resulting in at least one jail sentence. These criminal subjects were all drawn from category three above.

Figure 1 presents a flow diagram indicating the methods of subject selection for this study. We determined to define criminals as individuals with jail sentences. Of the 1400 cases, 242 of the fathers had only a record of minor criminality; these cases were dropped leaving 1158 cases where the father had either a serious offense or no listing. By dropping sons with minor offenses and fathers and sons with serious offenses but no jail sentence, we reduced the subgroup "fathers with serious offenses" down to 92, where the father had at least one jail sentence. In 56 of these cases the sons were unknown to the police; in 36 cases they had at least one jail sentence and an additional police record. These two groups both include distinctively criminal fathers; in one group the sons are at least equally criminal; in the other the sons have no police record.

The same procedure was followed in the case of the two groups with fathers with no police record, yielding groups with and without criminal

Figure 1
Flow diagram for Subject Selection

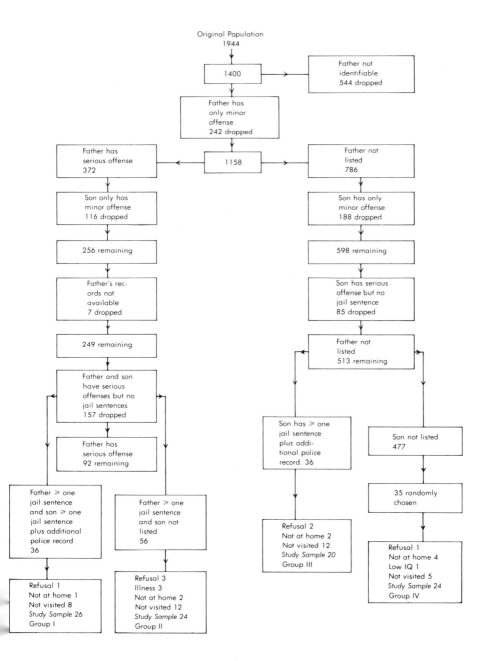

sons. Sons residing in Copenhagen were brought to the laboratory for intensive examination. Four subjects were excluded because of illness and low IQ (74).

The four groups were, of course, automatically matched for sex and age. Wherever possible, subjects were chosen to maximize the equivalence of the groups for social class of the father at the time of the birth of the son.

None of the subjects was in jail at the time of the study. Almost none was out of work (1972–1973).

In the case of the sons it was possible to check the NPR information on criminality by obtaining PR reports from the police district where the son was born. The two registers agreed perfectly in defining a subject as criminal. This check was not done for the fathers, because for some of them the information on birthplace was not readily available.

The final groups selected consist of:

Group I   Criminal father—criminal son ($N = 26$)
Group II   Criminal father—noncriminal son ($N = 24$)
Group III   Noncriminal father—criminal son ($N = 20$)
Group IV   Noncriminal father—Noncriminal son ($N = 24$)

Testing procedure.   After identification, subjects received a letter stating that they have been selected for a follow-up examination because they were part of the birth cohort born at Rigshospitalet in 1936–1938. They were informed that a physician would be visiting them soon and would invite them to our laboratories for an examination. A psychiatric resident (J.K.) interviewed them regarding their social development and status and scheduled their laboratory testing. Seven of those contacted refused to participate.

The subjects arrived at the laboratory at 8:30 a.m. and went through the following examinations in this order:

Psychophysiology
Psychiatric interview
Lunch
Perceptual tests
Avoidance testing
Psychological tests (including abbreviated WAIS)

It should be noted that all examiners were blind regarding the group identification of the subjects except for the psychiatrist who interviewed the subject in his home.

Intelligence testing.   The similarities, vocabulary, block design and picture arrangement subtests of the Danish adaptation (Hess, 1973) of the WAIS were chosen for evaluation of the intelligence level of the subjects. These subtests were chosen because of their high correlation with full IQ and their representation of verbal and performance intelligence. The subtests were administered in accordance with the WAIS manual's (1955) instructions.

Psychophysiology. Psychophysiological recording was made using an Offner-Beckman Type R Dynograph using couplers built especially for this project. Three channels of physiological information were collected: Skin conductance, skin potential, and electrocardiogram. Only skin conductance results are described here. For skin conductance, unilateral bipolar recording was made continuously from the nondominant hand. In addition, levels were obtained from the other hand during the rest periods. The procedure involved the constant voltage method advocated by Venables and Christie (1973) using a coupler designed by them.

The stimuli consisted of 14 orientation tones each of 1 sec, 400 Hz. This was followed by a rest period of 10 minutes. After the rest period a series of 36 stimuli comprising a conditioning, generalization and extinction schedule followed.

The stimuli used were

Conditioned stimulus 1	1 kHz 60 db 12.5 sec
Unconditioned stimulus	
(occured only with C.S. 1)	noise 96 db 4.5 sec
Conditioned stimulus 2	500 Hz 60 db 12.5 sec
Generalization stimulus 1	1311 Hz 60 db 12.5 sec
Generalization stimulus 2	1967 Hz 60 db 12.5 sec

This part of the procedure took approximately 25 minutes.

Results

It will be recalled that 544 of the original population of 1944 live male births were dropped because the father was not fully identifiable. We were able to check the information on the criminality of the mothers and sons with such fathers. Of the 544 women, 42, or 7.7% evidenced serious criminality. Of the remaining population of 1400, 61, or only 4.4%, evidenced serious criminality. The women with not fully identifiable mates were significantly more criminal χ^2 (1) = 7.81, $p < .01$). The sons of the not fully identifiable fathers had records of serious criminality in 15.3% of the cases (83 of 544). Of the 1400 sons, 13.6% (190) evidenced serious criminality, a nonstatistically significant difference. The 544 families dropped apparently were a bit more criminal than the remainder of the population.

Fathers' and sons' criminality in total sample

Table 1 presents the percent of fathers with criminal sons, sons with

Table 1

Percent of fathers with sons at three levels of criminality, (NPR data)

		SONS' FORM OF REGISTRATION			
		Serious Transgression	Minor Offenses	Not Listed	N
Fathers' Form of Registration	Serious transgression	40.0	31.3	21.5	372
	Minor offenses	16.3	18.0	17.1	242
	Not listed	43.7	50.7	61.4	786
	N	190	371	839	1,400

Note: Percentages in the cells are column percents.

minor offenses, and sons not listed in the NPR. Note that the severity of registration of the father is in a rough way mirrored in the severity of registration of their sons; of the 190 sons who have a record of serious criminality, 40% of their fathers are serious criminals. It is clear from this table that the criminality of the sons and fathers is interdependent (χ^2 (4) = 50.6, $p < .0005$).

Study sample

Some characteristics of the four selected groups and their parents are presented in Table 2. Note that the noncriminal fathers of noncriminal sons have a higher mean age than do the fathers of the other three groups. This group of 24 was drawn from the 35 randomly selected out of a group of 477. At the time of the birth of these sons, these 35 fathers had an average age not different from that of the other three groups (28 years). By some mischance the psychiatrist happened to visit and invite

Table 2

Identifying Characteristics of Study Sample

	CRIMINAL FATHERS		NONCRIMINAL FATHERS	
	Criminal Sons	Non-Criminal Sons	Criminal Sons	Non-Criminal Sons
Number of cases	26	24	20	24
PARENTS' CHARACTERISTICS AT BIRTH OF CHILD (MEAN VALUES)				
Father's age	29	28	28	33
Mother's age	25	26	24	29
Father's social class†	1.3	1.4	1.6	1.6
SONS' CHARACTERISTICS (MEAN VALUES)				
Number of years of schooling	8.0	8.6	7.9	8.1
Social class†	1.31	2.33	1.45	2.21

†Svalastoga (1959)

as subjects those individuals in this subgroup with relatively older fathers. In other words, the higher age of the noncriminal father with noncriminal sons is not a reliable characteristic of such fathers but actually resulted from unfortunate chance selection factors. Our knowledge of the total population characteristics spared us from reporting and interpreting this "finding."

It should be pointed out that the criminal father—noncriminal son group achieved the highest level of education. This difference was not significant. The criminal sons attained a significantly lower social class level than the noncriminal sons ($F = 10.95$, $1/92df$, $p < .01$).

Criminality of sons

Some information on the criminal careers of the sons is given in Table 3. There are no significant differences between those with or without criminal fathers. It is interesting to note that the criminal sons with noncriminal fathers tend to be a bit more violent and recidivistic. Almost

Table 3

Criminality of Sons

	Criminal Sons Criminal Father	Criminal Sons Noncriminal Father
Type of sentence		
Conditional	57%	58%
Unconditional	43%	42%
Type of criminal career		
Episodic or beginner	65%	45%
Periodic or chronic	35%	55%
Type of offense		
Property	92%	90%
Violence	35%	45%
Sexual	19%	25%

Note: Episodic or beginner refers to less recidivistic criminality. (For details see Hurvitz and Christiansen, 1968)

half the members of each group of criminal sons were diagnosed as psychopathic. This diagnosis was reached as a consensus between the interviewing psychiatrist, using the CAPPS computer-derived diagnosis (Endicott and Spitzer, 1972), and Dr. Irving Gottesman, who interpreted the MMPI. The following criteria were used in the diagnosis:

1. Poor impulse control.
2. Poor feelings of responsibility.
3. Emotional immaturity.
4. Lack of ability to learn by experience.
5. Very poor work habits.

Intelligence test scores

WAIS mean scaled subtest scores and IQs are presented in Table 4. The verbal IQ was calculated on the basis of the vocabulary and similarities subtests. The performance IQ was calculated on the basis of the block design and picture arrangements subtests.

On the block design subtest the criminal sons performed more poorly than the noncriminal sons ($F = 8.26$, $1,92\,df$, $p < .01$). This is in large part due to the superior performance of the noncriminal sons with criminal fathers. The interaction of fathers x sons was significant ($F = 5.56$, $1,90$

Table 4

Mean WAIS IQs and subtest scale scores for four groups

				MEAN WAIS SCORES				
		Similarities	Vocabulary	Block Design	Picture Arrangement	Verbal IQ	Performance IQ	Total IQ
Criminal father	Criminal son	10.8	10.2	8.1	9.5	102.7	96.1	99.8
	Noncriminal son	12.6	12.7	10.9	10.5	115.3	108.5	113.0
	Total criminal father	11.7	11.4	9.4	10.0	108.7	102.1	106.1
Noncriminal father	Criminal son	12.1	10.6	9.0	10.0	107.6	101.0	105.0
	Noncriminal son	11.4	11.4	9.3	9.5	108.3	100.4	104.6
	Total noncriminal father	11.7	11.0	9.2	9.7	108.0	100.7	104.8
	Total criminal son	11.4	10.4	8.5	9.7	104.8	98.2	102.0
	Total noncriminal son	12.0	12.1	10.1	10.0	111.8	104.5	108.8

df, p < .05). The criminal sons also performed relatively poorly in the vocabulary subtest (*F* = 12.78, 1,92 *df, p* < .01). On the similarities subtest the criminal father—noncriminal son group performed best of the four groups; the father x son interaction was significant (*F* = 6.14, 1,90 *df, p* < .05).

On the verbal, performance and total IQ scores the criminal sons performed more poorly than the noncriminal sons (verbal IQ, *F* = 7.00, 1,92 *df, p* < .0l; performance IQ, *F* = 5.89, 1,92 *df, p* < .05; total IQ, *F* = 7.39, 1,92 *df, p* < .01). Mainly because of the superior performance of the noncriminal sons with criminal fathers, significant interactions of father x son were observed for the verbal, performance, and total IQs (verbal IQ, *F* = 5.19, 1,90 *df, p* < .05; performance IQ, *F* = 6.70, 1,90 *df, p* < 0.5; total IQ, *F* = 7.81, 1,90 *df, p* < .01).

The reported IQs are based on United States norms. Consequently, these absolute levels cannot be interpreted in the usual manner. Norms exist for a Danish edition of the WAIS for 50- and 70-year-old men. Hess (1973) has reported on the WAIS testing of 698 Danes who were 50 years old, including 391 men. Kyng (personal communication, 1975) has tested 70-year-old Danes. These authors point out that the IQs reported for Danes that are based on United States norms do not have a mean of 100, but, instead, a mean of 107. In large part, this difference is ascribed to higher scores for Danes on the information and vocabulary subtests. The Danish authors suggest that this is most likely due to easier items being substituted in the Danish form of these subtests.

Psychophysiological tests

The analysis of the psychophysiology data is not complete. Certain trends in electrodermal functioning, however, seem clear and are listed below:

1. The *son criminal, father noncriminal* group is most distinctive, psychophysiologically. They evidence low basal conductance level, low amplitude, small numbers of individual responding, and slow rate of recovery. These findings are exaggerated in the case of those in this group diagnosed as psychopathic.

2. The *son criminal, father criminal* group, surprisingly, evidences a very high level of responding.

3. The *son noncriminal, father criminal* group evidences remarkably fast EDRec.

DISCUSSION

Intelligence

The criminal sons achieved lower IQ scores than the noncriminal sons. This result is in good agreement with that of previous research, cited before. This supports our hypothesis that good intelligence would tend to protect against engaging in a criminal career. The specific hypothesis concerning the noncriminal son reared in a criminogenic milieu suggested that high intelligence would tend to protect him from a criminal career, perhaps by presenting him with rewards for law-abiding behavior within the school setting. This hypothesis was supported by the relatively high IQ scores achieved by this group. It should also be noted that this group completed more years of school than the other three groups.

We also hypothesized a lower IQ in the criminal son—noncriminal father group. This hypothesis was not supported; the IQ scores for this group are not unusually low. Low intelligence cannot be cited as a personal characteristic increasing the likelihood of criminality of sons in a noncriminal milieu.

It is possible to suggest that perhaps the most intelligent group (noncriminal sons of criminal fathers) is not registered for criminality, because they are too clever to be caught by police. However, the average IQ scores of the noncriminal sons of noncriminal fathers seem not to support this explanation. Also, West and Farrington (1973), using self-report data in a prospective design, found a negative correlation between delinquency and intelligence.

It should be emphasized that these subjects stem from a well-defined birth cohort. None of them was in jail at the time of the study. This suggests that low intelligence test scores found in criminal groups in previous studies may not have been due to the fact that these studies were conducted in jail settings.

Psychophysiology

The rather classic psychopathic skin conductance pattern evidenced by the criminal sons of noncriminal fathers is quite striking. This pattern supports our general hypothesis that personal characteristics might help explain criminal behavior in the relative absence of clear socioenvironmental criminogenic forces. It also supports the specific hypothesis of the role of ANS factors, including recovery, in the etiology of criminal behavior. Other studies supporting this specific hypothesis are reviewed by Siddle (See Chapter 12).

The high ANS responsiveness of the criminal son—criminal father group deserves some comment. These individuals form a large portion of the serious criminals in this population (40%; see Table 1). It seems likely that paternal criminality was a factor influencing the sons' asocial behavior. If their ANS hyperresponsiveness predated their asocial behavior, then it was not sufficient to prevent it. (This group is also marked by moderately slow EDRec.) Their ANS hyperresponsiveness may also be a result of the demands or sociolegal consequences of their asocial behavior.

The law-abiding group with paternal criminality is especially remarkable for its members' very fast EDRec. This might again be seen as supportive for the general frame of reference of this study and for the specific hypothesis regarding ANS recovery. The very fast ANS recovery may be seen as supplying an excellent aptitude for learning to inhibit asocial behavior. This aptitude perhaps helped protect these individuals from committing asocial acts despite the criminogenic parental influence.

Comments on research design

The authors are, to some extent, aware of the superficial nature of the definition of criminogenic environment represented by "parental criminality." Despite this superficiality, however, some interpretable relations are emerging from the data analyses. Also, fathers' registered criminality is easily defined and ascertained and is empirically justified as a criminogenic influence. It is hoped that future research will bring more sensitive socioenvironmental criminogenic factors to this same research design.

The data suggest that personal characteristics (such as ANS recovery or intelligence) may be useful in helping understand law-abiding or asocial behavior in those circumstances where they exist in the face of opposing environmental forces. This finding is consistent with Christiansen's report of a greater expressed genetic contribution to criminality in environmental circumstances (e.g., higher social class, rural environment) which are relatively less criminogenic (see Christiansen, Chapter 5). Christiansen explains this interaction in terms of Sellin's theory of "Group resistance to crime" (1938). In our laboratory we have observed that slow EDRec is highly related to criminality only in the lower-middle and middle classes. In the lowest class less relationship is observed. This suggests that the environmental pressures are critical in the lowest classes, and that individual factors have some importance in the middle classes.

Perhaps it is worth emphasizing that these criminal subjects stem from a well-defined birth cohort. They probably represent the serious criminality as it would exist in any Danish male birth cohort. This fact increases our confidence in the representativeness and generalizability of the reported findings.

Chapter Three

Crime and behavioral epidemiology. Concepts and applications to Swedish data

Gösta Carlsson

CRIME, EPIDEMIOLOGY AND THEORY

A broad spectrum of methods and styles of theorizing have been applied to crime, with a varying but mostly limited degree of success. At the risk of oversimplification, one may distinguish between two major traditions running through the history of the subject that are still vital today. One is the interest in theoretical schemes of high generality, far-ranging visions of crime and its origins. The other is a concern with the detailed facts about law-breakers and their transgressions, what may be called the descriptive side. There is nothing startling in this or, indeed, unusual, for the distinction surely has its counterpart in other fields. What is more disconcerting is the weakness of the link between theory and description, and the difficulties met in specifying what theories are incompatible with what facts (Hirschi, 1969).

Ill-defined rules of testability are not a sign of health, and the usefulness of much of existing theory of the more ambitious type may thus be questioned. We cannot, on the other hand, go on collecting elementary data and rely on undigested statistical tabulations to guide us. The philosophy behind the present effort is to look for a middle ground between all-too-lofty theory and overly factual studies. Or, put a little more precisely, we shall try to use population models of crime, and to raise some basic questions about the distribution of criminal activity. This means that assumptions have to be made about reality that could turn out to be false, in contrast to accounting, or pure measurement, not as such subject to confirmation or confutation.

Swedish data are used, not only for illustration but as pointers to a state of affairs that may prevail more generally. It is the writer's belief that proper methods of evaluating data and putting them in perspective will do much to remove the apparent babel of conflicting interpretations in the field of crime. For this, however, we may have to pay the price of recognizing that epidemiological effects are often quite weak, and that much of the observable variability in human behavior is still left unaccounted for. Recent cynics (Nudelman et al., 1975) have defined the correlation coefficient as a way of proving that we can explain from 2 to a staggering 22% of the variance, and 22% may well mark the upper limit for what is mostly attainable. More is said about this situation later.

THE DISTRIBUTION OF CRIME

A fundamental question in the analysis of any behavioral phenomenon like crime is the degree to which it is concentrated, whether it is "produced" by relatively few, or widely dispersed and produced by many. Thus the identical number of offenses (per 100,000 population per year) may be the result of a small minority, each of whom is committing a large number of offenses, or a large part of the population violating the law sporadically at the individual level, with an obvious infinity of cases between the extremes. No matter what our moral feelings may be and no matter which case is judged the more disturbing from a social point of view, it is important to be clear which one actually obtains. Such knowledge, although it will not automatically prove one theory of crime or completely rule out others, will, nevertheless, have a bearing on the wider issues of theory and make certain solutions look less promising than others.

Thus widely dispersed crime, a relatively "egalitarian" distribution, will rather argue against "kinds-of-people" interpretations and lead us to explanations in terms of temporary situations, or perhaps strictly macrosociological perspectives. A high degree of concentration of criminal activity, on the other hand, implying high predictability at the individual level, will point in the direction of stable personal attributes of one kind or another. As is discussed later, a process of "labeling" or growing "commitment" to crime could also yield a high degree of concentration.

As a start, two methods may be used to get further in this matter;

they should be regarded as supplementary and not as mutually exclusive. The first is to construct simple but not wildly improbably progression models, describing how persons move to a first offense, from the first to the second, from the second to the third, and so on, and with what probabilities or progression ratios. The consequences of such models with respect to the distribution of crime may then be examined. The second method is to look at the empirical evidence on the issue, with full awareness of its likely imperfections.

As the writer has reported on this phase of the epidemiological enquiry into crime in other publications (Carlsson, 1975, 1976) it is sufficient to set forth the procedure and results in the barest outline, beginning with the progression model. Figure 1 shows its structure and the meaning of symbols used.

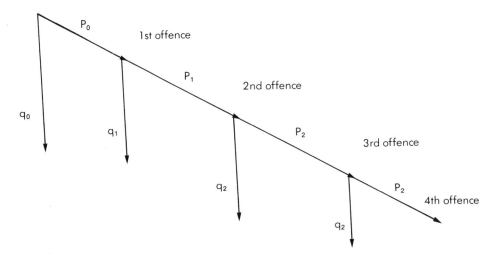

Figure 1. Progression models and risks. There is a *first-offense risk* p_0, which is the probability of a person changing from the never delinquent to the ever-delinquent status (to borrow terms used in demographic analysis). The complementary probability $q_0(p_0+q_0=1)$ refers to the probability of desisting from crime altogether. Having committed a first offense the person may continue to a second with probability p_1, progression risk, or desist with probability q_1, again the two probabilities add to unity. After the second offense he may proceed to a third with probability p_2 or desist with probability q_2. Usually, it will not be necessary to differentiate further according to order of offense, probabilities p_3, p_4, . . . will be assumed equal to p_2. Indeed, for many practical purposes p_2 can be assumed identical with p_1. First-offense risk and progression risk to second offense will always be assumed different, with p_1 typically greater than p_0.

An example of a similar analysis of progression can be found in the cohort study of Wolfgang, Figlio, and Sellin (1972). The progression risks or ratios are analogous to parity progression ratios in fertility analysis (Spiegelman, 1968: 257). Granted the assumptions above, the distribution by number of offenses (x) can be derived easily. We have for the first few values of x, that is to say, none, one, two, and three offenses:

0   q_0
1   $p_0 q_1$
2   $p_0 p_1 q_2$
3   $p_0 p_1^2 q_2$

Of the entire population, q_0 never commit an offense; $p_0 q_1$ just one; $p_0 p_1 q_2$ two offenses; and so forth. At this point two remarks need to be made, the first dealing with the problem of units. No difficulty is encountered as long as we are ordering individuals with respect to number of offenses. However, the population total is not identical with the total number of crimes reported in police statistics, even if we decide to leave out altogether unreported crime. Several individuals may participate in the same crime. The population total or mean obtained from the distribution above refers to a new unit, "crime incident," an occasion where an individual commits a crime alone or is one of several participants. The number of crime incidents, in this sense, is greater that the number of reported crimes, probably by a factor of 2 to 3.

Let K denote the population mean number of incidents. It can then be shown that following relation holds:

$$K = \frac{p_0}{q_2} (p_1 + q_2) \tag{1}$$

which reduces to

$$K = \frac{p_0}{q_1} \tag{2}$$

on the further assumption that $p_2 = p_1$. Even with Eq.1, one may say that we are nearly dealing with a system with two degrees of freedom, for one can assume that p_2 is as high or somewhat higher than p_1. Essentially, then, K may be inferred from knowledge of p_0 and p_1 (bearing in mind that $q_1 = 1 - p_1$). Or, knowing K and p_0, the value of p_1 may be inferred.

On the basis of Swedish data from the 1960s one can estimate the magnitude of K for a recent cohort to be 10 to 20 cases. In other words, in a lifetime perspective a cohort may be assumed to contribute 10 to 20 incidents per person of cases of participation in recorded but not necessarily cleared crime. For this level to be attained p_1 and p_2 must be fairly near to unity, almost regardless of what the value of p_0 might be. This in turn creates a very skewed distribution; the model does not readily yield normal or even unimodal frequency curves. A small part of the population or cohort will be responsible for a large proportion of all incidents.

The second remark to be made concerns the fit between model and reality. This clearly remains to be determined. Although good data are hard to come by, some are presented in a later section. No claim is made that the fit is a very close one, only that the model is a useful device in that it generates distributions in rough agreement with observational data. To anticipate slightly, crime distributions seem indeed to be quite skewed, so that there is no contradiction between facts and model, with its implied high concentration of criminal activity.

DETECTION AND IMMUNITY

Epidemiological use of data from known offenders, say, persons arrested or sentenced, immediately raises the thorny question how representative these are of the universe of all offenders, detected as well as undetected. Low clear-up rates speak for low detection risks, so there is certainly room for legitimate doubts here, clear-up rates being quite low for many types of crime. Indeed, warnings against inferences from identified to all offenders belong to the commonplaces in criminological literature. It is, of course, a warning easier to utter than to heed, for there is usually no workable alternative to relying on data from known offenders. In the following, the analysis is centered on the never-delinquent/ ever-delinquent dichotomy, that is to say, on the situation in which we study the properties of individuals who become known to the police or the courts up to a certain age limit, say, 21 years, with no regard to the number of times they have been arrested or convicted or for what number of offenses. If the upper limit is death, this amounts to the determination of lifetime risks. In the present case we denote it as *long-term risk*, with the proviso that there should be considerable room for variation in what we decide to call "long." Sometimes this may be as little as a year or two, sometimes the entire length of life or a good part of it. With this understanding we may proceed to look at the consequences of moderate to low detection risks.

As noted by several writers, and no doubt by many more criminals, low detection risks for isolated offenses confer only a temporary immu-

nity (cf. Walker, 1965, pp. 12-13). If a person is active in crime and con-
tinues to commit offenses, his luck will fail him sooner or later, even if
the odds are in his favor for any single incident. He will be arrested or
otherwise become known for at least one offense, and accordingly
counted as ever-delinquent. The long-term risk of becoming thus
known, perhaps only for one out of many offenses, is denoted Y_x. It
appears reasonable to assume that Y_x will grow monotonically with
creasing values of x, the number of offenses (incidents) that have really
occured. To get any further, a primary detection risk π has to be introduced. This is the risk of detection directly resulting from a given incident. The concept, it will be seen, differs somewhat from the conventional clear-up rate (cf. McClintock and Avison, 1968; pp. 120-125).

Now, a simple model of increasing long-term risk with increasing
number of offenses used by Walker, and by McClintock and Avison (*op.
cit.*) is the following:

$$Y_x = 1 - (1 - \pi)^x \tag{3}$$

As π obviously takes a value between 0 and 1, Y_x will rise from 0 (when
$x = 0$) to values near unity when x is high. Even with quite low values of
π, say, of the order of 0.1, the long-term risk Y_x will be high for persons
with a high number of offenses. To take an example, if $\pi = 0.1$ and
$x = 20$, Y_x will be 0.88.

From these assumptions it follows that studies relying on known
offenders will draw a disproportionate number of persons who are
highly active in crime, with a large number of offenses, known and
unknown, behind them. The occasional offender is much less likely to
be included. Combined with the progression model described earlier, it
means that known offenders are probably responsible for a fairly large
part of all crime. In fact, we have

$$V = 1 - \frac{q_1^2(1 - \pi)}{(1 - p_1(1 - \pi))^2} \tag{4}$$

following the notation used earlier and with V denoting the proportion
of all crime (meaning incidents) cleared up or not, which is the work of
persons who eventually become known as ever-delinquent though
perhaps only for one or a few of their offenses. With some length of time
covered, V will reach high values, easily above 75%. The implication of
skewed crime distributions and increasing long-term risk is a high degree of visibility of crime in the sense that much is due to offenders
sooner or later officially registered as such. Again, it should be noted
that the progression model may not fit actual distributions to perfection,
so that a margin of approximation has to be allowed for.

The upshot of all this is that customary "clinical" data, from police or court files, may well fail to give an adequate impression of the element of one- and two-timers (still speaking of real incidents, not cleared-up crimes); they will be much more influenced by frequent repeaters and hard-core offenders. All things considered, the well-worn iceberg metaphor does not seem particularly apt, for a good deal more is observable of the iceberg than one tenth, at least if offenders are weighted by their production of crime.

DISTRIBUTIONS: MODEL AND REALITY

Table 1 shows the distribution of Swedish males born in 1953 with regard to the cumulative number of "registrations" for penal-code crimes before December 1975 (when most of them had reached the age of 22). The unit is nearer to adjudication than single criminal offense; thus the average for the entire cohort comes out at a modest 0.34. Also shown are the frequencies to be expected on the assumption of a Poisson (random) distribution, and on the basis of the progression model described earlier and parameters given below the table.

It can be seen that the Poisson model with one adjustable constant gives a poor fit and fails entirely to reproduce the long tail of individuals with a high number of adjudications, the record in the present case being no less than 37. The progression model, here with two adjustable constants, fares better; it cannot be said to be completely successful either.

The failure of random or Poisson models should cause no surprise. A close parallel, certainly as far as statistical criteria are concerned, is found in accident research and the long controversy around the concept of accident-proneness (Shaw and Sichel, 1971). Here again simple models of random distribution with equal probabilities are often out of touch with the observational data, the range of observations far exceeding what can be expected on the random hypothesis. It is desirable to move beyond the progression model, which is largely a descriptive device, and find generating schemes more clearly of a causal nature. Only in this way can we hope to throw light on underlying mechanisms. Unfortunately, there are two modes of thinking capable of explaining large individual differences in terms of number of offenses or accidents. One is to assume initial differences in risks. Some people are more accident or crime prone than others right from the beginning, and the risk differences are relatively stable. The other solution is to posit aftereffects of events on probabilities. Even though individuals start with identical

Table 1

Cumulative Number of Registrations for Penal Code Offenses for Swedish Males Born 1953:
Empirical and Theoretical Distributions

Number of Adjudications	Observed	Poisson[a]	Progression Model[b]
0	0.839	0.713	0.840
1	0.097	0.242	0.075
2	0.028	0.041	0.040
3	0.013	0.004	0.021
4	0.007	—	0.011
5	0.005	—	0.006
6 and and	0.011	—	0.007
Total	1.000	1.000	1.000

[a] Mean and variance = 0.34
[b] $p_0 = 0.16$ $p_1 = p_2 = 0.53$ K = 0.34

risks to meet with an accident, or commit a crime during the next period of time the outcome, offense or no offense, will permanently affect risks for subsequent periods.

Both models, initial stable differences and probability aftereffects, can be related to important hypotheses in criminological theory, the first to constitutional, personality, or stable-environment explanations, the second to theories of reward and punishment, commitment, or stigmatization. They are by no means to be looked at as mutually exclusive, either in the formal-statistical or the sociological sense. Nevertheless, testing one will help to reach a decision on the other. Should we find very little evidence for the first, we would be more inclined to turn to the second, and it would win by default. Hence the importance of establishing the existence or absence of initial differences, for instance, by relating crime to facts outside the sphere of crime and observable earlier than the start of a criminal career. This brings us to the study of epidemiological effects, which forms our next main subject. In due time we return to the statistical models with some final comments.

EPIDEMIOLOGICAL EFFECTS: EVALUATION STANDARD

As mentioned earlier, there is no shortage of data on the characteristics of law-breakers and their environment in the literature. If all this fails to produce a clear picture of crime causation, at least one of the explanations lies in the difficulty of comparing different sets of data and in the bewildering variety of statistical approaches. There is need for a common standard of evaluation and for some degree of consensus on what is to be counted as a strong or as a weak epidemiological effect. Here, as before, "epidemiological effect" refers primarily to a statistical association without any necessary presumption of a specific causal nexus. The solution to be put forward is by no means new. On the contrary, we return to the old and elementary concept of normal correlation and judge associations, even when qualitative classifications are involved, as if they had arisen from a normal correlation surface. Essentially, this is the method of tetrachoric correlation, that is to say, correlation estimated from fourfold tables, although only a graphic technique will be used. The model on which the method rests cannot be fully tested within any concrete application; it must be judged by its success in leading to a coherent view of different sets of data over a wide range of applications. In due course evidence is presented that it meets this requirement.

When dependent and independent variables are continuous, or can be thus treated, no special problem is met if one wishes to determine the strength of a relationship. A coefficient of correlation may be determined and the regression tested for linearity if necessary. However, when we are concerned with crime and deviant behavior, a far more typical case is one with a dependent variable or response that is discontinuous in nature, indeed, that is mostly of an all-or-none character (dichotomous). Thus boys become known as ever-delinquent before the age of 15, or they do not, or a person has been registered as having a drinking problem, or he has not. In fact, much the same can be said for epidemiological studies of disease and of behavioral epidemiology in general; response is often scored in categorical terms, and a dichotomy is typically found to be the easiest or only feasible solution. With the independent variables, which are often indicators of environment, both continuous and discontinuous-categorical cases occur. Crime, alcoholism, mental illness, and for that matter political voting, fertility, and life styles may be related to income and used as a continuous variable, or to social class, which is usually treated as discontinuous. On the whole the discontinuous case is the rule here, too, and our attention will therefore be centered on this.

An often employed method of expressing a relationship is through the *relative risk.* This is the quotient formed by taking the risk in a special category, the critical stratum, as the numerator and a suitable reference risk as the denominator. Let p_j denote risk in the critical stratum, where the subscript is a reminder that there are often many alternative ways of defining that stratum with a corresponding variation in risk. Thus one may observe the number of boys who become delinquents relative to all boys from working-class homes, or make the same computation for a middle stratum, or again combine these two strata, or define the critical stratum as broken homes.

In epidemiological research it seems customary to define the reference risk as that of an unexposed or most-favored stratum. Thus mortality in lung cancer for heavy and moderate smokers may be related to that among nonsmokers. However, when one is dealing with crime and similar phenomena, the idea of unexposed stratum loses much of its meaning, and the definition of a most-favored stratum to serve as an anchoring point becomes largely a matter of convention. Partly for this reason and partly to simplify calculations, the reference risk is here defined as that of the total population, *including the critical stratum*. This risk (or probability) is denoted p_o, and the relative risk then becomes p_j/p_o. It should be stressed that choosing total population rather than unexposed stratum for reference purposes is a technical solution without deeper significance. The logic of relative risks remains the same regardless which method one favors.

As is shown presently, the relative risk p_j/p_o can be determined quite easily, even when the overall risk p_o is unknown. Let m_j be the proportion of all individuals within the deviant category who come from the critical stratum, and n_j the proportion within the entire population who come from the identical stratum. Then

$$\frac{p_j}{p_o} = \frac{m_j}{n_j} \tag{5}$$

To take an example, suppose that 65% of all delinquent boys come from a working-class stratum, whereas independent evidence, such as census data, points to 50% as the best estimate of the working-class element among boys in general (including deviant boys). Then $m_j = .65$ and $n_j = .50$; accordingly $p_j/p = 1.30$. It can be seen that relative risks often can be computed quickly by combining information for some special (deviant) group and matching population data. Frequently, such computations can be carried out on the basis of published data not originally designed for this purpose.

Unfortunately, we need to take the magnitude of the overall risk p_o into the account to be able to say how strong an association is. Figure 2 illustrates the reasoning behind the normal-correlation analysis of relative risks. In the graph the abscissa represents the independent or predictor variable, the ordinate the dependent response. Both are assumed essentially continuous variables on which a dichotomy has been imposed by the dividing lines L_1 and L_2. Of these, L_1 divides the population into critical stratum and remainder, whereas L_2 divides it into responding and nonresponding units, for example, deviant and nondeviant

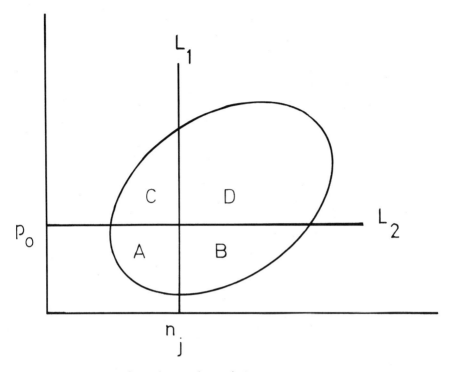

Figure 2. Relative risks and normal correlation.

cases. The A, B, C, and D stand for the numbers falling in the four quadrants defined by L_1 and L_2.

Now, the overall risk p_o is obviously $(A + B)/(A + B + C + D)$, whereas p_j, the risk within the high risk stratum, is $A/(A + C)$. We then have for the relative risk

$$\frac{p_j}{p_o} = \frac{A(A + B + C + D)}{(A + C)(A + B)} \qquad (6)$$

or

$$\frac{p_j}{p_o} = \frac{\dfrac{A}{A + B}}{\dfrac{A + C}{A + B + C + D}} \qquad (7)$$

$A/(A + B) = m_j$ and $(A + C) / (A + B + C + D) = n_j$; thus Eq. 7 expresses the same relation as Eq. 5. The value of p_j/p_o, the magnitude of the relative risk, depends on three factors:

1. The underlying correlation coefficient
2. How extreme the cutoff point for the independent variable is. Other things being equal, the more extreme the dichotomy, which is to say the smaller n_j, the greater the relative risk.
3. How rare or frequent the dependent behavior is. Other things being equal, the smaller p_o the greater the relative risk.

With regard to point 2, the size of n_j, we often have a choice, and we can try various possibilities. The risk within a most-exposed stratum can be studied and related to the overall risk, or the most-exposed and next-most-exposed strata can be lumped together and treated similarly. It is always assumed that a start is made with the most extreme stratum, and the line of dichotomy moved from there. Thus one would start with the very lowest income stratum (if the low end is the high-risk end), determine the value of p_j, and then add to this the next lowest and determine p_j for the combined category, and so on.

As to p_o, the overall or population risk, there may not seem much of a choice. However, one may sometimes have an option by using, say, different stipulations regarding seriousness of crime, age limits, and so forth, making the behavior more or less common. The important point is to realize that relative risks depend not only on correlation level (as we want them to do) but also on stratum size and population risk. Seemingly impressive values of relative risk may be caused by a rare behavior or an extreme stratum. Broadly speaking, if one starts with the high-risk end of the scale, relative risks will fall in the range 1-3 in the great majority of cases. It follows, then, that a value of 1.5 in one study may indicate a closer association than the value 2.0 in another.

To facilitate evaluation, special graphs may be prepared, but this technique can be more suitably described as it has been applied to authentic Swedish data on juvenile delinquency.

EPIDEMIOLOGICAL EFFECTS: DATA

Having laid the groundwork in the previous section, we are now ready to turn to a quick survey of some results pertaining to crime, beginning with (and spending most of the space on) certain recent Swedish data. In a study of juvenile delinquency, young offenders were selected who became known to the police between the ages of 12 and 15, with no previous record. The offense in all cases was a property crime, mostly trivial thefts and the like. The overall risk level (p_o) can be estimated at 0.05. There were about 200 delinquents and a control group of nondelinquents of about 100. The latter were matched with respect to age, social class, family type (complete-broken), and neighborhood. However, by use of independent data, values of the entire population of boys could be inferred; figures from the control sample have been standardized to give population estimates unaffected by special selection procedures. Hence we get from the delinquent group values of m_j and after standardization, a value of n_j from the control group. This means that relative risks may be determined by use of Eq. 5.

A graph may now be prepared (Figure 3) containing relative risks, n_j, and different levels of correlation. The graph is only valid for an overall risk around 0.05 as indicated. If one is working with a given set of data and fixed overall risk, this is no great inconvenience; no matter what the specific risk may be, a similar graph can be prepared by means of bivariate tables found in handbooks of statistical tables. Any relative risk may be entered very quickly and the degree of association read off by looking at the curves showing correlation level. One has, of course, to bear in mind that sampling errors may influence observed risks and quotients.

In the graph several indicators of environment and behavior-personality characteristics have been entered. For a fuller description of data and methods the detailed reports may be consulted (Swedish Council for Crime Prevention, 1976). The "stratification factor" shown is a combined classification by social class, family type, and neighborhood, for which several cutoff points were tried beginning with the least-favored stratum.

It is apparent that environment in the sense of social class or income is a relatively poor predictor, although there is some correlation. Even social handicap as here understood gives only a moderate effect. A similar scale was used by Gibson and West (1970) on British data and the degree of association seems to have been about the same. With measures of the boy's own behavior or personality we get somewhat stronger relationships, as witnessed by school data and personality assessment. Here two remarks are in order. Predicting crime from school adjustment, behavioral tendencies, or personality traits means attacking the problem at a different level from early environment in such structural terms as family social class, income, housing standard and the like. The two kinds of analysis should not be seen as competing and not used polemically one against the other. The second remark concerns personality and psychological disorders as an explanation of crime and delinquency. What the results of the Swedish study bear out is *not* the thesis that aberrant personality development in general confers a higher risk. Neurosis does not appear to create much of a danger in this regard; thus mental health as a general concept will not take us very far. But one particular type of deviant personality or psychological disorder defi-

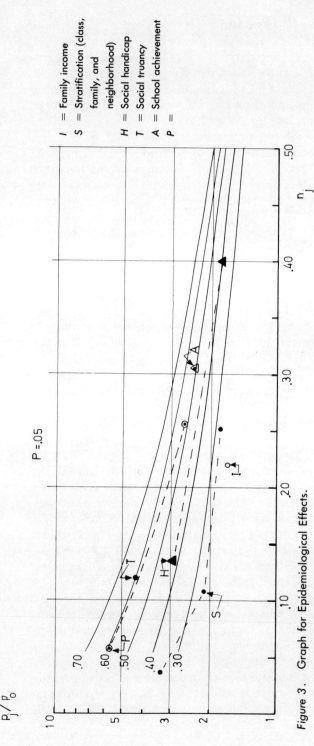

Figure 3. Graph for Epidemiological Effects.

"Social handicap" refers to a combined classification including registration of parents for crime or alcohol problems, social relief or action on the part of the Child Welfare Board (other than measures due to the crime for which the boy may have been selected for the study). "Personality factor" is a classification into a number of types or clinical patterns, the extreme one being the impulse-driven, acting-out type. This was done by means of projective tests by two psychologists working without any knowledge of criminal record, if any. Remaining items in the list probably need no explanation.

nitely carries with it a higher risk. This is the acting-out type of boy just mentioned, often called "psychopaths" or "sociopaths" in the literature. (Robins, 1966; Glueck and Glueck, 1950).

As far as can be judged from comparisons with other enquiries, inside and outside Sweden, there is nothing remarkable in the level of association demonstrated for standard environmental indicators. In Jonsson's (1967) study of delinquent boys from the Stockholm area, both weaker and stronger associations are found, but the average level does not differ materially from the one that emerges from Figure 3. His delinquent group represents more serious deviance and presumably a lower overall risk (p_o) for which allowance has to be made. In the Philadelphia study cited earlier (Wolfgang et al., 1972) the relationship between social class and delinquency among white boys (by far the largest category in the community) was quite weak, with a correlation level under 0.30. Here the population risk (for whites) is 0.29, and the results have been evaluated accordingly, not by means of the contours shown in Figure 3. The fact that the usual relation between social class and delinquency sometimes fails to materialize in a set of data should cause no surprise; a weak correlation may be upset by sampling errors or special local factors.

Nor is there anything unusual about these results viewed against the background of behavioral epidemiology in general and sociological field studies outside crime and delinquency. Though it has been customary to stress the deterministic aspects of such features as social stratification or the urban-rural dimension, it is rare to find more than 10% of the variance accounted for with regard to a broad range of dependent behaviors, corresponding to a correlation near 0.30. Before we look closer at the theoretical implications of this state of affairs there is a practical side to it that deserves to be discussed.

SCREENING AND EARLY PREDICTION

Perhaps something could be done about crime if we were able to sense the early warnings and intervene at the individual level before a deviant attitude has hardened into a style of life not easily changed. There are many if's in such a proposition, for instance, the real danger of causing harm through labeling people as high-risk cases. Also, it is quite doubtful if any sound program of remedial action exists or can be put together. It will, nevertheless, be instructive to enquire whether the first condition, the *sine qua non* of such a policy is met, the ability to mark out with sufficient accuracy, and well in advance, persons likely to become delinquents, especially serious criminals. The problem is more or less identical with the medical screening problem, currently a much-debated subject. In the medical application a test is sought that will tell medical workers what persons should be referred to a more careful, time-consuming, and expensive examination, and perhaps treatment. The prospects for the screening strategy do not seem altogether bright in medicine, and the findings just reported for delinquency are not calculated to instill optimism. Correlation levels of 0.30 or 0.40 are simply not enough; there will be too many false positives and false negatives. Three times the population risk may seem high for a stratum, for instance, defined by a plurality of family problems. But should the population risk be 0.05, the great majority of cases selected for counteraction by this criterion represent a sheer waste of time, and perhaps worse. If the overall risk increases, relative risk usually declines. Also, there will be a large number of future delinquents who go undetected and untreated.

It is not necessary to rely on the normal-correlation model to see this; the required computations can be made directly from overall and stratum risks, taking into account also stratum size. The trouble with high-risk strata is that they tend to be small, and their contribution to the problem group therefore limited.

It may be possible to build on *behavioral symptoms*, or personality measures closely related to behavioral disorders. But then the question arises if the warning we get is enough in advance to give hope for successful intervention.

A Danish study of children with adjustment problems (Vedel-Petersen, 1975) led to much the same conclusion. "The study has proved that as regards several family background characteristics, the socially disadvantaged families contained a relatively high number of problem children. However, a closer look at these differences revealed that they had relatively insignificant value as causative variables and as indicators for investigative work."

A numerical example (now again based on normal-correlation reasoning) will make it clearer what we are up against. Suppose we are interested in prediction and perhaps countermeasures against some undesirable behavior for which p_o, the overall risk within the population, is approximately .16. This is a higher risk than found for early police contacts in the Swedish sample but not atypical of other such risks having to do with crime, alcoholism, etc. Now, if we have an early "sign" that correlates .50 with the outcome (a rather optimistic assumption) what are the consequences? Let us further suppose that the sign admits of gradations so that we can pick a smaller or larger proportion for treatment. Under these conditions, if we were to select the 10% worst off according to the sign, their risk if untreated would indeed exceed the overall risk considerable. More precisely, it would be around .45. We would still be treating a group the majority of which would never be affected by the "disease" even if left alone. And we would only have found .10 times .45, that is .045 out of .16, in other words less than one third of the target group. To find about half we would have to work on nearly 25% of the total population; as a consequence, a clear majority would never have developed the behavior if left untreated. Such, or often worse, is the outlook for screening and early intervention if environmental indicators are to be used as pointers to individuals more than others worth treating.

RISKS AND BEYOND

If epidemiological effects mostly turn out to fall somewhere within the weak-moderate range, is this because we have slipped in our methodology? There are several ways in which this could happen, and it is worth the trouble to review them quickly and point to needed improvements.

There is first the temporal aspect and the weakening of relationships that could arise because we observe present but not past environment. If behavior is shaped by a sequence of environmental conditions with substantial variability through time for many individuals, looking at present conditions could give a poor grasp of the "effective sum" of these influences. A similar difficulty is met in medical research, for instance, in the study of lung cancer (Cairns, 1975), and there is little doubt that it needs to be taken seriously in behavioral research. Perhaps it is a little less acute in delinquency studies, as we are dealing overwhelmingly with young persons with a correspondingly limited freedom for such variability to obscure patterns of causation. In the Swedish delinquency study referred to earlier, some attention was paid to changes in family situation, with no decisive results.

Perhaps more striking is the spatial or network (group) analogue to variability through time. Just as the acting person is affected by what has happened to him in the past, not only today or yesterday, he is also affected by what happens to his friends and members of the social network to which he belongs. In this sense *their* environment is *his* environment, although presumably in a weakened form. There is no question that there is at least the semblance of marked group effects in crime and delinquency. Delinquent acts are often committed together with other persons of roughly the same age, and delinquent boys often mention as friends other boys with delinquent habits. Some of this may be the outcome of selective group membership rather than real group influence, but common sense, not to mention sociological theory, argues for a strong element of real group pressure. This granted, it follows that we ought to determine family, social class, and the like of the given boy but also the identical factors for his friends. To translate this principle into field operations is not easy, because we have little to fall back on in the way of established methodology, surprising as this may seem. It should be noted that the objective ought to be environmental factors for network members, not only or even chiefly their response. To explain the delinquent behavior of a certain boy by reference to delinquent behavior among his friends is a solution the hollowness of which is quickly disclosed when social trends and historical change are to be interpreted.

So far we have followed one of the main roads of epidemiology, to examine variation among individuals in terms of environment and response, and found the neglect of the temporal and group contexts a shortcoming. It is perfectly possible that causal influences are missed or underestimated in this manner. If this is so, an alternative strategy might be to abandon the search for factors at this level and look instead at rates or proportions for different populations, trying to find stronger relations at the aggregate level. Epidemiological workers in other fields, such as disease, are perfectly willing to do this as occasion demands, and it ties in well with themes in criminological theory. It is only in this way, it could be argued, that social structure in its full sense can be related to crime. To some extent, criminologists have long followed this path, for example, when they deal with urban and rural crime rates. With more ambitious versions of this idea the obstacles are formidable, not least the paucity of comparative data across national and cultural borders.

All things considered, there is justification for the view that "environment" is both loosely defined and poorly handled in observational data. To find that social class, income and the like are only weakly related to many behaviors is a far cry from disproving the effects of environment generally. Especially sociologists, "environmentalists" almost to a man, have a special obligation to develop and experiment with new concepts of environment. This also means that new observational methods have to be tried. As usual, it is easier to find fault with existing practices than propose new ones sure to be more productive. But there is no doubt that some hard thinking along unorthodox lines is called for. A beginning might be made by casting "environment" in terms of a stream of stimuli, or perhaps causal "quanta", rather than in structural terms as is now the rule.

Perhaps one or another of the innovations discussed so far will do the trick and make epidemiological effects more distinct. Yet it would be unwise to place a high degree of confidence in this outcome, to the neglect of other possibilities. At this point let us see where we stand and sum up the empirical evidence in a few words. In the first part of the analysis it was shown that crime as an activity, its "production," is probably quite unevenly localized and that relatively few produce a relatively large part. This means stability through time in behavior at the individual level. The findings from the epidemiological analysis reported later, that certain behaviors (other than delinquent) and personality traits give a shade stronger relations to delinquency, are consistent with the finding of individual stability. But such differences have proved resistant to explanation by means of structural indicators of environment in that correlations are often quite modest. At the same time, environmental correlations cannot be neglected; although they leave much out of the account, they are nevertheless a part of the story. Theoretical schemes must have a place for their persistence as well as their moderate size.

It is time to return to the two process models sketched in a previous section, one based on initially existing, stable differences in probabilities, the other on probability aftereffects of events. A high degree of success in predicting delinquency from early family environment would have supported the first one of the two. What we now have is presumptive evidence for the second model, at least for the presence of aftereffects in some degree. The evidence, of course, is far from conclusive, nor need the two models be taken as excluding one another completely. Indeed, they are not entirely different in what they imply for one says that individuals are different in their behavioral propensities "from the beginning," the other that they gradually become different. It is obvious that we could mean different things by "beginning" in the case of delinquency. What are relatively stable differences at the age of 15 may have started as a much less predetermined process with probability aftereffects at the age, say, of 5.

It is the writer's belief that progress in the area of crime causation cannot be made unless we are prepared to investigate the properties of such stochastic processes more carefully, and their fit to observational data. They are likely to introduce an element of random walk in human development (Carlsson, 1972), precisely the kind of mechanism that will produce the seemingly paradoxical case of stable tendencies hard to explain in environmental terms. But here most of the work remains to be done.

Chapter Four

A review of studies of criminality among twins

Karl O. Christiansen

In this chapter the criminological twin investigations by Johannes Lange, A. M. Legras, A. J. Rosanoff and others, Friedrich Stumpfl, Heinrich Kranz, C. A. Borgström, Shûfu Yoshimasu, Pekka Tienari, and Odd Steffen Dalgaard and Ejnar Kringlen are critically examined. In addition, the criminologically relevant cases, known by the present author in which monozygotic twins have been reared apart, are reviewed.

JOHANNES LANGE

The first application of the twin method in criminological research is found in the Munich doctor, Professor Johannes Lange's book *Verbrechen als Schicksal* (1929, 1931).

1. Material

Lange examined 37 same-sexed pairs of twins. The material was collected in (a) the Institute for Criminal Biology at Straubing Prison

(*Kriminalbiologische Sammelstelle am Zuchthause Straubing*) in Munich, (b) all twins among prisoners in Bavarian prisons at a certain time, including brothers and sisters who were twins, and (c) twins among psychopaths registered in the genealogical department of the German Research Institute for Psychiatry (*Deutsche Forschungsanstalt für Psychiatrie*).

The sample is described as complete in the sense that it includes all same-sex twin pairs found in these registers who had reached the age of criminal responsibility. Of the 37 pairs found in this way, seven were excluded, because none of them was criminal.[1] There is some indication of an increased crime rate among monozygotic twins. Penal certificates were collected for all of the probands. The twins who were in the prisons were examined by Lange personally. All penal and police records including information from the prisons were scrutinized; furthermore, many civil documents were collected and studied. A number of examinations of the twins within the rest of the sample were performed by some of Lange's colleagues, but they were not informed of the specific purpose of the investigation (p. 40). There is no information about the time of investigation, but the latest data appears to refer to 1927, so it seems probable that the collection of the material continued until one or two years before the publication of the book.

2. Zygosity diagnosis

Regarding the zygosity diagnosis we are only informed that in "a large number of cases" Lange had "exact measurements," and in almost all the cases several photographs as well as "in a lot of them" duplicate examinations and fingerprints (p. 40). A case of doubt (*Garkoch*) with amazing similarity regarding measuring results, photographs, and characteristics of rare occurrence is regarded as dizygotic, as the twins never are mistaken for each other. They are concordant (pp. 53-60).

3. The concept of concordance

The concept of concordance is not defined, but it appears from the description that it is based on the occurrence of sanctions, including deprivation of liberty, although the number, length, and kind of such measures have not been taken into consideration. Among the 10

[1]Lange's book was published with the title "Crime as destiny" (London, 1931) pp.38–41. All the following page references regarding Lange are from this edition; the quotations, however, are based on the German edition. In the following sections page references refer to the principal work named in the introduction to the section.

monozygotic pairs who are described as concordant, there are two pairs in whom there is no concordance according to the above criteria, as only one of them has been punished. In pair 8 both the brothers were homosexuals, but were not carefully examined. In pair 9 the two sisters "have not yet been punished" but they lead an immoral life and had both "mysterious conflicts with the law." These two pairs are included because their life careers in many deviating aspects show a great similarity. Furthermore, it must be mentioned that the concordance is only weak in pair 6. Lange emphasizes that the two brothers are not criminal in the normal sense of the word, whereupon he concludes—definitely not convincingly, and rather surprisingly—that it is common, deeply rooted characteristics in the predisposition (*die Anlage*) which have brought them into conflict with the law.

4. Results

Among Lange's 30 twin pairs, 13 were monozygotic, and out of these, 10 were considered concordant, but out of 17 dizygotic, only 2 were concordant. After this Lange concludes: "As far as crime is concerned, monozygotic twins on the whole react in a definitely similar manner, dizygotic twins, however, behave quite differently. In accordance with the significance of the twin method we must conclude from this that heredity (*die Anlage*) plays a quite preponderant part among the causes of crime" (p. 41). Lange's conclusion is not surprising. A few pages previously he has described twins as "brothers and sisters born together, and who in the majority of cases have grown up together; consequently in the decisive years of development they have common experiences and have been subject to uniform educational influences" (p. 34).

5. Interpretation

The manner in which Lange interprets his main result is expressed a bit more cautiously at the end of the book. " . . . .under our present social conditions heredity does play a role of preponderant importance . . . . certainly a far greater role than most people feel inclined to admit" (1929). In a formulation like this, the correctness of the statement cannot be denied.

Of course, from his basic view, Lange must regard it as justified to use the results of twin studies to "examine the question whether, and if so, to what extent, biological phenomena of the most different kind are determined by our predisposition" (p. 37). Therefore, it is also obvious

to use the twin method for illustrating the question of *how far* the influence of the predisposition reaches in the genesis of crime. If the hereditary predispositions were without significance, a comparison would not
show any difference between monozygotic and dizygotic twin pairs. The
greater significance the predisposition has, the more there has to be
concordance in the monozygotic pairs. It should not be overlooked that
Lange also points to the importance of the environment. He admits that
the predisposition is not the only reason for crime. The distance from
perfect concordance in monozygotic twins permits us to estimate the
extent of the social crime factors. Influence from the environment must
play a part, as approximately one-fourth of the monozygotic are discordant. Expressed another way, crime is not a purely biological phenomenon; it also presents a social picture and as such must also have a social
background. We could easily imagine societies in which many acts we
consider as misdeeds and crimes would not be defined as punishable
offenses. It is not only the biological standards by which a human being
gets classified under the category, law-breaker. Therefore, one might
object that we have used a scientific method in a field where it is completely irrelevant. However, the objection is not valid. "No serious person really doubts that we must look for significant causes of crime in the
criminal, i.e., in biological conditions" (pp. 173-174).

    Discordant monozygotic pairs constitute a special problem. In two of
Lange's three pairs, organic brain damage is ascribed a decisive significance (pp. 154 and 175). One pair had an intelligence defect, and one of
the twins suffered from traumatic epilepsy. The other pair had different
damages caused by a difficult birth; one of the twins had a brain damage
which (according to Lange) caused a constitutionally conditioned
homosexuality, but the other twin was heterosexual. In the last of the
three pairs (p. 165) the offense of one of the twins was a typical
nonhabitual offense, but here, too, the predisposition was ascribed a
decisive significance. The social position of the criminal, abuse of alcohol, higher intelligence, livelier temperament, and better eloquence
have played a part; but the social conditions, although they cannot be
ruled out, are supposed to play a very modest part (p. 176). Lange's
previously expressed expectation that in such pairs there would be
ample opportunities of studying the influence of the environment is not
realized.

    Johannes Lange's pioneer study on criminality among twins is the
achievement of a scrupulous and hard-working scientist. About the
zygosity diagnosis he writes: "Whenever I suspected myself of being
prejudiced, I endeavoured to bring in other helpers, whom I entrusted
with clearing up the question of similarities without, however, informing them of the criminal records. In this way I think I did all I could to

keep the investigation free from subjective influences" (p. 40). But Lange was also a child of his age and culture. German psychiatry in the 1920s and 1930s was certainly biased regarding the problem of heredity and environment. As a scientifically trained biologist, he would not be able to deceive himself in questions of zygosity. For the benefit of a scientifically sound assessment of his results, however, his classification of the twin pairs as concordant or discordant is most doubtful in at least two cases. Also, it should be noted that his interpretation of the relative influence of heredity and environment is that of a biologist educated in German psychiatry at the beginning of this century.

AUGUSTE MARCEL LEGRAS

At the beginning of the 1930s, inspired by Lange, Auguste Marcel Legras performed an examination of psychosis and criminality on a few Dutch pairs of twins. The results were published in 1932 in the dissertation *"Psychose en criminaliteit bij tweelingen"* (Psychoses and criminality among twins). A summary in German can be found in *"Psychosen und Kriminalität bei Zwillingen"* (1933, pp. 198-222).

1. Material

Legras' material consists of 24 pairs of twins, collected in this way: 6 pairs in the psychiatric-neurological clinic in Utrecht, 14 pairs through a questionnaire sent to Dutch mental hospitals, and finally 4 pairs in prisons and similar institutions. The leaders of these institutions were asked the following questions: (1) Are there among the patients, the internees or the pupils any who are known to be twins? (2) What is known about the other twin? (3) Is there any similarity between them?

Regarding the criminals, only twins of the same sex were included. Those cases where one twin had died young, the cases where there was no information about the life history of one of the twins, or about the similarity of the twins, were excluded from the investigation. Legras found four monozygotic pairs who were concordant and five dizygotic pairs who were discordant with respect to criminality.

2. The zygosity diagnosis

The polysymptomatic resemblance method was applied, as well as a blood group examination (1932, p. 30). In each case the results of the comparisons are thoroughly explained.

3. and 4. The concept of concordance and the results

The concept of concordance is not defined, but it is illustrated through the description of concordant pairs (p. 103). The first pair are two 13-year-old boys whose behavior disorders (among these petty thievery) resulted in reform school placement. They make Legras think of the old term "delinquent nato." The other pair are two 58-year-old tramps addicted to alcohol who both repeatedly had been placed in state workhouses because of smuggling, vagabondage, begging, and mal-treatment. The third pair are two 24-year-old sisters who—together and singly—committed several thieveries from department stores. Both were sentenced to 3 months' imprisonment at the age of 23 years, and one of them to an additional 2 months' imprisonment. The last pair are two 36-year-old brothers; of these two, one was sentenced to 1 month's imprisonment for theft at the age of 33 years, and, 2 years later, 1 year's imprisonment for blackmail. The other had, at the age of about 25 years, two sentences of 1 and 1½ years' imprisonment for theft. They both explained their thefts by their being very easy to influence.

Of the criminals in the five discordant pairs, only one has been sentenced to a serious punishment, namely 6 years' imprisonment for grave maltreatment.

5. Interpretation

Legras admits that the concordance of the monozygotic pairs may be a consequence of mutual impressionability (induction) as the twins in the four pairs have grown up together. As the five dizygotic pairs, however, are all discordant, he concludes that it has been the genetic disposition that has been the decisive crime factor in the monozygotic pairs (p. 104).

Legras' sample was collected in a rather haphazard way, and the careers of most of the criminal twins are only studied superficially.

AARON J. ROSANOFF, LEVA M. HANDY, AND ISABEL
AVIS ROSANOFF (LATER ISABEL ROSANOFF PLESSET)

Rosanoff, Handy, and Rosanoff's American examination "Criminality and delinquency in twins" (1934), is one among an extensive series of
articles concerning the occurrence of mental disorders in twin pairs
where at least one of them is affected by one of the deviations which has
been the subject of examination. A more detailed report has been published in 1941 under the title *The Etiology of Child Behavior Difficulties,
Juvenile Delinquency and Adult Criminality with Special Reference to their
Occurrence in Twins.* This review is based mainly on the last work.

1. Material

The authors examined 1008 twin pairs in 1934. There is no information regarding how these pairs were selected. The collection of material
started around 1930. The two earlier European examinations of criminal
twins (Lange and Legras) are briefly mentioned in the 1934 publication.
In 1941 the studies of Kranz and Stumpfl are mentioned. Surprisingly
enough, the 1941 study does not contain any reference to their 1934
article.

The material is the largest which until that point had been examined
from a criminological point of view. It includes 409 pairs of twins with
behavior difficulties, delinquency, or criminality. This includes 108 pairs
with adult criminality (sentenced after the age of 17), 113 pairs with
juvenile delinquency, 120 pairs of preneurotic- and prepsychotic-type
behavior difficulties, and 68 pairs with behavior difficulties of the so-
called predelinquent type. The two last groups are not dealt with in
great detail here.

The 108 pairs with adult criminality consist of 38 male and 7 female
monozygotic; 23 male and 4 female dizygotic pairs of the same sex; and
36 pairs of opposite sex. The 113 young delinquents include 29 male and
12 female monozygotic pairs, 17 male and 9 female dizygotic pairs of the
same sex, and 46 dizygotic pairs of the opposite sex. The 68 pairs with
child behavior difficulties include 8 male and 14 female monozygotic
pairs; 9 male and 19 female pairs of the same sex, and 18 opposite sex
twins (1941, p. 8).

2. The zygosity diagnosis

In 1934 the expressions "same-sex twins, probably monozygotic," "same-sex twins, probably dizygotic," and "opposite-sex twins, dizygotic" were used. In 1941 the term probably was left out. The expression "identical twins" has been rejected. "Monozygotic twins are as a rule more alike than any two persons that may be otherwise selected; but they are never identical; and sometimes they present physical, intellectual, and temperamental contrasts which may be said without exaggeration to make all the difference in the world." (1934, p. 930). It is not explained anywhere in the above-mentioned studies how the zygosity was diagnosed. There is, however, no doubt that the authors have used some kind of polysymptomatic resemblance method. But it is doubtful whether the diagnoses of zygosity and of concordance with respect to behavior difficulties, delinquency, and crime have been made independently of each other.[2] The number of same-sex MZ pairs is considerably higher than that of same-sex DZs; on the other hand, Conrad has suggested that some MZ pairs have been misclassified as DZs (loc. cit.).

3. The concept of concordance

Adult criminality is defined as having been convicted and sentenced, after the age of 17 years, at a criminal court to serve a term in a city or county jail or in a state or federal prison, or having been granted probation. Delinquency is defined as having been brought, before the age of 18, before a juvenile court because of some offense and thereafter committed to a correctional institution or placed under probation. About child behavior difficulties it is only mentioned that such cases "were found in child-guidance clinics, school clinics, neurological clinics, and in special classes for problem children in public school" (1941, p. 6). It is not mentioned how the persons who began their careers as young delinquents and later continued their criminality are classified; probably they are considered adult criminals. "In many of our cases of adult criminality, the clinical histories show that such criminality was preceded by juvenile delinquency and, earlier, by predelinquent traits in the shape of child behavior difficulties". (1941, p. 6). Nor is it stated how concordance is determined if one of the partners in a pair is sentenced young and the other when adult.

There is much overlap among these groups, and between them and cases with "so-called constitutional mental disorders" (ibid). The problem is touched upon at the very beginning of the 1941 paper, but the

---

[2]Gottesman and Shields, 1966, p. 19.

authors do not consider clear definitions of such concepts useful (1941, pp. 5-6). Concordance, which is also termed "both affected," refers not only to similar affections in both of the partners, but also to affections "representing both quantitative and qualitative intra-pair differences." For instance, one of the twins in a pair may have presented one of the principal behavior difficulties dealt with in the monograph, whereas the other may be free from such types of deviation, but suffers from "mental deficiency, epilepsy, or psychotic disease" (1941, p. 9). This type of concordance is, however, named partial, and in the case stories the authors describe intrapair differences regarding both kind and degree of the deviance.

However, a distinction is made between "criminalism" and "criminality." The last term (including mild or merely incidental offenses) is judged as normal. Criminalism covers cases of abnormal personality make-up, whether of hereditary, traumatic, or infectious etiology which manifests itself under different circumstances as a more or less persistent tendency toward antisocial behavior and which is not, to a high degree, the result of inner conflicts or external pressure. Criminality, unlike criminalism, appears more often in only one of a pair of monozygotic twins (1941, p. 178). No statistic is mentioned for documentation of this allegation, but a case which illustrates the fact is mentioned.

4. Results

The results of the study on the basis of the 1941 work (p. 8), is summarized in Table 1.

Concordance rates are with one exception higher in monozygotic than in dizygotic pairs; the negative case is juvenile delinquency among females, with 92% concordant among monozygotic and 100% among dizygotic pairs in groups with small absolute numbers. The MZ-DZ difference among males is significant both for adult criminality and juvenile delinquency.

The differences in the concordance percent in monozygotic and dizygotic pairs are, as can be seen, larger for male and female adult criminality than for juvenile delinquency, the concordance frequency being relatively large in both male and female dizygotic delinquents. The discordant monozygotic pairs are thoroughly discussed. As with Lange, some of these cases are explained by organic damage (especially brain damage) in one of the partners of a pair, or by differences in cerebral birth trauma, to which great importance is attached (1941, pp. 163-173, and 183).

Two more results, concerning age and sex, deserve to be mentioned.

Table 1

**Pairwise Concordance Percentages for
MZ and DZ Twins
(Rosanoff et al.)**

| | PAIR-WISE CONCORDANCE PERCENTAGE | | | | | |
| | Adult Criminality | | Juvenile Delinquency | | Behavior Difficulties | |
	%	N	%	N	%	N
MZ Male	76	38	100	29	100	8
DZ Male	22	23	71	17	56	9
MZ Female	26	7	92	12	100	14
DZ Female	25	4	100	9	42	19
DZ Opposite Sex	8	36	28	46	50	18
Total		108		113		68

Antisocial behavior generally has its onset in childhood, adolescence, or early adult life. In 36% of the cases the behavior disorders appeared before the age of 10 years, and in 90% before age 20 (1941, pp. 168 and 183). Unfortunately, concordance is not related to the age of the occurrence of the first observed symptoms of deviant behavior.

Rates of concordance are by and large the same for both sexes. But based on comparisons of the crime rates of brothers and sisters in the opposite-sex twins, as the authors underline, that sex is of "overwhelming importance" in the causation of crime and delinquency. A small part of this contrast is explained by "the greater vulnerability of the cerebral tissues in males as compared with females, with their resulting greater liability to suffer cerebral birth trauma" (1941, p. 1985). In crime, as elsewhere, the male shows "his venturesomeness, initiative, aggressiveness and instinctive interests as gatherer and provider; the female, her passivity and preoccupation with the love aspects of life" (p. 186).

5. Interpretation

The conclusions concerning adult criminality are close to those of Lange, Legras, Stumpfl, and Kranz (1941, p. 182). This does not mean that hereditary factors alone suffice to produce crime, as shown by the relatively high figures of discordance in monozygotic pairs (app. 25%). However, juvenile delinquency is considered to be predominantly socially conditioned because of the high rate of concordance among dizygotics. Here criminalism rarely occurs. The last fact is probably rather a consequence of the definition of this concept. Generally it is underlined that hereditary factors are not always present, and, consequently, not essential in the etiology of child behavior difficulty, juvenile delinquency, or adult criminality (1941, p. 183).

The influence of social factors is still further demonstrated by the fact that dizygotic twin brothers of criminal probands present concordance in 47% of the cases and twin sisters in 36%, whereas the corresponding figures for single-born siblings are 24% and 12%, respectively. The "enormous relative excess of concordance" in the twins can be attributed only to nonhereditary factors, influencing both twins of a pair *whether monozygotic or dizygotic* (1941, p. 183).

Summarizing, the authors mention the following explanations that might have contributed to the occurrence of discordance in monozygotic pairs: (a) incidental criminality (being determined mainly by environmental rather than by constitutional factors) occurs under special conditions to which only one twin of the pair is exposed; (b) inequalities of the original division of the early embryo or inequalities of development during intrauterine life may account for differences in constitutional make-up; (c) some factors, such as head injury, alcoholism, or diffuse syphilitic disease of the cerebral cortex existing only in one twin of the pair, may destroy controlling or inhibiting mechanisms and thus lay bare a previous latent antisocial component in his temperament; (d) concealment of a criminal tendency in one of the twins by a conspiracy for that purpose among informants may erroneously raise the percentage of cases in which only one twin is affected; (e) mistaking a pair of dizygotic for monozygotic twins may also erroneously raise the percentage of cases in which only one twin is affected (1934, p. 932). The reverse possibility is not mentioned.

The work of Aaron J. Rosanoff and his assistants is one of the results of their endeavor to throw light on a number of genetic problems in the fields of psychology, psychiatry, sociology, and criminology by means of the twin method. It was initiated and the first report on crime in the twin sample published before the studies of Kranz and Stumpfl, but it is much influenced by Lange. However, the authors paid more attention to the influence of a number of social factors studied by American criminologists as S. and E. Glueck and C. R. Shaw and his co-workers. It is probably for this reason that the conclusion presents a more balanced view on the problem of heredity and environment in the genesis of crime than one will find in the German studies.

The weakest point in the exposition is the way in which the concept of concordance was defined and applied. Interested colleagues suggested that the authors try to clarify this and similar concepts by clear-cut definitions. It seemed to them that this "would serve but to increase the fog of an atmosphere which is already much befogged. Although they have an appearance of rigid, scientific demands, their effect could be only to divert attention from the clinical material presenting the problems under consideration and to send it off into avenues of speculation instead" (1941, p.6). Here we shall let the authors have the last word, and only add that the avenue they chose has made impossible any direct comparison with concordance rates from other criminological twin studies.

FRIEDRICH STUMPFL

In 1936 two books about criminal twins were published in Germany. One of them was Friedrich Stumpfl's *Die Ursprünge des Verbrechens. Dargestellt am Lebenslauf von Zwillingen* (The origin of crime. Based on the careers of twins); the preface is dated March 27th. Stumpfl had the previous year (1935) published *Erbanlage und Verbrechen. Charakterologische und psychiatrische Sippenuntersuchungen* (Hereditary disposition and crime. Characterological and psychiatric investigation of families), in which he compares 195 serious criminals (Schwerkriminellen), that is, recidivists with at least five sentences to prison or hard labor and 166 nonserious criminals (Leichtkriminellen) only punished once, and with at least 15 succeeding sanction-free years.

The 1935 publication consists of family investigations, among other things conversations with 1734 relations and 600 other persons. According to Stumpfl this investigation showed that "an inherited coincidence of certain character traits and character abnormalities was of importance as an endogenous cause of crime. Criminals who were inclined, and criminals who were not inclined to relapse, displayed each their own particular, mutually exclusive character traits and character abnormalities." In the study of twins this fundamental point of view is repeated. Besides, Lange's influence is obvious.

1. Material

Stumpfl's basic material comprises 550 pairs of twins, of which at least one is criminal. It includes several complete series from prisons in Bavaria, Württemberg, Baden, Hessen, Braunschweig, Mecklenburg, and Oldenburg. In addition, it includes a complete series from the Criminal-biological Institute in Bavaria (Bayrischen Kriminalbiologische

Sammelstelle) and from the same source, twins selected on certain days as well as twins who consecutively were reported to the author. From this basic material 65 pairs were selected, 18 monozygotic, 19 same-sex dizygotic, and 28 opposite-sex pairs. The selection was made merely from a traveling-convenience point of view. With a few exceptions, all twins were visited by Stumpfl personally. Furthermore, the parents and sisters and brothers were examined, and information was obtained from mayors, teachers, priests, and the like.

2. Zygosity diagnosis

The zygosity diagnosis was made "with absolute certainty" in all cases on the basis of photographs. Apart from the small number of pairs who were not examined by Stumpfl personally, all the monozygotic twins were measured anthropologically (nine facial and cranial measures, color of hair and eyes) and examined for special and ordinary constitutional characteristics. Fingerprints were not taken at the examination, but if both had previous offenses, the fingerprints could be used in cases of doubt (1936, p. 17).

3. The concept of concordance

Stumpfl has made an analysis of the concept of concordance. His description (pp. 17, 104 and 171), which is not particularly thorough, can be characterized as follows:

If one starts from the criminality that is objectively described in the criminal records (Straflisten), then pairs with two registered twins will be concordant, and pairs with one registered and one unregistered twin will be discordant. The determinant factor is that they are included in the register. However, because other forms of similarity or dissimilarity in the social behavior of the twins may occur, Stumpfl introduces a distinction between different concordance levels or stages (Konkordanz-stufen). He uses the expression "concordance of the first degree" (erster Stufe) or general concordance if both twins have been entered in the penal register.

Sanctions for minor offenses (e.g., small traffic offenses) are not regarded as sentences. Slander is only considered an offense if the sentence has involved more than 6 days imprisonment. On the other hand, offenses against property, including begging, as well as sexual offenses and crimes of violence are included, even if the sentence were a small one. According to Stumpfl, this boundary line provides an unambiguous distinction between what is the essential and what is not the essential (p. 18).

"Concordance of second degree" concerns similarity regarding the severity of the crime (*Konkordanz der Schwere der Kriminalität*) which is, in fact, similarity of the criminal careers of the co-twins. It is established when both parties are only punished once or both are punished several times.

"Concordance of third degree" concerns the similarity regarding the way in which the crime has been committed. Similarity at this level is established when both partners predominantly are punished for the same crime. The main stress is laid on the kind or type of particularly serious crimes and on the most frequent crimes committed by the twins' partners. Moreover, the twins are not called discordant in cases in which only one of the twins has committed a more serious crime, for example, a sex crime, which does not occur in the other twin's criminal record, if the similarity is otherwise great. There is such a large amount of hidden criminality within offenses against property and sexual offenses that Stumpfl considers this point of view necessary. The same is the case regarding less serious offenses, for example, slander, also when these occur more than once in one of the twins.

"Concordance of fourth degree" is established when the twins' daily social behavior (outside the punishable area) is similar. Such a similarity must be well demonstrated on the basis of documents and other information.

"Concordance of fifth degree" is established when there is a complete similarity regarding the deeper character traits (*Wessenmerkmale*, which is specified as content, structure, and type of character, as defined by Klages) as well as regarding character abnormalities. Consequently, concordance of the fifth degree in psychopathic twins is tantamount to concordance regarding form or type of psychopathy.

It can be seen that concordance of fourth and fifth degrees are not defined criminographically and do not indicate anything about concordance with respect to criminality. They can contribute to explaining the types of similarities described in the three first-concordance degrees, but their occurrence cannot strengthen the weight of the evidence of an already established similarity with respect to crime or criminal career. Furthermore, the higher degrees of concordance only partly presuppose the existence of concordance at the lower level, and this actually makes Stumpfl's level-terminology (*Stufen*) misleading. Of course, there has to be concordance of first degree, if there is a second- or third-degree concordance, but the way in which the crime has been committed can be the same (third-degree concordance) in a twin who is only punished once and in his recidivist partner. In such a case second-degree concordance does not exist. (See Tables 2 and 3 on p. 172).

4. Results

The main results of the examination can briefly be described as follows:

Of 15 monozygotic male pairs, 9 evidence first-degree concordance. Of 3 monozygotic female pairs, 2 are concordant. The concordance rate in the monozygotic twins is thus 61%. The discordance in monozygotic twin pairs (7 out of 18), Stumpfl himself calls "a relatively frequent phenomenon which comprises almost half of the cases."

Among 17 dizygotic male same-sex pairs there are 7 concordant, and among 2 female there are none. The concordance percentage is 37%. The 28 opposite-sex pairs include 2 concordant pairs (7%). The low concordance frequency in this group is, according to Stumpfl, first of all due to the sex differences.

The criminal twins are divided into serious or grave criminals and nonserious criminals and, furthermore, into early criminals (early beginners) and late criminals (late beginners), defined by an age limit of 25 years (p. 138).

An offender is regarded by Stumpfl as a serious criminal if he has at least two jail sentences of a duration of several months and if it can be concluded from the criminal career that the antisocial conditions to a certain extent can be characterized as "habitual," that is, "representing a lasting state." Instead of conflict-provoking external circumstances that may lead to occasional criminality, the career of the serious criminals is determined by an abnormal character degeneration (psychopathy, as defined by Kurt Schneider). If the abnormality is serious it may be "the sole, lasting cause of crime" (p. 163, see also p. 155). This is especially noticeable in those cases in which the criminal career has started early.

The nonserious criminals include two subgroups: conflict criminals and late-criminals. About the first it is said that the criminality stems from an inner conflict or struggle "which under certain conditions could appear in anybody, and independently of whatever his psychic and physical qualities might be, could be activated and lead to action" (p. 165). Compared to the serious criminals, the late-criminals appear as "quite preponderantly normal of character or at least come close to normal personalities" (p. 167).

Because Stumpfl finds that in monozygotic twins there is always concordance regarding serious criminality, whereas they can be discordant if the index case shows petty criminality, especially conflict criminality, he considers it proved that serious criminality is a consequence of innate tendencies. He formulates his results as follows: In a group of male monozygotic pairs, who are characterized by early and serious criminality, a thorough concordance (almost 100%) will appear, whereas the concordance rate is only 45% among the dizygotic twins where the

index case displays serious criminality (pp. 172-73). Late-criminals and
female offenders are, without regard to the zygosity, almost always
discordant (p. 98). If the different degrees of concordance are examined,
there will appear in monozygotic pairs with serious criminality an increasing and, at the end, a complete similarity contrary to the dizygotic
twins in which the concordance rate stays the same on all levels (p. 171).

5. Interpretation

By means of the concepts conflict and late criminality, Stumpfl explains what to a biologist must be a tricky fact, namely, the discordance
in monozygotic twins. However, Exner doubts that this is a proof of the
stated 100% concordance in the early-starting, serious-criminal
monozygotic pairs. In a survey of Stumpfl's, Kranz's, and Lange's material he finds at least 15% of cases that must be considered exceptions
from Stumpfl's assertions.[3] In addition, the classes of serious and nonserious, early and late criminals are so vaguely and variably defined that
it is not surprising when Stumpfl in several places maintains that these
concepts are as difficult to define as other classifications of human
phenomena. Thus about conflict criminality it is stated: "The concept of
conflict criminality cannot be defined no more than can any other biological phenomenon, you can only learn to see it" (p. 167). And about the
distinction between nonserious and serious criminality: "A determination is only possible through the spirit, not through the letter" (p. 170).

There are not many reservations regarding the limitation of the twin
method in Stumpfl's book. It should, however, be mentioned that he
ends his chapter about the environmental influence by pointing to "the
greater similarity of the environment of monozygotic twins compared to
the dizygotic." Thus we cannot ordinarily draw a sharp line between
serious criminality due to adjustment difficulties in childhood and
youth, and genetically conditioned serious criminality "From the complete concordance of early beginning serious criminals among the
monozygotic twins it is not possible to conclude that all previously
punished recidivists are completely unsusceptible to external influences" (p. 131).

The radical difference between monozygotic and dizygotic pairs in
the intrapair similarity regarding the most deep-seated psychological
characteristics are, however, maintained. As expressed once and for all
by Goethe: "Abilities are presupposed, they must be accomplished into
skills." Stumpfl takes it for granted that abilities means the same as
inborn tendencies. There is no intermediary transition between the two

[3]Exner, 1939, 173 f.

extremes. One observes "everywhere a cleavage between the very great differences among the dizygotic twin partners and the comparatively microscopic differences among the monozygotic twin partners. (p. 129).

It is the merit of Stumpfl that he—together with Kranz—has initiated an analysis of the concept of concordance, but it must be added that his book is the most unreadable of the criminological-twin works. It is badly arranged, which among other things is illustrated but not illuminated by some strange errors in the page references in the table of contents. It is not free from vagueness, repetitions, and sometimes contradictions. The career descriptions contain general, often valuable characteristics of parents, sisters, and brothers, but they are not as thorough as Lange's. The criminality is only described summarily, so that the way it is classified does not always appear convincing. If it did not contain an insinuation, one might ask whether it had not been more important for Stumpfl to have his book published before Kranz's came out than to have it considered and edited in the same sober way as *Erbanlage und Verbrechen* from 1930.

HEINRICH KRANZ

In 1936 another German dissertation about criminality among twins saw daylight. Lange's pupil, Heinrich Kranz, published *Lebensschicksale krimineller Zwillinge* (Life careers of criminal twins). Kranz had, in 1935, published an article *"Discordant soziales Verhalten eineiiger Zwillinge"* (Discordant social behavior in monozygotic twins), about one of the main problems of criminological twin research. It was based on parts of the material that constituted the empirical basis for the major work.

1. Material

Kranz's basic material consisted of four series of twins. The first had not been collected by himself personally. It was supposed to include all the prisoners serving sentences in Prussian prisons on a certain day. Kranz did not receive the list until 1 year later. Evidently he did not rely on its completeness, and he supplied three additional series. The two following series originated from four Prussian penal districts (*Strafvollszugsbezirke*), where half the prisons one day and the other half another day carried out an inquiry regarding twin births among the prisoners. The fourth series developed in quite a different way. Six prisons, for one year, systematically asked all the new prisoners whether they were twins. Some pairs might have been overlooked, but it is certain that when ascertaining these twins no biasing consideration was taken as to whether they were concordant or discordant. Because of this, Kranz felt entitled to include them (pp. 3-5).

The basic material consisted of 552 twin pairs, 426 of which were rejected: (a) 127 because they were not twins, (b) 202 because one had died before reaching the age of criminal responsibility, and (c) 97 because two important conditions were not fulfilled: (1) the zygosity diagnosis and/or the concordance decision could not be determined, (2) or because one or both twins could not be traced, as the criminal records in question no longer existed (p. 4). Even if one accepts Kranz's basic material as being a complete twin population (although it does include a large number of nontwins), one could question whether this still holds true after the considerable reduction. Kranz thought there was a much larger possibility that the nontwins would state that they were twins than the reverse. This, however, seems doubtful. One could imagine that an offender who has an unpunished twin brother would hide this because of the fact that the brother was unpunished and had done better than the proband himself.

Kranz emphasized that the ideal would have been to require birth certificates from all the prisoners, but this work was insurmountable. Instead, the certificates for the prisoners who stated they were twins were obtained. This, however, excluded prisoners who actually were twins but attempted to hide it. As mentioned, Kranz considered their number to be very small.

Kranz's reduced sample included 32 monozygotic, 43 dizygotic, same-sex, and 50 dizygotic, opposite-sex pairs (p. 23). As mentioned earlier, one of them can also be found in Stumpfl's material.

2. The zygosity diagnosis

The most important zygosity criteria were shape and color of hair, color of eyes, physical type, genotype of the papillary lines, and blood groups. In addition, attached ear lobes, shape of nose, tongue furrows, shape of ear as a whole, teeth, shape of head, and outline of face was taken into consideration. All characteristics were rated in four degrees of similarity: strong similarity, moderate similarity, moderate difference, and strong difference. The blood type was considered of special importance. Of 75 same-sex pairs, 16 were examined together at the same time, 33 separately. Five pairs were examined by other experts. The remaining 21 pairs (among which, with a few exceptions, at least one of the partners were examined) were diagnosed on the basis of various kinds of information and photographs (p. 6).

Kranz emphasized that a diagnosis made in this way must be treated with special caution, but the skepticism should not be exaggerated. When the same information is received independently from several sources, it can be relied on, especially when good photographs are available. Here, experience from the usual twin diagnostic methods helps distinguish what is reliable and what is not (loc. cit.)

Finally, Kranz gave a detailed explanation for seven cases in which the diagnosis caused trouble. Furthermore, he carefully went through 11 monozygotic and 13 dizygotic twin pairs where the diagnosis was not made on the basis of his own examinations of both partners in the pair (pp. 6-23).

3. The concept of concordance

Kranz used a formal concordance concept as a starting point. It was defined as both co-twins having been previously punished. (Discordance meant that only one of the pair had previously been punished.) According to this, he examined to what extent the criminality in the twins was similar regarding the frequency of crimes, the kind and length of punishment, the kind of crime, and age at the onset of criminality. These criminality criteria were partly dealt with individually and partly in combination. For the last purpose Kranz constructed a common index (Chapter IV).

a. Frequency of crimes. It is obvious that concordance/discordance cannot simply be measured by the difference in the number of penalties or the number of offenses.

Kranz (following von Verscheuer) calculated the difference thus:

$$\frac{\frac{1}{2} \times \text{Diff.} \times 10}{M}$$

Where "Diff." is defined as the difference in number of offenses and M the mean of the twins' number of offenses. According to this formula, the differences vary between 0 and 9.9. A score of zero means that both had the same number of convictions; a score of 9.9 means that the difference regarding the number of convictions was very large. If one of them had never been punished for an offense, the value would be 10, that is, the pair was discordant.[4]

On the basis of these values the twins were divided into three concordance classes with values between 0-3.3, 3.4-6.6, and 6.7-9.9.

[4]In a previous work Kranz used the number of punishments as a basis for a similar calculation.

b. The kind and length of the sentence.   In an analogous way, similarity regarding the sentence was calculated. However, it was not described in further detail how different kinds of crime were combined in a single index; it was only mentioned that the different types of deprivation of liberty, fines, and punishments involving loss of civil rights had been made comparable, according to a system of points (*Punktzahlsystem*).

Here, too, the limits for the concordance grades were 0-3.3, 3.4-6.6, and 6.7-9.9. These figures regarding the punishments are considered less reliable than the figures for the frequency of offenses, because more subjective factors enter into the fixing of the sentence.

c. The kind of crime.   Similarity concerning the kind of crime cannot be expressed in figures. Kranz defined three categories: In "strong similarity" the co-twins had essentially committed the same kind of crime, although a few unimportant offenses might have been different. In "some similarity" the offenses were partly of the same kind in the co-twins. In "slight similarity" the co-twins had essentially committed different kinds of crimes; some unimportant offenses, however, might have been common.

d. Age at the beginning of the criminal career.   Comparisons of the age of delinquency (or crime) were measured in years and grouped in the following way: Age difference 0-3 years, 4-10 years, and above 10 years.

e. Total evaluation of similarity.   Finally, a calculation was made of all four values (a-d) combined, with an index figure varying between 4.0 and 0. They were divided into the following three groups: 4.0-3.0 (strong similarity), 2.5-1.5 (some similarity), and 1.0-0 (slight similarity).

4. Results

The main result of Kranz's investigation was that 21 of the 32 monozygotic, 23 of the dizygotic and 7 of the 50 opposite-sex pairs were concordant in the broad sense of the word. This gave the following concordance rates: 66% for monozygotic, 54% for dizygotic, and 14% for opposite-sex pairs. It is the smallest ascertained difference between MZ and DZ pairs with respect to concordance rates that has been found in investigations of criminality until recently.[5] More important, however, was Kranz's convincing demonstration of the differences in concordant monozygotic and concordant dizygotic twins regarding the frequency of crimes, the number of offenses, the length and kind of punishment, and the age at the beginning of the criminal career. Con-

---

[5]cf. however, Dalgaard and Kringlen, below.

cordant monozygotic pairs are essentially more alike than concordant dizygotic.

The results from the analyses of the various degrees of concordance are shown in Table 2. In most cases the figures speak for themselves. Because most recidivists were polytrope (*Warstadt*), it was natural that the middle group was strongly represented independent of zygosity. Kranz emphasized that not only did monozygotics commit the same type of offense, but their motivation for and execution of the crime were strikingly similar.

Table 2

	N	Strong Similarity	Moderate Similarity	Slight Similarity
(1) NUMBER OF CRIMES *(KRANZ)*				
Monozygotic	21	43%	38%	19%
Dizygotic, same-sex	23	39%	17%	44%
Dizygotic, opposite-sex	7	0	28%	72%
(2) KIND AND LENGTH OF SENTENCE				
Monozygotic	21	33%	19%	48%
Dizygotic, same-sex	23	17%	9%	74%
Dizygotic, opposite-sex	7	0	14%	86%
(3) KIND OF CRIME				
Monozygotic	21	43%	33%	24%
Dizygotic, same-sex	23	26%	30%	44%
Dizygotic, opposite-sex	7	14%	43%	43%

(4) AGE AT BEGINNING OF CRIMINAL CAREER				
	N	0–3	4–10	Above 10
Monozygotic	21	71%	19%	10%
Dizygotic, same-sex	23	52%	39%	9%
Dizygotic, opposite-sex	7	43%	43%	14%

(5) COMBINED EVALUATION OF SIMILARITY				
	N	Strong Similarity	Middle Similarity	Slight Similarity
Monozygotic	21	52%	29%	19%
Dizygotic, same-sex	23	22%	44%	34%
Dizygotic, opposite-sex	7	0	43%	57%

From Table 2 it is clearly seen that concordance with respect to crime does not mean the same for monozygotic as for dizygotic twins. Concordant monozygotics resemble each other "twice as much" as concordant dizygotics. However, Kranz did add that "the dead figures of statistics" only give a rough picture of reality. For example, among the four (19%) monozygotics with only slight similarity, a pair was found in which the criminal "valence" (*Wertigkeit*) of the co-twins must be almost the same. Kranz also pointed out in his general comments that the criminal partner in discordant monozygotic pairs relatively often, and more often than in the dizygotics, was heavily punished (*Schwerbestraffter*).

In the third part of the book a survey was given of what may perhaps be called releasing and forming crime factors (*Gestaltende Momente*). Birth order and birth trauma seemed very seldom to play any part. Among the diagnosed exogenic illnesses, syphilis had exercised an essential criminogenic importance. Some illnesses seemed to have a crime-preventing effect (e.g., tuberculosis). Brain traumas were not mentioned in the survey (p. 230).

The influence psychiatric illness and deviations exercised stands out more clearly. Low intelligence did not determine the kind of criminality, apart from sexual offenses against children committed by mental defectives. Those deficient in intelligence were capable of committing any crime. In the discordant dizygotic it was usually the more backward of the two who became a criminal. The type of psychopathy was, as a rule, similar in monozygotic and very different in dizygotic pairs. This was especially true regarding self-asserting (*Geltungssüchtigen*) swindlers (*Gemütlosen*) "enemies of society" and also—although more doubtful—certain types of spineless and infantile psychopaths. For these character traits heredity seemed to play a dominating part (p. 232).

Kranz ascribed great importance to alcoholism. Here, too, there was frequently concordance in monozygotic and discordance in the dizygotic pairs. Among the latter, it was usually the alcoholic who became a criminal. Several cases were mentioned in which drinking periods and criminal periods coincided. In most of the cases, however, it was not alcohol as such that caused a person to commit crimes; in the predisposed it had only a releasing influence on criminality (pp. 236-238).

In some pairs, both monozygotic and dizygotic, the fathers or other members of the family were criminal to such an extent that Kranz (with Gruhle) talked about "a family tradition of crime." Differences in the upbringing often occurred, and sometimes it was the partner with the strictest (most brutal) upbringing who became a criminal; but in most cases, rearing discipline did not seem to make a great difference. Kranz emphasized that family tradition could be the releasing factor, but it was difficult to decide whether it was the bad family environment or an especially dangerous genetic disposition that had accumulated in these families (p. 238).

The occupational training and career might now and then, although not always, be regarding as a symptom of personality traits. Here it again appeared that concordant monozygotic twins had often stayed at the same social level and normally also in the same environment. In one single discordant monozygotic pair, one of the twins' choice of occupation seemed to have been of importance for his criminality. Kranz had also observed that a bad marriage could be a contributory cause for offenses, just as a good one could prevent criminality. None of these factors had, according to the author, exercised a decisive influence in his material. The forms of sexuality and the choice of husband/wife was more likely an expression of personality characteristics rather than accidental environmental conditions (p. 244).

Monozygotic pairs were inclined to identify with each other; they could (especially when it was supported by the environment) experience a we-feeling (*Wir-Gefühl*), which Lange mentioned earlier. Kranz had a few typical examples of this among the monozygotic pairs. Among these examples were cases in which one could not disregard the possibility that this tendency had influenced the criminality. Some of this was also seen in the dizygotic pairs, although less frequently. "The effect of identification is consequently more an indirect influence springing from the internal tendencies common to the MZ twins than it is a direct effect of the external similarity" (p. 248).

5. Interpretation

It could not be a great surprise that Lange's student presented the problems in the manner of his master. He drew attention to the fact that there could be considerable differences in monozygotic twins regarding certain physical characteristics, such as the occurrence of exogenic-determined illnesses, including head trauma. The discordance in one monozygotic pair was assumed to be due to "different forms of appearance of the same psychical deviance." Kranz maintained that the environmental similarity within the twin pairs was not the same for monozygotic and dizygotic twins. It was assumed that the greater environmental discrepancies for the DZ were largely determined by gene differences. All this, however, did not shake the accepted thesis that monozygotics and dizygotics grow up under *approximately* similar environmental conditions.

Kranz's conclusion corresponded completely to what Lange stated in his less-categorical formulation. The genes must be ascribed a larger part in the genesis of crime than previously. Can one in every single case consider the genes as dictating an inevitable destiny? It depends on which meaning one gives the word destiny. It can cover both genes and the experiences the individual goes through. The existence of discordant and only slightly concordant MZ twins proves, however, that the destiny which in individual cases is expressed in criminal or noncriminal careers also depends on other factors than the hereditary dispositions (p. 250).

Kranz concludes his book by citing Schröder: "There is no such thing as *the* criminal, and there exists no born criminal, whose dispositions, physical traits, hereditary succession, and educability, etc. we can study in general. However, there exist people with tendencies and a preparedness towards particular kinds of behavior and reaction patterns which may be socially auspicious as well as felonious, by their character and personality (*Wesensanlage*)" (p. 251).

Kranz's work is the most solid among the criminological twin studies of the prewar period. It is clear in its basis; it presents the problem in a less biased way than the other criminological-twin investigations from Germany and Holland. The concept of concordance is analysed on the basis of four well-defined, relatively objective criteria, all of which concern criminality. The choice of factors from which the concordance is described is, however, equally arbitrary in the two German books from

1936. It should, however, be added that Stumpfl has taken conditions into consideration which may lead to a blurred presentation of the problem and interpretation of the results, whereas Kranz discusses the concordance problem on the basis of relevant criminographic criteria. Stumpfl's levels of concordance are more vaguely defined than those of Kranz, and this implies that his classification depends on less well-defined, subjective evaluations.

Kranz's descriptions of the life careers are full and well organized. They contain generally a clear and well-planned account of the criminality. His work can be characterized as the most comprehensive and thorough among the hitherto published criminological twin studies, partly because of his analysis of the concept of concordance, partly because of its careful investigation and discussion of the impact of environmental crime factors.

C. A. BORGSTRÖM

In 1939 the Finnish physician C. A. Borgström published a dissertation *"Eine Serie von Kriminellen Zwillingen."*

1. Material

With permission from the Finnish prison authorities Borgström sent out, in the middle of October 1933, circular letters to the directors of all the prisons in the country requesting them to question the current prisoners if they had a twin brother or a twin sister, and in such cases inform the Ministry of Justice every time a twin was taken into custody. At the end of February 1936 this sample included 29 pairs of twins. Of these, 19 pairs were monozygotic and 10 pairs dizygotic. The documentary material, which was received until October 1938 in the penal register, formed the basis of Borgström's study. The sample was heavily reduced, among other things because the author did not personally get the chance to examine 10 same-sex pairs. It thus consists of 9 same-sex and 6 opposite-sex pairs. Of the 9 same-sex pairs, 4 were monozygotic and 5 were dizygotic.

Slater states that Borgström's material apparently involves a representative series. It cannot be a complete sample, however, as it seems to be too small to include all the twins who in the years in question have passed through the Finnish prisons.

2. The zygosity diagnosis

The monozygotic pairs were, whenever possible, examined by Borgström personally, but this only happened in the case of 7 pairs. In 2 additional pairs the zygosity diagnosis could be made, even though only one of the twins was examined. Of the remaining 18 pairs of the basic sample, the author for practical reasons was only able to examine, at most, one of the twins in the pair. In some of the cases the zygosity diagnosis could probably have been made with a certain degree of confidence, but the author preferred to consider the diagnosis uncertain and left them out. These cases involve 2 concordant and 7 discordant pairs as well as a pair where one of the twins had died.

The zygosity diagnosis was made on the basis of the following characteristics: blood groups; papillary pattern; shape of face; color of eyes, color of eyebrow; shape of ear and nose; color of hair on the head, its size, shape and limitations; size of teeth, skin character and color, and so forth. No further explanation has been made for the zygosity decision in every single case, but the material is accessible at the Genetic Institute of the University of Helsinki.

3. The concept of concordance

By concordance Borgström meant that both twins have been convicted for some crime or offense and are included in the penal register. Inclusions for offenses against the Prohibition Act, which was abolished in 1932, were not included.

4. Results

The main result of the investigation was that three of the four monozygotic pairs were concordant (75%), whereas this only applies to two of the five dizygotic (40%). The author described the rationale of the investigation only briefly. It seems to be the same as the German investigations. Borgström, too, reported an example of brain damage in one of the co-twins in a discordant monozygotic pair.

SHÔFU YOSHIMASU

In Japan Shûfu Yoshimasu, psychiatric expert to the Ministry of Justice, has for a number of years collected material on two samples of criminal twins. In 1941 *"Psychopatie und Kriminalität. Die Bedeutung der Erbanlage für die Entstehung von Verbrechen im Lichte der Zwillingforschung,"* an article of 76 pages, was published. In 1947 "Crime and Heredity, Studies on Criminal Twins" appeared. The first of these two works includes 18 monozygotic and 15 dizygotic pairs, the second 10 monozygotic and 3 dizygotic pairs. These two samples were followed up and the results published together in 1961 under the title "The Criminological Significance of the Family in the Light of the Studies of Criminal Twins." In a later work, "Criminal Life Curves of Monozygotic Twin-Pairs" (1965), a renewed evaluation of the concordance frequencies has been undertaken on the basis of graphical representations of the criminal careers. The following survey of these studies is regarding methodology primarily built on the very full account from 1941, and the results are cited on the basis of the two latest articles.

1. Material

Yoshimasu's first series includes, in part, twin pairs he found during his 10-year period as psychiatric expert in Tokyo's prisons and penitentiaries, and, in part, pairs reported to him from prisons all over Japan during the period 1938-1941. He pointed out that many opposite-sex twins have dropped out, because in Japan a superstition exists that opposite-sex twins "do not easily let themselves be loved." This increases the probability of one of them being adopted. Seven of the reported pairs were not at all twins. The material in the first series thus included 18 monozygotic, 20 dizygotic, and 5 opposite-sex pairs. All the monozygotic twins have personally and carefully been examined by Yoshimasu.

The other series was collected during the war. It includes 10 monozygotic pairs and 3 dizygotic, same-sex pairs.

2. The zygosity diagnosis

Yoshimasu personally examined all monozygotic twins. He underlined that he made the zygosity diagnosis with the greatest meticulousness. He relied on the method of Siemen and Verscheuers, building on the occurrence of anthropological characteristics that probably are hereditary; in almost all the twins he was able to determine the blood groups. Furthermore, he used fingerprints in most of the cases, and he ascertained the gene types of the papillary lines according to Bonnevie-Geipel's method. He explains the large number of monozygotic pairs by the fact that in Japan more monozygotic than dizygotic twins are born.

Table 3[a]

Summary of Twin-Criminality Studies

	MONOZYGOTIC		DIZYGOTIC	
	Number of Pairs	Pairwise Concordance Percent	Number of Pairs	Pairwise Concordance Percent
Lange (1929)	13	76.9	17	11.8
Legras (1932)	4	100.0	5	0.0
Rosanoff et al. (1941)				
Adult criminality	45	77.8	27	22.2
Juvenile delinquency	41	97.6	26	80.8
Stumpfl (1936)[b]	18	64.5	19	36.8
Kranz (1936)	32	65.6	43	53.5
Borgström (1939)	4	75.0	5	40.0
Yoshimasu (1962)[c]	28	60.6	18	11.1
Dalgaard and Kringlen (1976)[d]	31	25.8	54	14.9

Notes:

[a]Tienari's results are not entered in this table because he has no group of dizygotic pairs.

[b]A monozygotic concordant pair is found in both Stumpfl's and Kranz's samples.

[c]The figures from Yoshimasu (1962) stem from two investigations in 1941 and 1947.

[d]Crime in the strict sense.

3. The concept of concordance

Yoshimasu's concept of concordance is not defined, but everything indicates that it is of a formal character. The monozygotic twins are alike, with almost no exception regarding frequency and kind of crimes.

It is clear from his first investigation that the biggest differences among the MZs regarding the number of sentences of the co-twins are 5-3 in one pair, and 11-7 in another pair. Among the crimes, stealing, which occurs in all monozygotic pairs, dominates. In one pair, one of the twins was also punished for stealing and bodily harm, violence and fraud; the other was punished for stealing, bodily harm, killing, robbery, fraud, blackmail, and embezzlement. Both of the brothers in another pair have been punished for stealing and robbery. The monozygotic twins were very close to each other regarding age at the first crime. The biggest difference is a case in which one of the twins got his first punishment at the age of 16, and the other at the age of 25. In the discordant monozygotic, three late-criminals were punished for the first time at the age of 40.

4 and 5. The results and their interpretation

In Yoshimasu's two samples of 28 monozygotic pairs, 17 were concordant, and of the 18 dizygotic pairs, two were concordant, corresponding to concordance rates of, respectively, 61% and 11%.

The first work. In the first work the following was concluded: Generally speaking character traits have a strong penetration; although these traits, even in monozygotic twins, can be expressed differently, one can always find deeper character traits that are consonant. Among the criminals, Yoshimasu found many monozygotic pairs who were concordant with respect to psychopathic personality traits. In one pair, however, one twin was slightly psychopathic, whereas the other was judged to be borderline normal; in another pair only one of the twins seemed to be slightly psychopathic, and the other was normal.

Yoshimasu's presentation of the problem and its solution is the same as that of the German researchers. He suggested that genes play an important role for the beginning of a socially harmful career of crimes. By the twin method, he asserted, it has been proved that the concordance among dizygotic pairs is only superficial and incomplete compared to the concordance among monozygotic pairs. Similarly, discordance in the monozygotic pairs is only external and as a rule accidental compared to the dizygotics' thorough dissimilarity. Therefore, it is necessary to examine the degree of similarity, not only with regard to the frequency and kinds of offenses, normal social behavior, and basic character traits. There is no doubt that hereditary dispositions for criminality to a high degree are correlated with certain types of psychopathy.

The later interpretation. Yoshimasu's early view changed because of more profound analysis in the course of the following 25 years. The diagnosis "psychopathy" was given up (1965) because it easily became subjective and moreover, was defined differently in various countries. In a certain sense "psychopathy" was substituted by schematized drawings of criminal life curves. These represent a criminological diagnosis based on the analysis of the registration in a large-scale social experiment. They are objective inasmuch as punishments are not inflicted arbitrarily. The life curves vary somewhat because of the influence of the environment during a lifetime, but for every individual they keep within certain limits. In this way every offender gets his own personal profile, determined by the age at which he began his criminal career, the type of his criminality, and the shape of the curve (continuous, remitting, intermitting, and suspensive). Despite environmental influence, the life curves show a striking resemblance in the monozygotic pairs.

On the basis of this, Yoshimasu made a renewed classification of his material and found 50% concordant among the 28 monozygotic pairs, but no concordance among the dizygotic pairs. Yoshimasu concluded that social factors exert the greatest influence on whether a person becomes an offender or not; but it is the basic personality traits that are attached to the genetic factors that decide the kind of criminality.[6]

Only a few other results from the 1961 article shall be mentioned. Almost all concordant monozygotic twins committed offenses before the age of 25 and repeated them many times (early recidivists). However, discordant monozygotic twins were either first offenders or late starters, that is, starting after the age of 25. Discordant pairs with early onset of recidivism were extremely rare among monozygotic twins, but occurred often among dizygotic twins. The agreement with Stumpfl and Kranz is clear. Each pair of concordant monozygotic twins resembled each other in their life curves to a considerably high degree.

All concordant, monozygotic, early-starting recidivists came from deviant families. Twins punished only once came from nondeviant families—regardless of the zygosity diagnosis. They were nonhabitual criminals, and neither hereditary dispositions nor the "personality's environment" played an important part. In late-starters, environment played a more important part than hereditary predisposition.

In general, Yoshimasu cautiously concluded that the difference in concordance in monozygotic and dizygotic twin pairs to some extent can be understood from the interpersonal relations in the family; on the other hand, such an explanation would not be satisfactory if it were not at the same time assumed that there was a difference in the hereditary factors.

Yoshimasu's continued analyses of the concept of concordance and especially his criminal career studies from the sixties has brought criminological twin research another step forward.

His own life career, at the beginning strongly influenced by German biological tradition and later by American sociological thinking, is an excellent example of a straight line pointing toward a steadily more profound understanding of criminality among twins.

---

[6]This is almost the reverse of Ferri's (1892) result. It is the social environment that decides the form of criminality, but the degree causes must be sought in biological (organic or psychic) antisocial tendencies.

OTHER JAPANESE TWIN STUDIES

Yoshimasu (1961) cites Sugmati's (1954) case study of 15 pairs of delinquent twins. The author of this chapter has not had access to this publication, but Yoshimasu summarizes it briefly in the following way:

10 uniovular twins: 8 concordant, 2 discordant
5 same-sex binovular twins: 1 concordant, 4 discordant

Mitsuda (1961) has published a similar study, the results of which also are reported by Yoshimasu in the same brief style:

15 uniovular twins: 11 concordant, 4 discordant
4 same-sex binovular twins: 3 concordant, 1 discordant.

Yoshimasu added that the high concordance rate with respect to juvenile delinquency in these two investigations is easily explained by "the similarity of their early environments and the mutual influence of impressionable minds" (Yoshimasu, 1961).

S. Hayashi, Director of Osaka City Child Welfare and Guidance Center, examined a sample of 15 male monozygotic pairs before the age of 20 years in which one or both were delinquent. It is published in Japanese with a short English summary, including an "Outline of Cases." 11 pairs were concordant, 4 discordant with respect to "delinquent behavior or criminal acts."

Hayashi underlines in his summary the following results:

1. Of 11 concordant pairs, 6 were chronic recidivists. They were considered to possess predetermined dispositions toward habitual criminality. Four other pairs showed delinquent behavior of much less disturbing kind; hence their social prognosis was judged to be favorable. In the remaining pair both were schizophrenics of the hebephrenic type.

2. In three of four discordant pairs, the delinquent behavior proved to be of a relatively mild degree. Some of the partners were noted to be "potential delinquents;" hence the discordance was only apparent. However, unequivocal discordance existed in one pair of the twins with respect to delinquency; it was presumably due to differences in psychological development and psychological milieu.

3. Factors to account for the discordance were analyzed in some detail from the viewpoint of the biological milieu, intelligence, personality, and psychological environment during the early stage of development.

It was concluded that factors interact with one another in a compli-cated manner, and further that a great role is played by differences in personality maturation resulting from the mutual interaction of biologi-cal, psychological and social environments.

PEKKA TIENARI

In Finland Pekka Tienari has carried out a large-scale study of twins (1963).

1. The starting sample comprised 1141 same-sex pairs, born 1920-1929. For various reasons 238 were excluded. (For details see page 25.) From the remaining 903 cases (in which both twins were traced and interviewed), two unselected samples were established. One consisted of 80 Finnish-speaking, identical pairs residing in the southwestern part of the country, where about half of Finland's population lived in 1959. The other sample consisted of 46 identical pairs from the other part of the basic material. In all pairs one or both of the co-twins had com-plained of psychic or nervous disturbances or were excessive users of alcohol or total abstainers according to the interview.

2. The zygosity diagnosis was made by similarity tests and, in all cases in which the zygosity was doubtful, serological types were deter-mined.

3. Concordance was defined (1) broadly: both partners being in pos-session of a criminal record, and (2) more narrowly: both being habitual criminals.

4. Results. Among 23 pairs with criminal records, 5 were concordant (21.7%) and 18 discordant. Among 5 pairs with habitual criminality, 3 were concordant and 2 discordant.

In a subgroup of 15 pairs it was possible to diagnose continued psychopathic behavior, including habitual criminality, abuse of alcohol, and poor adjustment. Of these six were concordant (40%) and nine discordant. In five pairs where one or both of the twins were classified as psychopaths in a narrow psychiatric sense, two pairs were concordant and three discordant.

5. Interpretation. No conclusion regarding criminality in the broad or the narrow sense of the word is presented. Concerning the small group with psychopathy in the narrow, psychiatric sense, it is stated that "the less adequately adjusted twin had had, in almost every case, a poor relationship with his parents."

ODD STEFFEN DALGAARD AND EINAR KRINGLEN

The latest among the studies of criminality among twins, "A Norwegian Twin Study of Criminality" by Dalgaard and Kringlen in Oslo was published in 1976.

1. Material

The sample studied is part of the Norwegian Twin Register, which was compiled by one of the authors (Kringlen, 1967). It comprises approximately 33,000 twin pairs born between 1900 and 1935. The sample studied included all 205 male twins born 1921-1930 where one or both twins entered the national criminal register with a conviction before 1967. Of these 205, 66 pairs were excluded. One or both of the twins died before the age of 15 years in 48 of the pairs; 10 pairs had unknown addresses; 4 pairs were inaccessible (living in the most northern part of the country or abroad). Two pairs could not be contacted and two were in fact not twins. The remaining group of 139 male twin pairs forms the basic sample of the investigation. The authors, characterize the sample as a complete and representative one.

2. Zygosity diagnosis

Visits were paid to all 278 twins to obtain blood tests and interviews. The zygosity diagnosis was in most cases based on blood and serum types. In the cases in which it was not possible to have blood samples from both twins in a pair, they were compared with respect to external appearance, color of eyes and hair, shape of face, and height; in all cases the authors had information regarding identity confusion as children.

3. The concept of concordance

The authors mention that the concept of concordance implies a dichotomy that is not always acceptable, and they present their results separately for a broader and a more strict or narrow concept of criminality. The broader included offenses against the penal code *plus* traffic offenses, military offenses, and treason during World War II. The more narrow definition included only penal code offenses, such as violence, sexual assault, and property offenses. Pairwise and proband concordance rates were calculated for crime in both the broad and the narrow sense of the word in the initial analysis.

4. Results

The two most important results appear from Tables 4 and 5.

Regarding the broad concept of concordance, there is only a minor, not significant, difference between MZ and DZ twins, the MZ:DZ ratio being 1.24 (pairwise rate), and 1.20 (proband rate). For the narrow concept the difference is somewhat higher, MZ:DZ ratio: 1.73 (pairwise rate) and 1.59 (proband rate), but the difference is not statistically significant.

Table 4

Concordance with Respect to Criminality, Employing a Broad Concept of Crime[a] (Dalgaard and Kringlen)

Zygosity	Total Pairs	Concordant Pairs	Discordant Pairs	Pairwise Concordance	Proband Cordance
MZ	49	11	38	22.4%	36.7%
DZ	89	16	73	18.0%	30.5%
MZ/DZ				1.24	1.20

[a]Including, for instance, crime according to the motor vehicle law, the military law, and cases of treason during World War II.

Table 5

Concordance with Respect to Criminality, Employing a Strict Concept of Crime[a] (Dalgaard and Kringlen)

Zygosity	Total Pairs	Concordant Pairs	Discordant Pairs	Pairwise Concordance	Proband Corcordance
MZ	31	8	23	25.8%	41.0%
DZ	54	8	46	14.9%	25.8%
MZ/DZ				1.73	1.59

[a]According to the criminal law, including violence, sexual assault, theft, and robbery.

Crimes related to theft and burglary show pairwise concordance rates of 19.1% for MZs and 18.5% for DZs. The difference is greater for violence, threat and robbery, and sexual offenses against children, but the absolute numbers are so small that no conclusion regarding concordance rate is warranted, "except that the general pattern seems to be that of discordance in both MZ and DZ."

The authors have, on the basis of information from the interviews, been able to classify the twin pairs according to "intrapair interdependence." It appears that the MZ pairs have more often been brought up as a unit and dressed alike, and much more often experienced a subjective feeling of emotional closeness and mutual identity than have the DZ pairs. From this comparison stems the most interesting result of the Norwegian study. Table 6 shows that MZ and DZ pairs with an extreme or strong degree of closeness have concordance rates that are virtually the same. If, however, the closeness degree is moderate or weak, the absolute numbers for MZ are so small (two concordant out of five) that a comparison is insignificant.

Table 6

Concordance for Crime in the Strict Sense in Twins with Respect to Intrapair Interdependence (Dalgaard and Kringlen)

Degree of Closeness	MZ		DZ	
	Concordance	%	Concordance	%
Extreme or strong	6/26	23.2	3.14	21.4
Moderate or weak	2/5	40.0	5/40	12.5
Total group	8/31	25.8	8/54	14.9

5. Interpretation

The interpretation of the results is obvious. Dalgaard and Kringlen concluded that the genetic disposition to criminal behavior is a weak one—if it exists at all. They added: "Even such a modest conclusion, however, is based on the underlying assumption that the environmental conditions for MZ pairs do not differ from those of DZ pairs, an assumption which today cannot be accepted." The difference in concordance could be partly explained by the more similar upbringing of MZs than of DZs. However, after having compared MZ and DZ pairs with the same degree of mutual closeness, the authors are no longer in doubt: ". . . *the significance of hereditary factors in registered crime is non-existent"* (emphasis by the authors).

A short discussion of a possible influence of some crimes being unreported and unconvicted leads to the result that there is no reason to believe that this affects the concordance rates between MZ and DZ twins.

The investigation by Steffen Odd Dalgaard and Einar Kringlen is remarkable because it is the first and only criminological twin study that discloses no clear difference in the concordance rates of monozygotic and dizygotic twins. Furthermore, when the samples are classified by degree of closeness of the co-twins, the small and insignificant difference disappears. The basic sample is a complete population of twins born between 1921 and 1930 in Norway. If all registered criminals are identified correctly, the discussion of criminality and heredity will certainly be affected by this study.

SUMMARY OF TWIN STUDIES TO DATE

Certain problems and results of earlier investigations can be summarized as follows.

1. Only one of the examined *twin samples* satisfied Luxenburger's demand of nonselected, complete twin populations, namely Dalgaard and Kringlen's study of male twins born between 1921 and 1930 in Norway. Even there, the rate of sample reduction is for various reasons 32%.

2. The *zygosity diagnoses* seem in the majority of cases to be made most carefully on the basis of the best of methods available at the time of examination. There is no explanation regarding the method in the investigations of Rosanoff et al., but there can be no doubt that the diagnoses have been made on the basis of general similarity tests. The designation "probably dizygotic" need not mean that the unreliability is greater in this investigation than in others. However, some doubt has been expressed regarding the contamination of the zygosity groups; it has been suggested that some MZ pairs have been misclassified as DZs.

Blood group comparisons have been used by Kranz, Borgström, Yoshimasu, Tienari, and Dalgaard and Kringlen. Still, practical difficulties have sometimes created doubt in individual cases. In Borgström they result in the elimination of approximately half of the pairs.

3. The *concept of concordance* in all investigations starts from some kind of similarity concerning registered criminality, generally defined as entrance in an official criminal register. With Lange, however, the criterion is imposition of a sentence of imprisonment.

Important progress in the treatment of the concordance problem is found in Stumpfl's, Kranz's, and, particularly, Yoshimasu's studies. Yoshimasu used a graphical description as the basis for an evaluation and comparison of the course of the criminal careers.

4. *The main results* of all of these studies are summarized in Table 3.

It can be seen that there are considerable variations in the pairwise concordance rates (in monozygotic from 100% to 25.8% and in dizygotic from 81% to 0%). In the investigations with larger samples, the monozygotic concordance rates hover around 67%, with the exception of Dalgaard and Kringlen, who found a rate of 25.8%. For the DZs the dispersion is considerably larger. This gives corresponding variations in the distance between the concordance rates of monozygotic and dizygotic pairs. The difference is significant in Lange $(P < 0.002)$, Rosanoff, adult criminality $(P < 0.001)$, and Yoshimasu $(P < 0.01)$. If Kranz and Dalgaard and Kringlen are excluded, it can be determined that the pairwise concordance rate for monozygotic is about twice that of dizygotic twins.

It is important to note that the results of Stumpfl, Kranz, and Yoshimasu give clear indications that the criminality of concordant monozygotic pairs is considerably more alike than that of concordant dizygotic pairs.

Dalgaard and Kringlen's study can obviously not be omitted from consideration. On the basis of a representative sample, a most reliable criminal register, and the important classification of the sample by closeness of the co-twins, they have demonstrated that the difference in concordance rates between monozygotic and dizygotic pairs is not statistically significant. It should be pointed out, however, that they are in the same direction as for the other investigations.

5. In the *explanation* of the findings, Lange's method of presenting the problem and his manner of interpretation have by and large been accepted and followed: The greater concordance of the monozygotic twins is a result of genetic influence. The fundamental assumption of this interpretation, namely that the intrapair similarity in environment is just as large in dizygotic as in monozygotic, is discussed by several researchers. None have acknowledged, however, that the twin method, as an attempt to throw light on the criminological hereditary problem, has been compromised by this problem.

Lange ascribed importance to environmental influences, but with him as with his successors, general reflections have led to a reduction of the weight attributed to the environmental factors. Real reservations regarding the genetic interpretation have been made by Kranz and Yoshimasu.

Dalgaard and Kringlen's study changes the picture somewhat. A most critical attitude toward this investigation would, consequently, be appropriate. The reduction of the original population by one third, that is, 66 pairs, is not especially large because it includes 48 pairs where one of the twins died before the age of 15, six pairs where both died, and two pairs who were in fact not twins. However, the results of the study are so important that the completeness of the original twin population and the reliability of the criminal register ought to be carefully checked once again, or—even better—a new investigation of criminality in another Norwegian twin population carried through.

Although it is an extremely unlikely interpretation, one must be aware of the possibility that some special conditions exist in Norway (e.g., highly variable relevant environmental influences) that would dampen the expression of genetic factors (see discussion in Chapter 9).

MONOZYGOTIC TWINS REARED APART:
AN ADDENDUM

The study of twins who have been separated early in life and have grown up in different environments offers special opportunities for clarifying the relative importance of heredity as opposed to the environment in the occurrence and development of physical and mental characteristics.

Newman et al. (1937) investigated 50 monozygotic, nonseparated and 19 monozygotic, separated pairs. The separated pairs were between 11 and 59 years of age and comprised 7 male and 12 female pairs. They found greater differences in intelligence in the separated than in the nonseparated pairs, but no important differences with regard to personality. The differences in intelligence, however, were largely due to 4 pairs whose education had been of a very different kind.

Shields (1962) investigated 44 pairs of monozygotic twins in England who were separated in childhood. His control group of 44 monozygotic pairs who had grown up together was matched for sex and age, but not for domicile. In each of the two groups there were 15 male and 29 female pairs. On the basis of his study, which was predominantly psychologically and sociopsychologically orientated, he concluded *inter alia* the following: (a) Intelligence is only slightly influenced by environmental differences. Hereditary influence seems clearly established in that the separated pairs were at least as similar as those brought up together. (b) The personality differences of separated twins were greater than those of twins brought up together, but the differences were statistically significant only in the case of females and in twins below 45 years of age. Age at separation did not manifest itself in greater personality differences. (c) Early family environment does not play as important a part in the development of intelligence and personality as was previously supposed; other factors, especially genetic ones, are judged to be of somewhat greater importance.

Shields provided a lengthy discussion of the objections that might be raised against the methodology and the sampling techniques used in his study. Two major problems are that first, the separated twins volunteered after the importance of the study had been explained on television, and, second, wide cultural differences between the separated twins were exceptional. Shields is, however, of the opinion that the following two conclusions are justified:

1. Family environment can vary quite a lot without obscuring basic similarity in a pair of genetically identical twins.
2. Even monozygotic twins brought up together can differ quite widely.

Interpretation of these results, according to Shields, will depend on which proposition is emphasized.

Juel-Nielsen (1965) compared 12 Danish monozygotic pairs of twins (9 female and 3 male) who had been separated at an early age. His results point in approximately the same direction, but differ from the English study on a few points which are of special interest to criminological research. The two authors reached almost the same conclusions about intelligence. Intelligence scores are determined to a limited degree by environment and formal education, but are "quite predominantly determined by genetic factors." Juel-Nielsen does, however, place rather a different emphasis on the relative importance of hereditary and environmental factors in personality. The clinically observed differences in personality were greatest for social characteristics such as ability to cooperate; need for social contact; form of social contact; attitudes on cultural, religious, and social questions; and sexual, marital, and other family problems. Other important differences were found in the fields of ambition, aggression, and spontaneous emotional reactions, and also in life styles, as exemplified by choice of occupation, interests, and personal taste. Personality differences as measured by tests were less marked. All the differences can be readily understood by looking at the psychological and interpersonal relations of the twins from childhood onwards.

Juel-Nielsen concluded that environmental factors play a decisive role in the development of the normal personality. He did not, however, ignore the existence of similarities in twins who had grown up in environments that were psychologically "more or less different."

Serious psychiatric disorders in Juel-Nielsen's sample appeared only in three pairs, both partners being affected. Minor neurotic symptoms, psychosomatic, and character traits showed both marked intrapair differences and marked similarities. The differences have "a meaningful association" with environmental differences. The author has drawn no conclusion regarding the relative importance of heredity and environment. Both sets of factors are of importance.

CRIMINALITY IN MONOZYGOTIC TWINS REARED APART

The author of this chapter knows of eight monozygotic twin pairs, brought up apart, in which one or both co-twins are registered as criminals. There are probably more. (The author would be most grateful for information concerning MZ pairs with some kind of criminality and/or deviance where the twins were separated at an early date and reared apart).

Lange (1929) found only one pair (No. 6) of monozygotic concordant twins in his sample. The partners were separated at 8 years of age. Both truanted from school, became vagrant and intemperate, and had illegitimate children. Both twins were convicted, F. being convicted several times and receiving long sentences, the other, L., receiving only a disciplinary punishment for truancy and 1 week's imprisonment during adolescence for exceeding the limits of what is permissible in self-defense. At the age of 33, L. was well-adjusted, sober, a respectable worker, husband and church-goer, which according to Lange, was due to an excellent, strong-willed woman whom he married at the age of 25. F. continued his antisocial way of life, which was marked by drunkenness and "association with loose women." Both are described as weak-willed (*haltlos*). Lange believes that this "inherited" character trait is the explanation for their respective life histories.

In the sample of twins examined by Newman et al. (1937) there is one discordant pair (Case No. XVIII). R. was described as incorrigibly asocial or criminal, whereas the other, J., who was brought up by steady and industrious people in a small town, seemed to be socially well adjusted. R. grew up in a family that avoided regular work and he went to school only when he pleased. He did not like to work in a factory because he felt it was too much like slavery. Newman felt it would not be fair to probe further into his less creditable experiences. J. went through high school, worked regularly, and enjoyed reading "improving literature."

Schwesinger (1952) found a Mexican, monozygotic, concordant, female pair who had been separated at 9 months of age. Elvira remained with her mother and stepfather, whereas Esther lived with her step-father's stepmother. At the age of 9 years, Elvira moved to a town, while Esther remained in the desert. The two people responsible for their upbringing were very different in personality. The twins seemed to be well adjusted until the age of puberty. Both girls then left their homes, independently of each other, "took to the streets" and became involved in juvenile crime, being put into institutions several times. After this they returned to live with their mother. Esther married shortly after-wards. Elvira planned to marry, but did not. Both seemed to have set-tled down. Esther, however, soon left home, joined a group of drug addicts, and some time later was found dead in her hotel room after an overdose of morphine. Elvira was managing quite well at the time of the study. The period of follow-up after her release from the institution was, however, short. Esther had shown behavioral disturbances at an early age. Later these grew more pronounced. Her IQ was 11 points above that of her sister. She was less aggressive, more mature, and more stable emotionally, but less confident and more tense.

Yoshimasu (1961) found two pairs of monozygotic twins, one pair being concordant, and the other discordant. The concordant pair (Case No. XVL) had been reared by various relatives but were together be-tween the ages of 16 and 19, and attended the same school. Toyohiko had stolen while a boy, but his criminal career started around the age of 18. He served four prison sentences and cheated and tricked his family on several occasions. He drank to excess and was unstable and emotion-ally cold. He died in prison at the age of 25. Toyosako's criminality first began after World War II. At the time of the study, when he was aged 35, he had only a conviction for larceny. He was, however, divorced and vagrant. His behavior before the war was favorably described by most of his relatives and neighbors, apart from one uncle who was interviewed at a later date and who said that the brothers had had the same un-trustworthy character. Yoshimasu concludes that both twins, though reared in rather different families from birth, showed the influence of their heredity in their essential criminality.

Yoshimasu's case of Kazuo and Takao Sano (Case No. XXIV) is an illuminating example of the influence of the environment. The twins were separated soon after birth, Kazuo, who was weak, remaining with the parents, and Takao being sent to foster parents in the same town.

Takao grew up in a poor environment and had bad company as a child. After the death of his foster mother, his pilfering from the home and vagrancy increased, and he was placed under the child welfare authorities. Around the age of 15 the two twins lived together for a year in their parental home. Later, Takao was again placed in a foster home and had various jobs which he soon left. In connection with one of these jobs, he committed embezzlement. At the age of 17 he received his first sentence, for theft, and was later sentenced three more times for theft (the sentences being 2, 1, 2, and 3 years hard labor, respectively). He died of tuberculosis at the age of 34. Yoshimasu diagnosed him as weak-willed and lacking in perseverence and stability.

Kazuo grew up in a cultured atmosphere of his parents' home. When he was 14, his mother died, which was a serious shock for him. He suffered from tuberculosis and stayed home from school for a year. After some time, he left home and was away for a year, until his father found him and brought him home again. In the meantime, his father had married a pious, Christian, Japanese woman. She had considerable influence on Kazuo, who began to study theology. He became a pastor, married, and, when Yoshimasu met him, was living a happy family life with his wife and three children. After the war he became a grammar school teacher in Tokyo. He was well spoken of by all, but was described as weak-willed like his brother. Yoshimasu, however, considers the "striking differences of their environment from the time of their birth" as the explanation of "the remarkable difference of their social character."

Shields (1962) also described a concordant and a discordant pair. The first pair (S m 4) were separated immediately after birth, but were together for less than a year at the age of 5. H. grew up with his grandmother and N. was adopted. Both suffered as children from enuresis. Both were persistent truants and had repeatedly started fires. Both had stolen during puberty. H. was sent to an approved school. N. was placed on probation and later sent to an institution. Although both showed early signs of schizophrenia, their premorbid personalities were markedly similar. This accounted, to a major degree, for their concordance with respect to asociality and criminality.

The other pair (S m 8), Edward and Keith, were discordant. Their parents were both alcoholics. The children were put in an orphanage, but were separated around the age of 2 because they quarrelled continuously. Several attempts were made to put them together again, but they soon had to be separated because of their quarrels and fights. This went on until the age of 20. After World War II, however, they met at least once every 1 or 2 years.

Both drank a lot. Both were described as hot-tempered, had difficulties in social contacts, and preferred to be alone. Keith was occupationally unstable; Edward was unstable in his family life and married twice; Keith's wife was very protective.

Keith stammered as a child, although this later markedly improved. He suffered a concussion at the age of 2 and was often ill during childhood and at later times. At the time of the study, however, Edward was the less well-equipped physically, suffering from hypochondria. Edward worked mostly in towns, whereas Keith spent much time working in the country. Keith coped better and became a foreman in a factory.

Edward admitted himself that he had always behaved badly, run away from home, played truant from school, and sought out bad company. At 19 he received a conditional sentence for breaking and entering. He was also charged with auto theft, but the case was closed. He has never been to prison, although he has said that he would like to see the inside of one, "try anything once." Keith was never convicted.

Shields concludes that Keith's stammer and wife and their respective occupations seem to account for some of the interesting differences between the twins.

Juel-Nielsen (1965) gives a detailed description of a monozygotic, discordant pair (Case No. V), who were separated not later than 9 months after birth and reared far apart in very different environments. Robert was adopted by a boatswain in Copenhagen, Kaj by a groom and trainer on a large estate in Jutland. They met for the first time at the age of 40. At 45 Kaj was a commercial traveller living in one of the suburbs of Copenhagen, and Robert was a draughtsman living in a provincial town on the coast of North Zealand. Kaj was sentenced to 8 months' imprisonment at the age of 19 for breaking and entering a private dwelling. He had previously been occupationally unstable and tended to steal. Later, charges of theft, collaboration in Denmark with the Germans, embezzlement, theft of 5000 Danish kroner, and so on, were all dropped for lack of evidence, but he was fined for violating rationing ordinances. Robert had no convictions.

Juel-Nielsen emphasizes important similarities in the patterns of their lives. Both had experienced great difficulties in adjusting to work and both were married three times. The main difference consists of the predominantly external conflicts of the criminal partner as opposed to the predominantly internal ones of the other. Both were classified as "characterologically deviating personalities." Kaj was more "psychopathic," whereas Robert was predominantly "neurotic" or "character-neurotic." Both were vacillating, imaginative, unstable, and unreliable. There were considerable differences in their childhood environments which may explain their personality differences and their attitudes toward authority and society.

SUMMARY

The total available cases of monozygotic separated pairs of twins who displayed criminal behavior thus comprises only eight pairs of which one pair (Lange, No. 6) was not separated until the age of 8. Of these eight pairs, four were concordant, four discordant.

The type of concordance used by Lange was almost of a formal nature. In one of Yoshimasu's pairs concordance was also limited. In one of Shield's pairs, it was closely associated with schizoid personality traits, both twins showing clear signs of schizophrenia. The most interesting case as far as the question of the association of criminality with genetic factors is concerned, is Schwesinger's pair. This pair, however, was not completely separated until 9 years of age. The reciprocal, apparently direct, criminogenic influence began when they were 17.

In the discordant pairs, clear manifestations of criminality were found in one twin of Yoshimasu's second pair and in the pair studied by Juel-Nielsen. Minor criminality was found in Shield's second pair. Newman et al.'s pair is difficult to evaluate.

The early environment of one twin does not appear to be radically different from that of the other twin, even though very different constellations of personality may be distinguished in the primary groups of the individual. Some of the more common background factors are also clearly different.

CONCLUSION

No study carried out up to now can be said to have provided conclusive evidence of the dominance of genetic over environmental factors in the genesis of criminality. Given the nature of the genetic and environmental facts, it is still an appropriate *a priori* hypothesis that *heredity and environment always interact in a dynamic fashion to bring about and shape criminal behavior*, and that both the mutual interaction and the mutual strength of the two factors form a continuous dimension for all persons and situations. It is the task of future research to establish the details of the correlations in this field.

Thus, in general, it must be maintained that criminality, defined as a sociolegal concept, can only be studied from a genetic point of view as long as it is closely associated with a well-defined somatic or psychological state.

Chapter 5

A preliminary study of criminality among twins

Karl O. Christiansen

INTRODUCTION AND METHODOLOGY

This chapter reports on a pilot study of crime among twins in Denmark. It utilized 3586 unselected twin pairs from the Danish Twin Register (Harvald and Hauge, 1965). The pilot study is being expanded to include all twins born in Denmark from 1890 to 1920, a total of about 13,500 twin pairs. This report of the pilot data aims at an analysis of concordance in relation to social background factors such as birth year, birth place, father's social class, and seriousness of crime. (See Chapter 4 for previous studies of criminality among twins.)

The twin method

To evaluate the results of criminological twin studies, the student must consider four questions: (a) the validity and reliability of the diagnosis of zygosity, (b) the content of the concept of concordance with respect to criminality, (c) the representativeness of the twin sample under investigation, and (d) the open or tacit assumptions leading to conclusions concerning the interplay of environment and heredity. I shall make a few general remarks about these problems.

(a) *The diagnosis of zygosity* was rather dubious for some twin pairs in the older studies. Today zygosity can be determined with a high degree of reliability through blood tests and the like. In the present study the zygosity was determined by means of a modified similarity test based on a questionnaire. The validity of this method was checked by comparing diagnoses for 165 same-sexed pairs with the results of a thorough examination of their blood and serum groups. Seven pairs were originally diagnosed as "uncertain;" the blood and serum tests made it probable that four of them were MZ. Of the remaining 158 pairs, one among 78 pairs classified as MZ pairs, and four among 80 called DZ had probably been given an erroneous diagnosis. Harvald and Hauge (1965) concluded: "Thus it turns out that our diagnostic procedure is sufficiently reliable."

It should be underlined that the diagnosis of zygosity was not known to the staff of the criminological study (including the author) until the coding and punching of the data were completed. The diagnoses were never entered in the case histories, only on the punch cards and the magnetic tapes.

(b) *The concept of concordance* varies from author to author, even if it is taken in its most formal sense, because "recorded in the official penal register" incongruities may exist. Definitional difficulties will not disappear even when concordance is defined more narrowly. Changes in the penal code over the years, as well as differences in the administration of justice, can well produce noncomparable results. Old offenses that correspond to similarly named criminal acts may in a new penal code be defined differently. Similarly, prison sentences of the same length do not necessarily mean that they correspond to penal sanctions of the same gravity in various jurisdictions within the same country. However, no radical changes seem to have taken place during the period covered by this study in Denmark.

In this study a number of different criminographic indices are compared, such as type of offense, seriousness of sanction, number of sanctions, maximum penalty, and criminal career.

In the following presentation offenses are classified in two main categories:

(1) Crime proper, defined as an act that has been sanctioned by some kind of conditional or unconditional deprivation of liberty; it includes juvenile delinquency but not acts committed below the age of criminal responsibility, which in Denmark is 15 years. Such acts are, as a rule, offenses against the penal code. In the following they are called crimes.

(2) Minor offense, defined as an act that has been sanctioned only by fines or less serious reactions, such as warnings. Such acts are as a rule offenses against the special laws.

When the seriousness of the offense is not specified, and when crime and minor offenses are combined into one category, the term *offense* or *criminality* is used.

Concordance includes three forms of similarity: (a) Twins are called concordant with respect to crime when both twins are registered for crimes (and either or both co-twins, perhaps in addition for offenses). (b) They are called concordant with respect to minor offenses when both partners are registered for minor offenses. (c) They are called concordant with respect to offenses when one of the twins is registered for crimes and the other for minor offenses.

Because the risk period of the twins is very long (35-65 years), changes in law and in the practice of criminal policy have created some alterations in the definition of the criminal group. Because the two twins of a pair are of the same age, it seems reasonable to believe that such changes must have affected the partners equally.

(c) Only one of the previous studies is based on a complete, unselected *sample* of twins. Borgström (1939) intended to collect an unbiased sample, but he did not succeed. Yoshimasu (1961) also made efforts to locate a complete series, but according to his own opinion the attempt was not successful. Dalgaard and Kringlen (1976) apparently succeeded in tracing all criminal twins in a complete sample from the Norwegian twin register.

Searching for criminal twins haphazardly may run a serious risk of an overrepresentation of concordant pairs because the probability of their being brought to the attention of the investigator is greater than with the less conspicious discordant pairs. As disclosed by the figures in some of the older investigations, more monozygotic than same-sexed dizygotic pairs have been found, although the opposite should be expected.

The basic twin sample analyzed in this study is, as mentioned, drawn from the Danish Twin Register, which was established primarily to obtain a complete sample of twins that would permit studies of "the relative importance of genetic determinants in normal and abnormal characters." It was founded in the 1950s by Bent Harvald and Mogens Hauge (Harvald and Hauge, 1965).

The Danish Twin Register includes virtually all twins born in Denmark between 1870 and 1920. It is based on the local birth registers kept by the church authorities in each of the approximately 2000 Danish parishes, data from the register of death in the same parish, and a special death register in Copenhagen; from the public register of the municipalities; from the local probate courts; and from information from relatives and other sources. It has been possible to trace a majority of the twins. Because it proved difficult to gather information about the causes of death and the zygosity diagnoses for twins dying at an early age, pairs broken by death before the age of 6 years were left out. However, "the working material comprises in principle all twin pairs born in Denmark within the years 1870-1920 in which neither partner is known to have died prior to the day when he or she attained the age of six years."

The basic sample analyzed in this study is drawn from the Danish Twin Register. It comprises 3586 twin pairs born in the eastern half of Denmark, that is, the Danish islands east of the Little Belt, between 1881 and 1910, in which both twins were alive at least until the age of 15 years.

Twin births from 1870-1880 were omitted from this pilot study because the Danish penal registers were not established until 1896. Members of the older generations who only committed minor offenses when they were young have not been included in the registers. Material for 1911-1920 was not yet complete when the criminological sample for this pilot study was derived from the Twin Register. The reduction of the geographical area was not complete for Jutland at that time. Twin pairs broken by death or emigration before the age of 15 years were omitted, because 15 years is the lower age limit of criminal responsibility and registration in Denmark. Consequently, the basic criminological sample consists of 3586 pairs which—within the limits defined above—must be characterized as an unselected twin population.

Criminality register search. For each of the 7172 twins three sources of criminality information were searched:

1. *National Police Register (Rigsregistratur).* This register maintains a national record of police contacts with the Danish population. For many minor types of criminality that do not lead to a court conviction, this register is the only possible source. Delinquent acts committed before the age of 15, traffic offenses, and a variety of minor offenses associated with alcohol can be ascertained only in this register. It also contains a record of the more serious crimes. It was established in 1930; for earlier years it includes a collection of local registers.

2. *Penal Register (Strafferegister).* This register consists of 57 archives that preserve a record of violations of the penal code resulting in court decisions against individuals born in the local district of the individual archive. From this register one can determine the sections of the laws which an individual has been convicted of violating and the precise sentence obtained. It was established in 1896.

3. *Police Report, Court Documents, and the like (Straffeakter).* These consist of all the reports prepared by the police in a criminal case, describing the crime in some detail, the police charge, data on the background and the situation leading up to the crime, and certain data about the family and the social conditions of the offender. They also include all the documents from the prosecuting authority, evidence from witnesses

and other sources, psychiatric statements, if any, the decisions of the court, and the grounds of the court judgments. Finally, information exists about how the sentence was implemented, and often there are short statements from the probation or prison authorities.

There are several important characteristics of the Danish law enforcement process that relate to its statutory uniformity regarding treatment of the offender and sentencing by the court. Police officers are legally *required* to report cases if they have a suspect. They are not permitted to make judgements in such matters. An elaborate court appeals system is aimed at achieving national uniformity of sentencing. The social status of a Danish police officer is comparatively high; they are regarded as being incorruptible.

Of the 7172 twins, 926 individuals belonging to 799 pairs were registered in one or both of these registers for crime, delinquency, or minor offenses. In 467 pairs, one or both of the twins were sentenced to a conditional or unconditional deprivation of liberty. These registers, used jointly, constitute the best source of registered delinquency and crime in Denmark, as far as type of offense, convictions, and so forth are concerned. The number of registered cases not included in any of the registers must be very low, probably only a small percentage, but, of course, a somewhat higher percentage in the older than in the younger generations. There is no reason to believe that the loss should be higher among twins than among other citizens, if anything the opposite would probably be the case. It is, however, more important that the two co-twins of a pair will have the same probability of being registered for an asocial act resulting in apprehension.

(d) The fundamental assumption underlying conclusions about heredity and environment that have usually been drawn from criminological twin studies is that the relevant environment of the two twins is (and has been) equally similar or equally different, regardless of zygosity. Stated in another way: intrapair environmental variations must be the same for MZ co-twins as they are for DZ co-twins. It is open to serious doubts whether this condition is fulfilled with respect to social behavior (Gottesman and Shields, 1972).

In the first place, it must be taken for granted that certain differences between twins and nontwins exist. Prenatal factors, differences in nutrition, premature birth, prenatal death, birth complications, and the like are supposed to be some of the conditioning factors. According to Tienari (1963) these differences are strongly connected with a tendency to develop a dominance-submissiveness relationship, which is more frequent and more pronounced among twins than among ordinary siblings. He also found that birth order and birth weight had no particular significance for differences observable later in life. Dencker (1963) conversely claimed that "dominance is due to a congenital difference of physical nature, of which one manifestation is a higher birth weight."

In the second place, it is generally accepted that the experienced environment of MZ twins is more similar than that of DZ twins. Since von Bracken (1933), a number of studies have confirmed this assumption. Among the various factors that have been considered to be of importance, a few are mentioned here. Monozygotic pairs tend on the whole to establish much more similar environments than dizygotics do; they spend considerably longer time together, follow each other to school, do their lessons together, and choose more often than dizygotics the same friends. According to their parents, the MZs were more closely attached to and dependent on each other than DZs. Their level of education and their choice of occupation are also more similar. They are more satisfied with being twins, and their index of devotion to each other is greater than among DZs (Husen, 1959). MZ twins cooperate, DZ twins compete; von Bracken (1933) speaks of a "tendency towards differentiation in dizygotic twins." Zazzo (1960a, 1960b) has mentioned that the mothers of dizygotic twins are on the average 2 years older than the mothers of monozygotic; consequently, the twins are placed later in the succession of siblings, that is, in more variable surroundings than monozygotic twins.

Defenders of the classical genetic interpretation of the results of the twin method now and then refer to factors which might imply that the far-reaching similarity of monozygotic twins is veiled. Most important are certain organic conditions in the natal phase, birth damages, later cerebral disturbances, and illnesses. Bronson Price (1935) attaches great importance to the mutual circulation of monochoric twins during gestation. "If as is here assumed, the intra-pair differences are greater in monochorial than in dichorial MZ cases, then the MZ differences observed in larger scale studies are due mainly to the presence of monochorial pairs among the MZ group."

Scarr (1968) found that MZ co-twins were "somewhat more similar than DZ pairs in their behaviors and in the parental treatment they received." She considers this to be a result of both genetic and environmental factors, and poses the question: But are MZ co-twins more similar mainly because of environmental pressures for similarity? Or is it a reflection of a greater genetic similarity, resulting in phenotypic similarity with respect to behavior? She compares MZ and DZ pairs who are misclassified by their parents as DZ and MZs, respectively, and finds that it is the correct classification that determines similarities and dissimilarities with respect to social maturity, dressing, early behavior problems, and early development. The data confirm the hypothesis that "genetic relatedness of the twins determines the similarity of parental treatment." This, however, does not prove that the degree of similarity in the treatment the twin receives from others, for instance teachers and peers, likewise is a consequence of the genetically determined similarity, and not of the perceived similarity. Most associates do not classify twins in terms of zygosity.

Burlingham (1952) on the basis of careful observations of three monozygotic twins explains their pronounced tendency of identification as a reaction against the strong feeling of mutual jealousy.

The fundamental aspects are divergent, but the confusion is not complete. Being a criminologist, I shall not commit myself by pronouncing judgement on this and related matters. It appears to me that a prudent point of departure might run as follows:

The twin method can throw light on the question of the interplay between environment and personality, in which personality, as a phenotype, must be considered to be a product of heredity and environmental influences. A greater frequency of concordance among MZ than among DZ twins means only that (more) similar heredity factors and/or (more) similar environmental (prenatal, natal and postnatal) conditions give a greater likelihood of similarity in social behavior than (more) disparate hereditary and/or (more) disparate environmental conditions.

Because the environment in a certain sense plays a double role, one might expect that the frequency of concordance among MZ as well as among DZ twins varies with environmental conditions. This very general hypothesis is examined below.

To draw conclusions from twin studies regarding the hereditary and environmental factors that play a role in the breaching of social norms would require an extra prerequisite that could be paraphrased from Gottesman and Shields (1972). If genes are important in the manifestation of criminality, MZ co-twins should be affected more often than DZ co-twins. Such a result proves the importance of genotype under two conditions: either that the MZ twins as such are not especially predisposed to criminality and/or that the environments of MZ twins are not systematically more alike than those of DZ twins in respects that can be shown to be of etiological significance for criminality. It must, however, be stated that it is extremely difficult to demonstrate that the second of these two necessary, *negative* conditions are fulfilled.

RESULTS AND DISCUSSION

The 3586 pairs were identified and the criminality registers searched. As mentioned above, a registration was found in at least one member of 799 pairs. Concordance rates were computed.

Table 1

Number of Twin Pairs (N), Criminal Pairs (Crim), Concordant (Conc) and discordant (Disc) Pairs, Pairwise and Proband Concordance Rates (PWCR and PRCR), according to Zygosity.

	MALE-MALE PAIR		FEMALE-FEMALE PAIR		MALE-FEMALE PAIR		UNCERTAIN ZYGOSITY	
	MZ	DZ	MZ	DZ	Male Criminal	Female Criminal	Male-Male Pair	Female-Female Pair
N	325	611	328	593	1547 [a]	1547 [a]	112	70
Crim	71	120	14	27	172 [a]	24 [a]	40	6
Conc	25	15	3	2	6 [a]	6 [a]	10	0
Disc	46	105	11	25	166	18	30	6
PWCR	.35	.13	.21	.08	.04	.25	.25	.00
PRCR	.52	.22	.35	.14			.40	.00

[a] Persons.

Concordance rates

The main results of the pilot study appear in Table 1. The pairwise rate of concordance, which has been used in all the previous criminological twin studies, is for MZ males, 35%; for DZ males, 13%; for MZ females, 21%; for DZ females, 8%. The differences between MZ and DZ pairs agree with earlier findings insofar as the concordance rate is higher among MZ than DZ pairs, but there is a clear discrepancy with respect to the absolute concordance rates. Although in the older studies about two thirds of the MZ pairs and about one third of the DZ pairs are concordant, this is the case for only one third of the MZ pairs and one eighth of the DZ pairs in the present study. It is also worthy of note that male MZs have a concordance rate that is almost 3 times higher than the DZs, the corresponding relationship being the same for females.

The lower concordance rate in the Danish sample deserves to be emphasized and, if possible, explained. However, first of all one must examine whether this result is reliable.

There is (at least) one possibility that the composition of the basic material has contributed to the lower concordance rates in this study. It appears (see Table 1) that there are 40 male-male twin pairs with uncertain zygosity diagnosis, among which ten are concordant. Harvald and Hauge judge that most of the ten are probably MZ pairs. On the other hand—judged from our concordance rates —it is most unlikely that all the concordant pairs should be MZs and all the discordant DZs. If, however, we accept this hypothesis as the extreme possibility, the concordance rates for males become 43.2 and 10.0%, respectively. This gives a greater difference between MZ and DZ pairs. These rates are still considerably below the average rate of former investigations, among which the lowest for MZs (60.6%) was found by Yoshimasu (1941).

Thus it seems safe to conclude that the problem we are facing is a real one. Taking into consideration how the Danish sample has been derived, it seems more reasonable to reformulate the question, and ask: What is the explanation of the *higher* concordance rates in the older twin studies? The answer which immediately presents itself is that none of these studies is based on complete or representative samples of twin pairs. The Danish material—as has already been mentioned—comes closer to Luxenburger's (1938) ideal of an unselected twin sample.

In the criminological twin investigations the degree of concordance is expressed by *the pairwise concordance rate*, which is defined as the ratio of concordant pairs to all criminal pairs, that is,

$$\frac{C}{C+D}$$

where C is the number of concordant pairs and D the number of discordant pairs.

The similarity with respect to crime may also be expressed by *the proband concordance rate*, which is the conditional frequency of one twin being criminal when it is known that the other *is* criminal. It is defined as

$$\frac{C + X}{C + X + D}$$

where X is the number of pairs in the sample represented by two independently ascertained index cases. In the present study, where every single twin is checked in the penal register, X is identical with the number of concordant pairs because in such pairs both partners will be found independently of each other. The conditional frequency can therefore be expressed as

$$\frac{2C}{2C + D}$$

For each zygosity group: monozygotic males—MMMZ; dizygotic males—MMDZ; monozygotic females—FFMZ; dizygotic females—FFDZ; different-sexed pairs—MF; unknown or uncertain male pairs—MMUU; unknown or uncertain female pairs—FFUU, as well as for a number of subgroups, tabulations of the type illustrated by two examples in Table 2 have been prepared.

Table 2

Cross Tabulation of Registration of Male Twin Pairs for Minor Offenses and Crimes

| | *MMMZ* Twin I | | | | | *MMDZ* Twin I | | | |
	No offense	Minor	Crime	Total		No offense	Minor	Crime	Total
TWIN II No offense	194	20	16	230	TWIN II No offense	420	33	43	496
Minor	29	11	6	46	Minor	34	4	7	45
Crime	16	8	25	49	Crime	44	11	15	70
Total	239	39	47	325	Total	498	48	65	611

It may be noted that the number of twin pairs registered for crime is for MZs $16 + 8 + 25 + 6 + 16 = 71$, and the number of concordant pairs 25, which gives a pairwise concordant rate of 35.2%. For DZs it is $44 + 11 + 15 + 7 + 43 = 120$, with 15 concordant. This gives a pairwise concordance rate of 12.5%. The MZs' rate is 2.8 times higher than DZs'. The difference is significant ($p < .001$); among females, with pairwise concordance rates of 21.4% for MZs and 7.4% for DZs, the difference is not significant. The number of criminals is, however, rather small.

The proband concordance rate is

$$MZs = \frac{25 + 25}{25 + 25 + 46} = 0.521$$

and for

$$Dzs = \frac{15 + 15}{15 + 15 + 105} = 0.222$$

Here MZs have a concordance rate 2.3 times higher than DZs.

The results for all the seven zygosity groups presented in Table 1 are based on similar tabulations and calculations.

It appears from Table 1 that (1) MZ male and female pairs have a higher pairwise and proband concordance rates than the corresponding DZ pairs, (2) female MZ pairs have lower concordance rates than male MZ pairs, and the same holds true of DZ pairs, (3) male-female (MF) pairs have lower rates than same-sexed pairs, (4) male-male zygosity uncertain (MMUU) pairs have rates between MZ and DZ males, and (5) none among six criminal female-female zygosity uncertain (FFUU) pairs are concordant.

The pairwise concordant rate differences are significant for male MZ and DZ ($p < .001$), and MMMZ and MF ($p < .001$), for MMDZ and MF ($p < .01$), and for FFMZ and MF ($p < .02$). The pairwise concordant rate for MMUU is neither significantly lower than for MMMZ ($p > .2$), nor significantly higher than for MMDZ ($p > .05$).

THE TWIN COEFFICIENT

To evaluate the influence of background factors on the concordance rates in various subgroups of twins it is necessary to compare the concordant pairs with the total twin population if the trait occurs with a relatively high frequency, as is the case of crime. The most expedient procedure is probably to relate the proband concordance rate to the expected crime rates in the same population.

The expected criminality rate (ECrR) in a group of concordant and discordant twins is

$$\frac{2C + D}{2S}$$

where C and D have the same meaning as above and S is the total number of criminal and noncriminal pairs in the sample. The ratio between the proband concordance rate and the expected crime rate of a group of twin pairs,

$$\frac{PRCR}{ECrR}$$

is a measure of specific properties attached to *the twin situation*, determined by similarities with respect to inheritance (gene-overlap), the general and specific social background, and, in cases in which the twins have committed their offenses together, maybe also some situational factors. It answers the question: How much does the probability of crime increase for a twin (as compared to the general crime rate of the twin group), provided the partner is criminal? In the following this ratio is called *the twin coefficient*.

For the zygosity groups mentioned above, the introduction of the twin coefficient changes the general picture seen in Table 1.

It appears from Table 3 that (1) the twin coefficient is higher in male and female MZ pairs than in the corresponding DZ pairs, (2) this coefficient is higher in female MZ and DZ pairs than in the corresponding male groups, (3) MF pairs have lower twin coefficients than same-sexed pairs, (4) MMUU pairs have an even lower twin coefficient than have MMDZ pairs.

The comparison of the twin coefficients reverses some of the results of the comparison of concordance rates: in female twins criminality is more inheritable and/or more directly or indirectly communicable than male criminality. The comparison of MMUU and MMDZ pairs, likewise, leads to a conclusion that is rather different from the corresponding conclusions based on comparison of the concordance rates.

Such results illustrate how important it is to relate the concordance rates to the frequency of crime within the various subgroups of twins. This is even more obvious from the analysis in the following section.

Table 3

Number of Twin Pairs (N), Criminal Pairs (Crim), Concordant Pairs (Conc), Proband Concordance Rates (PRCR), Expected Crime Rates (ECrR) and Twin Coefficients (TwCoef), according to Zygosity.

| | MALE-MALE PAIR | | FEMALE-FEMALE PAIR | | MALE-FEMALE PAIR | | UNCERTAIN ZYGOSITY | |
	MZ	DZ	MZ	DZ	Male Criminal	Female Criminal	Male-Male Pair	Female-Female Pair
N	325	611	328	593	1547 [a]	1547 [a]	112	70
Crim	71	120	14	27	172 [a]	24 [a]	40	6
Conc	25	15	3	2	6 [a]	6 [a]	10	0
PRCR	.52	.22	.35	.14	.04	.25	.40	.00
ECrR	.15	.11	.03	.03	.11	.02	.22	.04
TwCoef	3.53	2.01	13.62	5.64	2.25	2.25	1.79	

[a] Persons.

THE TWIN COEFFICIENT
IN VARIOUS POPULATION GROUPS

A very general hypothesis was advanced earlier, according to which concordance differs in different population groups. Having introduced the concept "twin coefficient," it is possible to be a little more specific and formulate it in this manner: The twin coefficient is a function of genetic factors (gene-overlap), similarities in past experiences (which together with genetic factors have molded the personalities of the co-twins), situational factors, and certain characteristics of the population group to which the twins belong. It is the influence of the last variable that is examined in the following.

In the analyses which follow, the 70 female pairs of unknown zygosity (with only six criminals) have been omitted.

Birth year

The population may be classified into two subgroups: pairs born 1881-1895, and pairs born 1896-1910, the borderline being arbitrary. It is assumed that during a span of 30 years a number of changes took place in the material and nonmaterial culture, and it cannot be excluded that some of them may have influenced the rates and forms of criminality. These include changes in technology, politics, the economical and occupational patterns, education, alcohol habits, the general attitude towards breakers of the social norms, and so on.

Table 4

The Twin Coefficient for Crime and Offenses, according to Zygosity and Birth Year

	1881–1895		1896–1910	
	Crime	Offenses	Crime	Offenses
MMMZ	3.88	2.31	3.29	1.79
MMDZ	2.37	2.20	1.80	1.54
FFMZ	12.74	8.47	12.44	7.03
FFDZ	10.32	8.67	4.74	1.63
MF	2.86	1.39	0.40	0.66
MMUU	2.21	0.94	1.38	0.74

The results of the analysis are presented in Table 4. It appears from Table 4 that the twin coefficients for crime as well as for offenses are higher among pairs born 1881-1895 than among those born 1896-1910 in all six subgroups. This means that the specific population factors that influence the twin coefficient have themselves been affected by the cultural changes around the turn of the century in such a way that the coefficient has decreased. The differences between the zygosity groups are by and large the same within the two generations, and the same as those shown in Table 3.

Birth place

The material is classified in twin pairs born in towns and twin pairs born in rural districts; towns comprise greater Copenhagen plus provincial towns, and rural districts comprise the rest of the country. The basic assumption corresponds to the assumption cited under "birth year:" a number of cultural differences between the two types of geographical area may have influenced criminality in the two areas in different ways.

The results of the analysis are presented in Table 5. Here we find that the twin coefficient for crime is higher among rural-born than among urban-born twin pairs in five of the subgroups. The exception is female monozygotic pairs, where the coefficients are 12.82 and 13.68, respectively. With respect to offenses, we find three exceptions to the main result, namely MMDZ, FFMZ, and MMUU pairs; whereas three out of

Table 5

The Twin Coefficent for Crime and Offenses, According to Zygosity and Birth Place

	TOWN		RURAL	
	Crime	Offenses	Crime	Offenses
MMMZ	3.33	1.95	3.79	2.00
MMDZ	1.67	1.79	2.67	1.34
FFMZ	13.68	7.98	12.82	6.25
FFDZ	5.28	3.29	8.22	3.70
MF	0.82	0.76	1.14	0.90
MMUU	1.50	1.04	2.08	0.70

the six subgroups show the highest twin coefficients among rural born. Because special weight must be attached to the results regarding crime, it may be concluded that specific population factors in the two geograph-ical areas differ in such a way that the coefficient is higher among rural-born than among town-born twin pairs. The differences between the zygosity groups are, again, by and large the same within the two differ-ent cultural areas compared here, and the same as the differences shown in Table 3.

Social status of father

The basic criterion of the classification according to social status is Svalastoga's nine-point prestige scale (1959). The dividing line is drawn between what is here called "higher social classes," that is, the upper-upper, middle-upper, lower-upper, upper-middle, and middle-middle classes, and "lower social classes," that is, the lower-middle, upper-lower, middle-lower and lower-lower classes. Omitted are 125 pairs in which the social class of the father is unknown. Again, the assumption is that cultural differences between the upper and the lower classes may influence the crime pattern of the two classes in different ways.

The results are shown in Table 6. In five out of the six subgroups the twin coefficient for crime is higher among pairs from higher social class homes than among pairs from lower social class homes. The exception is MF pairs. The same holds true for offenses (without exception). The differences for the six subgroups defined by zygosity and sex are by and large the same, and they correspond with the distribution in Table 3.

Table 6

**The Twin Coefficient for Crime and Offenses,
According to Zygosity and Social Class of Father**

	HIGHER		LOWER	
	Crime	Offenses	Crime	Offenses
MMMZ	3.79	2.56	3.27	1.83
MMDZ	3.43	1.82	1.51	1.67
FFMZ	20.00	12.15	14.81	8.62
FFDZ	50.00	6.31	3.57	3.88
MF	0.72	0.84	1.11	0.71
MMUU	2.56	1.08	1.62	0.78

A POSSIBLE EXPLANATION

The foregoing analyses have clearly demonstrated that the specific twin milieu, which is a product of inheritance and environment, influences twin pairs of different zygosity as well as pairs with different environmental backgrounds differently. Certain subgroups of twins depend more strongly on the twin milieu than do their counterparts. This information is summarized in Table 7.

Table 7

Key Diagram of Subgroups of Twin Pairs, According to Size of Twin Coefficient

Higher Twin Coefficient	Lower Twin Coefficient
Monozygotic	Dizygotic
Females	Males
Females in male-female pairs	Males in male-female pairs
Same-sexed twins	Different-sexed twins
Older generations	Younger generations
Rural born	Urban born
Father: higher social class	Father: lower social class
Crime	Offenses

To find an explanation of these differences we might start by looking to urban and rural crime. Investigations from a number of different countries and periods have shown that the crime frequency is much higher in towns than in the country. The explanation for this difference has been sought in various psychological and social factors. Towns, and especially the high-delinquency areas of the big cities, are supposed to attract a negative selection of the population, people who are mentally abnormal or deviant, for example, the mentally defective and mentally ill as well as psychopaths and neurotics.

In ecological studies a great number of sociologists have pointed to the economically determined conditions of such underprivileged areas— poor education and housing and high rates of delinquency, illness, infant mortality, and so on.

Sellin, in his well-known book *Culture Conflict and Crime* (1938), discusses a similar problem in terms of culture conflict, that is, conflict of cultural norms, which undoubtedly characterizes most societies with high crime and delinquency rates, and, more specifically, in terms of group resistance to crime. This last concept seems particularly relevant to our problem.

The group's resistance against breaches of the accepted norms is partly expressed through legal sanctions, but conduct norms are not necessarily embodied in law. Conduct norms also come from institutions such as the family, the church, and colleagues and are effective through the actual attitude of the community to the individuals, through ridicule, estrangement, ostracism, and the like.

The group's resistance against criminality is determined by the strength of the sanctions connected with conduct norms. They raise a barrier against violations.

Group resistance is, however, experienced differently by different people, depending on the internalization of the norm and on the existence of conflicting norms absorbed from other groups. The psychological experience of group resistance can often be reduced in a community with a heterogeneous population.

Group resistance may also be described in purely sociological terms as the group's publicly expressed disapproval of violation of the norm. Group resistance, then, depends on at least the following conditions: (a) the number of persons in the group who directly or indirectly disapprove of the violation of the norm, (b) the emotional strength of resistance of such individuals, (c) the stronger or weaker organization of the persons who take part in the group resistance, and (d) the way in which the disapproval is expressed (privately, informally or publicly, officially).

In this sense group resistance may be regarded as a sociological term combining several closely integrated social factors that influence the rate of criminality.

Strong group resistance involves—all other things being equal—a smaller number of criminal acts, and weak group resistance, a greater number of criminal acts.

Group resistance also seems to have an influence on the selection of persons who become criminals. Sellin recommends that criminological research concentrate on persons who have violated norms: (a) with high resistance potentials, (b) incorporated as personality elements, (c) that possess strong emotional tone. "Offenders who have overcome the greatest and most comprehensive group resistance probably disclose more clearly than others the type of personalities which are important to our aims of research."

Consequently we may postulate: Strong group resistance involves—all other things being equal—a greater frequency of socially or psychologically deviating persons among those who under such circumstances become criminals, and weak group resistance involves a selection of offenders who socially and psychologically come closer to the average population. This implies that strong group resistance is more easily overcome by persons who because of *mental* deviations feel the resistance less strongly, or by persons who because of unfortunate *social* conditions are living under special pressure.

When the twin coefficient for certain subgroups of twins is higher than in certain other subgroups, then the co-twins will be more alike than in subgroups in which the twin coefficient is low. This is true, not only with respect to criminal behavior, but also with respect to background factors. Therefore, we may expect that the subgroups with high twin coefficients (placed in the left column in Table 7) have acted against a greater group resistance than their counterparts (in the right column). Is this assumption founded in reason or, even better, in facts?

The answer must, as far as the author can see for most of the subgroups, quite clearly be in the affirmative. The resistance against deviating behavior, and particularly crime, is considerably higher in the country than in towns, within the older generations than within the younger, in the higher social classes than in the lower, for women than for men, and higher against crime than against minor offenses. It may suffice to refer to the outcome of a few investigations that support this assumption.

Inghe (1941) in a study based on forensic psychiatric statements on persons convicted of various crimes in Sweden concluded that mental deviations of convicted persons are found more frequently in women than in men, in the old than in the young, and in urban than in rural populations, among sexual offenders and persons convicted of the more serious crimes of violence and arson rather than among the other types of offenders.

In a similar way Dahlberg (1948) has proved, also from Swedish data, that frequency of mental deviations is higher among criminals in the country than in the towns, among women than among men, and in the age groups where the risk of criminality is small, i.e. among older offenders than in high risk age groups, that is, among juvenile delinquents.

In a study of Danish citizens who during World War II collaborated with the Germans, a similar connection between group resistance, frequency of collaboration, and frequency of social deviations in various population groups was disclosed. Group resistance toward collaboration with the Germans was least among the German minority in South Jutland, greater among Danish Nazis, and greatest, although not complete, among the rest of the population. Corresponding to this, the greatest frequency of male collaborators was found within the German minority (25%); it was less among the Nazis (10%); and least among the rest of the population (0.4%). On the other hand, the relative frequency of social deviations among the collaborators grew with increasing group resistance. Measured by illegitimacy, broken homes, educational level, occupational training, unemployment, increase of income by recruiting as collaborators, civil status, previous criminal career, and social status, it was least among the collaborators from the German minority and greatest among the rest of the population, those who had neither national nor political affinities with the occupying power (Christiansen, 1968).

So far, the hypothesis regarding the influence of group resistance on the frequency of deviating norm breaches and on the twin coefficient has gained support. It should, however, be emphasized that at the same time other factors may also influence the twin coefficient.

First of all, we must reject the assumption that group resistance against criminality is higher in the milieu of monozygotic than in the milieu of dizygotic twins. The group's attitude toward criminality may exert a different influence on the co-twins in MZ pairs, and especially in DZ pairs, but this does not imply that the general attitude within the milieus of the two zygocity groups is different. Other factors must be decisive. We are brought back to the classical problem of inheritance and environment.

The twin coefficient is not supposed to be a measure of heredity. It is an index that expresses something about the impact of the specific twin situation, whether it is determined by environmental factors or factors in the personality, which are basically a product of heredity and environment. Consequently, a greater frequency of concordance among MZ than among DZ pairs only means that similar hereditary factors and/or similar prenatal, natal, or postnatal environmental conditions result in greater likelihood of similarity in social behavior than disparate hereditary factors and/or disparate environmental conditions.

The first condition of discriminating between the two sets of basic factors is, according to Gottesman and Shields (1972), that MZ twins are not especially predisposed to criminality. This condition is definitely not fulfilled. In MZ pairs the frequency of crime is 14.8%; in DZ pairs it is 11.0%. This source of error, however, is eliminated by comparing MZ and DZ pairs with respect to the twin coefficient, a fraction in which the frequency of criminal persons in the corresponding twin population is introduced as the denominator.

The second condition, that is, that possible crime factors in the environments of MZ co-twins are not systematically more alike than those of DZ co-twins, is probably not fulfilled. At any rate, it has hitherto not been possible to demonstrate that it must be the case. This can hardly surprise anybody. Because crime is defined as a sociolegal concept in which the sociological element plays an important role, it could not be expected that criminal acts, as such, are heritable entities unless they are closely connected with well-defined, somatic or mental heritable traits. This, however, is not the case according to our present knowledge.

Chapter 6

Psychopathy: Heredity and Environment *

Fini Schulsinger

Nothing indicates that the disease or condition we today call "psychopathy" has not been prevalent as far back in the history of mankind as have psychosis, mental retardation, and neurosis. Once psychosis and mental deficiency had been delimited, psychiatrists became interested in describing and classifying those conditions that could not be ascribed to either psychosis, mental deficiency, or gross neurological damage.

The real pioneer of today's psychiatry, Philippe Pinel (1801), contributed to the concept of psychopathy, which he described as *manie sans délire*—insanity without symptoms of delirium or delusions. Pinel wrote: "I was much astonished to observe several insane persons who never presented any lesion of their intellect and who were dominated by a sort of instinctual rage, as if the affective abilities alone were damaged."

Esquirol and other French psychiatrists developed Pinel's concept further. The culmination was Morel's 1859 treatise in which he outlined a hierarchy of hereditary degeneration: If the first generation of ill people showed even a simple increase of their parents' nervous temperament, then the following generations would be worse and worse. The fourth generation would include the most defective individuals, idiots

*I am greatly indebted to Irving I. Gottesman and L. Erlenmeyer-Kimling, who suggested a number of valuable procedures during the preparation of this paper, and to Sarnoff A. Mednick for his assistance in statistical problems. Thanks are also due to Miss Agnethe Beck, who did the register searches; Mrs. Lene Kold and Mrs. Karen Nyboe, who did the secretarial work; and Jytte Villadsen, M.D., and Joseph Welner, M.D., who participated in the reliability study. This chapter is reprinted with the kind permission of the editors of the *International Journal of Mental Health*, 1972, 1, 190-206.

and cretins. Psychopathy, as defined today, would probably appear in the second generation.

Pritchard (1835), in his treatise on insanity, described a special form, "moral insanity," a term that has continued to be synonymous with psychopathy far into the twentieth century. Pritchard's concept was rather broad and included a collection of disparate conditions that should be ascribed to a variety of psychoses, as borderline or latent forms.

The modern use of the term "psychopathy" was coined by the German psychiatrist Koch (1891) in his book *Die psychopatische Minderwertig-keiten* (*The psychopathic inferiorities*). Under this heading he included "all, be they inborn or acquired, mental abnormalities that influence the life of a human being but that, even in severe cases, do not provoke psychosis and in the affected persons, even in the best cases, do not let them appear as being in complete possession of mental normality and capacity." Thus, Koch's concept was also rather broad, and many of his cases would today be included among neuroses and organic brain syndromes.

Kraepelin (1915) conceived of the psychopathic conditions as circumscribed infantilism or circumscribed development inhibitions. He described and subclassified the psychopathic conditions into seven groups and presented their sex distribution and prevalence on the basis of a hospital population.

Kahn (1931) and Kretschmer (cited in Schneider, 1934) both tried to correlate psychopathy with other aspects of personality. Kahn described 16 types of psychopathy, which he then assigned to either a drive, a temperament, or a characterological aspect of the personality. But these aspects of the personality were further elaborated, which again had the sad effect of enabling very few patients to be assigned more easily to one of Kahn's subclasses than to several of the others. Kretschmer's typology was more dynamic; it was based on four psychological stages: "the uptake," "the retention," "the working through" and "the release." A person's way of experiencing something could vary from sthenic to asthenic, which made three forms of reaction possible: the primitive reaction, the expansive reaction, and the sensitive reaction. Each of these three forms of reaction were characterized by a different constellation of the above-mentioned four psychological stages.

Obviously, the classification of psychopathy is an intricate problem. Inasmuch as we have been unable to classify psychopathic disorders according to well-known etiologies, the most useful compromise has been to classify them purely on the basis of clinical description. This is what Kraepelin did, and it is what Schneider (1934) called a "system-free typology." Schneider improved Kraepelin's typology to some extent because he added to Kraepelin's mainly transgressive psychopaths some

groups of personality deviations that did not necessarily lead to antisocial behavior. Schneider aimed at a concept and classification free of
moral values. He conceived of psychopaths as deviants from average
norms. The deviations caused the affected individual and/or his environment to suffer. Since the only behavioral norms clearly outlined are
those that can be deduced from the penal code, it is difficult to imagine
how Schneider could settle on norms without making a choice based on
his own moralistic equipment (Vanggaard, 1968). Apart from this
philosophical weakness, Schneider's typology has been relatively easy
to apply; and it has, to a large extent, pervaded European and other
schools of psychiatry.

Up until 1939, British psychiatry favored a concept of psychopathy
mainly as a moral disease. Since then, Henderson (1939), Curran &
Mallinson (1944), and Craft (1966) have made classifications of
psychopathy on a purely descriptive basis, but in a much less elaborate
way than their German colleagues. None of the British authors specified
more than three classes. In England the urge for systematic classification
has been much less intense than in Continental Europe; and the forensic
aspects of psychopathy have been in the foreground, partly because of
the existence, until recently, of the death penalty. For this reason, and
because of the strong position of social psychiatry, British psychiatrists
have focused more on the treatment aspects of this disorder than has
been usual in most of Continental Europe.

In the United States, Benjamin Rush (cited in Craft, 1966) wrote:

*There are many instances of persons with sound understanding and some of
uncommon talent who are affected with this disease in the world. It differs from
exculpative, fraudulent and malicious lying in being influenced by none of the
motives of any of them. Persons with this disease cannot speak the truth on any
subject.*

Rush thought of psychopaths as having an originally defective organization "in those parts of the body which are occupied by the moral
faculties of the mind." He called the condition "moral derangement,"
and he considered it a valid entity for treatment by physicians.

In the twentieth century, American interest in psychopathy has
taken a course that differs in some ways from the European traditions.
First, the application of research methods has been more common,
perhaps because psychologists and sociologists have had greater
academic prestige in the United States than is common in Europe. Second, psychoanalytic theory and practice were integrated into mental
health practice much earlier in the United States than in Europe, where
it was delayed partly as a consequence of the opposition of the German
Nazis to psychoanalysis. The result has been a vast body of more or less

sociologically oriented surveys in America on large populations of delinquents and criminals many of whom were psychopaths. Another result has been several, very different attempts at unifying psychoanalytic and descriptive principles in relation to the concept of psychopathy (Greenacre, 1945; Karpman, 1947; and others). Partridge (1930) proposed the term "sociopathic personality," which has become the official American term for psychopathy—a term possibly adopted for operational reasons, but with an unavoidable moralistic content, which does not make it easier for modern criminologists to fight the spirit of retaliation in the penal systems.

Alexander (1930) supplied a comprehensive description and explanation of the "neurotic character," which was the old-time analysts' term for psychopathy. His psychodynamic interpretations of case records are not easy to evaluate from a scientific viewpoint, but his clinical descriptions add much to the otherwise usable, system-free, descriptive classifications of Kraepelin and Schneider. Alexander's description of the "neurotic character" makes the concept of psychopathy a coherent one. Its focus is on personality traits that are also common, to a large extent, to Kraepelin's and Schneider's subgroups, which then become more meaningful. The essence of Alexander's description is that "neurotic characters" show a consistent pattern of acting out and that this acting-out is mainly of an alloplastic nature (except, perhaps, for some alcoholics and a few others).

This very sketchy and condensed review of such a huge topic as the concept of psychopathy does not pretend to do justice to all facets of the subject and all the authors who have written about it. I find a relatively simple, descriptively based concept of psychopathy the most useful tool in research; and, as will be evident later, Alexander's description has proved most tempting and also operationally useful to me.

ETIOLOGY

Genetics

The very special eugenic ideas of the Third Reich involved some German psychiatric geneticists in the classical type of family studies on relatives of psychopathic probands (Berlit, 1931; Riedel, 1937; Stumpfl, 1936). Their work was carried out in the same neat way as other, respectably intended, genetic work from the famous Munich school. The results of these studies unanimously indicated that heredity plays a role in the etiology of psychopathy.

The nature-nurture problem has always been particularly pro- nounced with regard to psychopathy, because therapists of all kinds have always been struck by the terrible environments to which many of their delinquent and/or psychopathic patients have been exposed. New- kirk (1957) stated: "As adopted delinquents permit research on the con- stitutional separate from the environmental element, thorough statistics on adoption and adopted persons including their ancestry should be devised and collected" (p. 54). Reiter (1930) tried to utilize this technique in a prospective design; but, for unknown reasons, nothing but a first presentation of the study has been published. Perhaps he feared Ger- man eugenics of the 1930s!

Brain Pathology

A number of electroencephalographic (EEG) studies on psychopaths, in different countries, have shown an excess of abnormal EEGs in psychopaths compared with the general population. The more violent or impulsive the psychopaths are, the greater is the number of their EEG abnormalities. The deviations have been shown to be of an unspecific nature, neither focal nor epileptic. Generally, these mild dysrhythmias are viewed as signs of immaturity. Otherwise it is difficult to interpret certain findings. How much of the abnormality is inherited, and how much comes from insufficient obstetrical care, or from series of minor cerebral concussions among the wildest of boys? This physiological cor- relate of psychopathy cannot yet, in any case, be ruled out as a possible etiological factor.

Cytogenetics

Among tall, violent lawbreakers, the prevalence of the XYY syn- drome is greater than among other offenders and the general population (Court Brown,1968; Nielsen, Stürup, Tsuboi, & Romano, 1969). Such findings are fascinating and encouraging. However, as only about 1% of severe criminal psychopaths in two psychopathic prisons showed this chromosome abnormality, a cytogenetic solution to the etiology of psy- chopathy is not to be expected in the near future. (See Chapters 10 and 11).

Deprivation in Infancy

Broken homes, loss of parents, hospitalization, lack of proper physical and emotional care, and institutionalization are all factors believed by many psychologists and psychiatrists to be of etiological significance in psychopathy, retardation of development, and other mental abnormalities occurring in childhood and later. This belief, or conviction, has been utilized in many countries to convince politicians and administrators of the value of humane and well-staffed children's institutions. Unfortunately, it is often difficult to provide proper care for children simply because they deserve it.

Writers such as Spitz (1945) and Bowlby (1951) have been influential in a positive way. From a scientific viewpoint, however, most of the classics on early experience and its later effects are more dubious, as has been shown in the more recent works of Clarke (1968), Heston (1966), and Pinneau (1955). A basic methodological error in the classical studies of institutionalization effects was that they were performed without proper genetic control. Heston's study has shown with reasonable certainty that the genetic variable is far more important than institution versus family rearing with regard to the later development of psychosis, personality deviations, and other manifest mental disturbances.

CURRENT INVESTIGATIONS IN DENMARK

Inasmuch as any pathological condition is a result of an interaction between genetic and environmental factors, the ideal research should aim at clarification of this interaction. The greater the knowledge about one of the two factors, the greater are the possibilities of planning investigations on the impact of the other factor.

The usual genealogical studies in psychiatry show that the closer the relationship between a family member and a mentally ill proband, the greater is the risk of mental illness for the family member. As already indicated, the relatives in the usual studies share with the probands not only genes but also environment. A realistic way to "isolate" the genetic factor is to conduct studies of probands who have been reared apart from their biological relatives and to analyze the prevalence of mental disorders among their biological and their foster relatives. This idea is not new, but the practical implications of this technique have generally discouraged possible investigators from making serious attempts.

In an investigation initiated by Kety, Rosenthal, Wender, & Schulsinger (1968) we explored the possibilities in Denmark of conducting such a study on schizophrenia. It turned out that studies of the desired nature were feasible in Denmark, for the following reasons:

1. Denmark has a central register of all adoptions, under the supervision of the State Department of Justice This department, understanding and appreciating our scientific goals, gave us permission to use its registers. (Of course, permission was granted only subject to several discretionary conditions.)

2. Denmark has a central register of psychiatric hospital admissions—meant for research purposes. This register goes back to 1916.

3. Denmark has maintained, since 1924, municipal population registers that make it possible to trace a person if one address from 1924 or later is known. By use of old census lists, it is possible even to trace people farther back—in some instances, as far back as the year 1800. In addition, the Danish population is relatively homogeneous, and there are few emigrants.

The schizophrenic probands in the first adoption study were found among 507 adoptees with psychiatric hospital records from a total pool of 5,483 adoptees, encompassing all the nonfamily adoptions in the city and county of Copenhagen between 1924 and 1947. All the case record material for these 507 adoptees with a record of mental illness was screened and reviewed by two Danish psychiatrists, the writer being one.

During this work I was amazed to find a relatively large number of adoptees who had been in contact with psychiatrists because of personality distrubances. Therefore, I planned to do a family study of psychopathy. The following criteria were subjected to reliability testing: separate hereditary from environmental factors. The study began in June 1967, and the collection of data ended in September 1969.

Procedures

The first step was to establish an operational and reliable definition of psychopathy. The following criteria were subjected to reliability testing:

1. A consistent pattern, lasting a reasonable period beyond adolescence, of impulse-ridden or acting-out behavior must be evident. This behavior can be (a) mainly active, expansive, or manipulating, or (b) mainly passive-asthenic. (Alcohol and/or drug abuse can be an expression of either a or b.)

2. The abreactions are inadequate in relation to the precipitating factors (of course, on the basis of very vaguely defined Danish behavioral norms).

3. The abreactions are frequently of an alloplastic nature.

These criteria are all positive. The negative criteria are the following:

4. Character neurosis must be excluded, i.e., a consistent pattern of neurotic restriction of activity and gratification.

5. Borderline psychosis must be excluded.

6. Cases in which acting-out is found in an otherwise psychotic person are excluded.

I think most psychiatrists would consider this definition of psychopathy adequate for most cases. (See also Chapter 12.)

Twenty cases were picked from the 507 mentally ill adoptees whom I had originally given a diagnosis of psychopathy in 1964, before the present study was planned and before the above definition of psychopathy was formulated. Twenty other cases with other diagnoses, but with the same amount of case record material and of the same sex and age as the 20 psychopaths, were selected from the same pool.

All the available sets of records for the two groups were then mixed into a common group and evaluated again blindly by two other experienced psychiatrists and me, following a discussion of the criteria. Each of the criteria was rated on a four-point rating scale. I now found 21 persons of the 40 who could be classified as psychopaths. The other psychiatrists considered 17 and 16 of these 21 cases, respectively, to be psychopathic. In 14 cases all three of us agreed upon the diagnosis of psychopathy; and as the raters had classified, respectively, 21, 22, and 20 persons as psychopaths, the over-all agreement among the three raters was 67%. However, one of the criteria, i.e., that the acting-out behavior should have lasted a reasonable time beyond adolescence, was applied differently by the three raters. An exclusion of the cases below 20 years of age from the screening raised the over-all agreement to 74% among the three raters. If agreement about absence of psychopathy were included, the over-all agreement would increase to 82%.

It turned out that the scoring system discriminated very well between psychopaths and character neurotics. Eight of the 40 persons were characterized by one or two raters as possibly borderline psychotics. The total scores of these eight persons were rather varied with regard to psychopathy, but none of them was high. As a result of the reliability testing procedure, the original definition was changed on one point: it was now required that the psychopathic symptoms should have lasted beyond the age of 19.

On the basis of the definition thus established, it was possible to select 57 psychopathic probands from the 507 adoptees with known mental disorders. Then, from the pool of nearly 5,000 adoptees who were not mentally ill, a control was selected for each of the 57 index probands. For every adoptee in this pool there was a form in the central register showing sex, age, and age at first transfer to the adoptive family;

names and birthdates of the adoptive parents; occupation of the adoptive father, his stated annual income and financial status, and his address at the time of the adoption; and the names, birthdates, occupations, and addresses of the biological parents. Starting with the form on the index proband, an alternating forward and backward search was made until four possible controls had been found. A control had to be of the same sex and born during the same period, to avoid the different influences of changing society. They were also matched for the age at transfer to the adoptive home and for the social class of the adoptive parents, on the basis of a Danish classification by Svalastoga (1959).

A pretransfer history was prepared for every index proband and his or her four possible controls—that is, a report of how long, with whom, and where each stayed until the transfer to the adoptive parents. In almost every one of the 57 cases it was possible to find a perfect control, with exactly the same age, social background, length of institutionalization, length of stay with biological relatives, and number of environmental shifts before the transfer. It was easy to match for social class, and in many cases to match even for the same section of the city of Copenhagen. The comparability of the two groups is evident in the following summary:

	Index Probands	Controls
Number of females	17	17
Average age of females (years)	35.8	35.8
Number of males	40	40
Average age of males (years)	36.7	35.8
Number of environmental shifts (Mean)	1.18	1.21
Months of institutionalization (Mean)	5.63	5.62

The total number of biological and adoptive relatives age 20 or above was 854. Their distribution in terms of relationship was fairly similar for the two groups, as the following figures* indicate.

	INDEX PROBANDS		CONTROLS	
Relationship	Biological	Adoptive	Biological	Adoptive
Half-sibs	169	12	156	8
Full sibs	25	8	16	11
Fathers	54	54	56	57
Mothers	57	57	57	57
Totals	305	131	285	133

Note:

Three biological fathers of index probands and one biological father of a control could not be identified. Three adoptive mothers of probands were unmarried at the time of adoption. Adoptive full sibs are offspring of both adoptive parents; adoptive half-sibs are offspring of only one of the adoptive parents.

Distribution of Mental Illnesses in Relatives of the Index Probands (1) and Controls (C)

	FATHER		MOTHER		SIBLINGS SISTER		SIBLINGS BROTHER		half-SIBLINGS MATERNAL SISTER		half-SIBLINGS MATERNAL BROTHER		PATERNAL SISTER		PATERNAL BROTHER		TOTALS	
Biological	I	C	I	C	I	C	I	C	I	C	I	C	I	C	I	C	I	C
Total number	54	56	57	57	13	11	12	5	35	33	35	33	46	51	53	39	305	285
Mentally ill	15	5	16	12	2	1	3	2	4	5	6	4	7	4	5	4	58	37
Spectrum disorders	15		7	2	2	0	3	3	2	5	3	6	3	4	4	4	19	
Core psychopathy	5	1	0	0	0	0	1	0	1	0	2	1	1	1	2	1	12	4
Adoptive																		
Total number	54	57	57	57	3	6	5	5	4	2	3	1	5	3	0	2	131	133
Mentally ill	7	3	9	7	0	0	1	3	0	1	0	1	1	0	0	1	18	16
Spectrum disorders	5	1	4	3	0	0	1	0	0	1	0	1	0	0	0	1	10	7
Core psychopathy	1	0	0	0	0	0	0	0	0	0	0	1	0	0	0	1	1	2

Findings

Mental illness among the relatives was found through a search for the names of all 854 relatives in the archives of all the psychiatric institutions in Denmark. A research assistant traveled throughout the country and spent several days at each institution searching the files (with greatly appreciated assistance from the local secretaries). I reviewed and summarized all the available case record material and did a diagnostic classification blindly, i.e., without knowing whether the person was related biologically or by adoption to an index proband or to a control. The findings on mental illness in the various categories of relatives are summarized in the table.

The distribution of mental illnesses of all types was as follows (total number of ill relatives, 129):

	Biological	Adoptive
Index	$\frac{58}{305} = 19.0 \pm 2.3\%$	$\frac{18}{131} = 13.7 \pm 3.0\%$
Control	$\frac{37}{285} = 13.0 \pm 2.0\%$	$\frac{16}{133} = 12.0 \pm 2.8\%$

It may be noted that the rates of illness are approximately the same in both groups of adoptive relatives and in the biological relatives of the controls. The over-all rate of illness for the biological relatives of the index probands, however, is higher than the rates for the other three subgroups of relatives.

The quality of the case record material, of course, varied according to the institution, the tradition of the time, and especially, the length of institutionalization. It therefore seemed most useful to operate with a *spectrum* of personality disorders, in which psychopathy was the "nuclear" disease. In some cases a diagnosis of psychopathy was rather likely, but the case record material did not permit application of all the criteria from the definition of psychopathy. These cases were classified as "observation for psychopathy" (probable psychopathy). Some cases were too mild or too inconsistent to be classified psychopathic according to the definition, and they were just classified as "character deviations." If the case record material was relatively sparse in such cases, they were classified as "observation for character deviation." A number of cases had to be classified as evidencing either criminality, alcoholism, or drug abuse, with no other clarifying diagnosis. (In my view, they probably belong to the spectrum of personality disorders more or less related to psychopathy.) A few cases had to be diagnosed as hysterical character deviation (but not conversion hysteria). These cases were counted within the psychopathy spectrum. A single case of an obsessive-compulsive character was not included in the psychopathy spectrum; nor were cases of completed suicide for whom there was no psychiatric information.

The figures that follow show the distribution of psychopathic spectrum disorders among the relatives:

	Biological	Adoptive
Index	$\dfrac{44}{305} = 14.4 \pm 2.0\%$	$\dfrac{10}{131} = 7.6 \pm 2.3\%$
Control	$\dfrac{19}{285} = 6.7 \pm 1.5\%$	$\dfrac{7}{133} = 5.3 \pm 1.9\%$

It is immediately evident that there is a great surplus of such disorders among the biological relatives of the index probands, more than 14% of whom have a psychopathic spectrum disorder compared with 5–8% among the other three relative groups. Among the biological relatives of the index probands, 76% of "mental illnesses of all types" belong to the psychopathy spectrum, compared with 44–56% in the other relative groups. The differences between the biological relatives of the index probands and the other relative groups would have been even greater if the diagnosis of hysterical character deviation had been omitted from the psychopathy spectrum.

Base rate figures for the expectancy of psychopathic spectrum disorders as classified here are not available for the Danish population. It may be seen, however, that the rates of disorder are again about the same in all of the relative groups except the biological relatives of the index probands.

The prevalence of the core disease, psychopathy, among the relatives is shown below:

	Biological	Adoptive
Index	$\dfrac{12}{305} = 3.9 \pm 1.1\%$	$\dfrac{1}{131} = 0.8 \pm 0.8\%$
Control	$\dfrac{4}{285} = 1.4 \pm 0.7\%$	$\dfrac{2}{133} = 1.5 \pm 1.0\%$

Psychopathy is certainly overrepresented among the biological relatives of the index probands.

This difference is even more marked when the distribution of psychopathy is compared in the four parent groups only.

PARENTS

	Biological	Adoptive
Index	$\dfrac{5}{111} = 4.5 \pm 2.0\%$	$\dfrac{1}{111} = 0.9 \pm 0.9\%$
Control	$\dfrac{1}{113} = 0.9 \pm 0.9\%$	$\dfrac{0}{114} = 0\%$

In fact, as none of the mothers in any group received the diagnosis of core psychopathy, the comparisons may be confined to the fathers only. Psychopathy occurs more than five times as frequently among the index probands' biological fathers as among their adoptive fathers or the biological fathers of the controls, as may be seen here:

FATHERS

	Biological	Adoptive
Index	$\dfrac{5}{54} = 9.3 \pm 4.0\%$	$\dfrac{1}{54} = 1.9 \pm 1.9\%$
Control	$\dfrac{1}{56} = 1.8 \pm 1.8\%$	$\dfrac{0}{57} = 0\%$

Referring back to the table, it will be noted that there is an over-all tendency for the psychopathic spectrum disorders, and for core psychopathy in particular, to appear more frequently among the male than among the female relatives. The sex differences, however, are not as marked and consistent in the sibling and half-sibling subgroups as in the parent subgroups. The table also shows that the differences between the biological relatives of the index probands and the controls do not increase consistently as one moves from the comparisons of rates of mental illness in toto to rates of psychopathic spectrum disorders to core psychopathy. The differences between the index and control relatives increase substantially, for example, as one goes from the psychopathic spectrum disorders to core psychopathy in the biological fathers, while in the biological mothers the increase occurs between the all-mental-disorders category and the spectrum-disorders category. It is not entirely clear from these preliminary analyses, therefore, whether the psychopathic spectrum as classified here is meaningfully related to the definition of core psychopathy. The difference in the patterns of the mothers and fathers may reflect the generally agreed upon fact that males are more likely than females to be classified as core psychopaths in Denmark. The symptomatology involved in the author's definition of psychopathy is more easily recognized in males who have to go to a hospital.

Assuming, however, that the psychopathy spectrum *is* appropriately classified, it is of further interest to examine the distribution of spectrum disorders on a family basis. The figures below indicate the distribution of the psychopathic spectrum disorders in the affected families, the presence of such a disorder in a biological or adoptive family being indicated by +, and its absence by −:

	NUMBER OF FAMILIES		
	Index	Control	Total
Group 1: biological +, adoptive −	27	11	38
Group 2: biological −, adoptive −	22	39	61
Group 3: biological +, adoptive +	5	4	9
Group 4: biological −, adoptive +	3	3	6
Totals	57	57	114

A chi-square test for this distribution (with groups 2 and 3 combined) results in $P < 0.005$.

DISCUSSION

The conclusion to be drawn from these findings is that genetic factors play an important role in the etiology of psychopathy. The definition of psychopathy that we used is purely descriptive, and, applied to case record material, it requires only a minimum of interpretation of the data. The definition has proven reliable, and it probably has face validity as well.

The selection of controls was made with due respect to possible etiological factors. Social background in the adoptive homes was matched, as was the period of birth. Even the possibility of deprivation during infancy was partially taken into consideration, as the controls and the index probands had been subject to the same number of environmental shifts, had spent the same amount of time in institutions, and had been with their biological relatives the same length of time before placement in their adoptive homes.

The assistant who visited all the psychiatric institutions to find the mentally ill relatives processed all the relatives as one group, without knowing whether they were index or control cases or adoptive or biological relatives.

I selected the index probands and the controls during 1967 and did not, at that time, make any notes about them. When I reviewed the case record material of the mentally ill relatives about two years later, I was unable to tell whether the relative belonged to an adoptive or biological family or to an index proband or a control, with few exceptions. In three cases I felt, because of very peculiar last names, that I could identify a relative as belonging to the biological family of an index proband. In a few cases I could identify relatives as adoptive relatives of probands, but did not know if these probands were controls or index cases. In each such instance, a note to this effect was made in the case summary. It turned out that these few cases of recognition had no influence on the results of the study.

Although the design of this study aims especially at demonstrating possible genetic factors in the etiology of psychopathy, this does not at all mean that the findings exclude environmental factors. However, the data indicate that the frequency of psychopathy and related disorders in the adoptive families can be excluded as an important etiological factor in this sample. Only three of the index probands had a unilateral prevalence on the adoptive side, and three of the controls also had this environmental load. Only five index probands and four controls had a bilateral load of psychopathic spectrum disorders.

Another possible environmental factor is deprivation during early infancy, as expressed in number of environmental shifts and lengths of institutionalization in early childhood. If this factor were to be tested in the study, it would have to be a test of, for example, the hypothesis that psychopathic spectrum disorders would be less frequent among the biological relatives of the index probands who were transferred late to their adoptive homes than among those transferred at an early age.

In order to make a statistical analysis of these data, it is necessary to take into account the great difference in the number of relatives between the biological families and the adoptive families. It is also necessary to take into account that fathers, mothers, and full siblings are first-degree relatives whereas the half-siblings are second-degree relatives. The following scoring system was used for our provisional analysis:

No disorder	0
Disorders other than psychopathy spectrum	1
Criminality, alcoholism, drug abuse	2
Character deviations and observations for psychopathy	3
Psychopathy	4

Each disease score was multiplied by one if the disorder appeared in a half-sib and by two if it appeared in a first-degree relative. Then the disease scores were totaled separately for each of the proband's two families (biological and adoptive), and the total score for each was divided by the number of relatives in the family group. In order to avoid 0 in the numerator, a score of 1 was added to the total disease score of each family before dividing.

$$\text{Family score} = \frac{\Sigma\,(\text{disease score} \times \text{relationship score}) + 1}{\text{Number of relatives}}$$

Fifteen index probands were one month old or less at the time of transfer to their adoptive home; 42 were older than this at the time of transfer. No significant difference in the frequency of psychopathic spectrum disorders among biological family members of the two subgroups was found when the biological family scores were compared by a t test ($P > 0.15$). In this study, therefore, early deprivation could not be held responsible for psychopathy in the index probands. Further, a repetition of this analysis, but with one year of age as the time of transfer as the separation factor, also revealed no significant difference ($P > 0.15$).

One of the possible etiological factors in psychopathy is brain damage. The case record material available for the relatives does not permit an evaluation of this factor, which would require a personal examination of all the relatives. However, a relevant factor could be pregnancy and birth complications. A search for the official midwife reports about the childbirths of the 114 probands and controls yielded 107 reports. Information on the births of 50 matched pairs of probands and controls was thus available.

The content of older Danish midwife reports is difficult to evaluate. There is some agreement in Denmark that not every complication is registered in these reports. On the other hand, if something is registered, one can feel sure that it really happened. In other words, the midwife reports yield minimum information. Every midwife report was rated according to a five-point rating scale devised in collaboration with Professor F. Fuchs, Chairman of Gynecology and Obstetrics at Cornell Medical School, New York. This scale, based on the relatively primitive type of information in the midwife reports, ranged from 0 (no complications) to 4 points (for severe complications); the total score could be 5 or more points.

The figures below compare the pregnancy/birth complications of the index probands and the controls:

	Index Probands	*Controls*
Number with birth records	53	54
Total scores	94	105
Average score	1.8	1.9

Number with birth records for both groups	50	50
Total scores	80	97
Average score	1.6	1.9
Number with score of 0	24	19
Number with 1-4 points	21	19
Number with 5+ points	5	9
Number with single scores of 3 and/or 4	8	5
Number with single scores of 4	6	3

This analysis does not establish a brain damage etiology of psychopathy, at least insofar as brain damage from birth complications is concerned. If there were such brain damage etiology, we could expect the index probands without obstetrical complications to have a more severe genetic load of psychopathic spectrum abnormalities than the index probands with complications. Twenty-four index probands had not suffered any pregnancy/birth complications (score 0), and 14 had a total score of 3 or above. To obtain a score of 3+, they had to have experienced one or more serious complications, or a combination of minor complications. Comparing the biological family scores for psychopathic spectrum disorders for the two groups, using the t test, we found no significant difference in the genetic load in the two groups ($P > 0.20$). Therefore, this analysis, too, failed to yield support for an etiological role of pregnancy/birth complications in psychopathy per se.

SUMMARY

In summary, this study of the 854 biological and adoptive relatives of 57 psychopathic adoptees and their 57 matched controls shows the frequency of mental disorders to be higher in the biological relatives of the psychopathic probands than among their adoptive relatives or than among either group of relatives of the controls. The difference is even greater when only psychopathic spectrum disorders are considered. The study supports a hypothesis of heredity as an etiological factor in psychopathic spectrum disorders. Deprivation during infancy and brain damage caused by pregnancy/birth complications were not found to be etiologically significant, at least as measured by the somewhat crude indices utilized in this investigation.

Chapter 7

Criminality in adoptees and their adoptive and biological parents: A pilot study

Barry Hutchings

and

Sarnoff A. Mednick

The importance of biological factors in the etiology of criminal behavior has received increasing attention in recent years (Hare, 1968; Shah and Roth, 1974; Mednick, 1975). This interest has stimulated a reevaluation of possible genetic factors that could be either directly or indirectly involved in criminality. The existing evidence is based largely on twin studies (see Christiansen's summary in Chapter 4). An adoption study in the United States has been reported by Crowe (1972, 1974). This chapter reports a retrospective investigation using archival material of registered criminality among adoptees and their adoptive and biological relatives. Adoption is regarded as an *ex post facto* experiment in which the hereditary influences, represented by the biological parents, and the environmental influences, as indicated by the adoptive parents, can be separated. If there is a genetic basis for criminality, then there should be an attendant correlation between the criminality of the biological parents and that of the adoptees. Furthermore, this correlation should be independent of the criminality of the adoptive parents.

The usefulness of genetic studies is often questioned, with the argument that even if a genetic factor exists, it can be but measured and noted, and little can be done about it. This is, of course, not true. Even where a large genetic component exists, environmental changes can

127

modify considerably the expression of the genetic effect. There are four
reasons for studying genetic factors in criminality research.

1. There may be at least some quite specific biological criminogenic
factors, for example, organic psychoses or extra sex chromosomes,
though such factors, it must be admitted, are unlikely to account for
more than an insignificant part of criminality.
2. If one does not take genetic factors into account, then studies on
environmental predisposing factors are confounded with hereditary factors. The delineation of environmental factors should ideally take place
in groups in which the genetic background is held constant. An illustration of this point is given later.
3. The demonstration even of considerable hereditary factors does
not preclude their control by environmental manipulation. Height is
generally regarded as being largely under genetic control. Nevertheless,
the average height of Danish males has increased by 4 cm. in the past 30
years (Andersen et al., 1974), and this increase has presumably taken
place because of environmental changes such as improved nutrition and
social conditions. By identifying points of interaction between genetic
and environmental factors in the etiology of a condition, and delineating
the reaction range of the genetic factors, it may be possible to act with
effect solely on the environment.
4. Understanding of biological factors, for instance, the role of the
autonomic nervous system, could result in more rationally designed
programs for the treatment of offenders.

Kety, Rosenthal, Wender, and Schulsinger, with the support of contracts between Copenhagen's Psykologisk Institut and USPHS, established a file of 5483 adoptees, encompassing all nonfamilial adoptions in
the City and County of Copenhagen between 1924 and 1947. The crea-
tion of this file is described more fully in Kety, Rosenthal, Wender, and
Schulsinger (1968). The study reported in this chapter centered on the
1145 male adoptees in this file who were born between January 1, 1927
and December 31, 1941. Thus the adoptees were between 30 and 44
years of age at the time their criminality was ascertained in 1971. This
would mean that the sample has passed through the greater part of the
risk period for criminality, especially for registration of a first offense. It
also has the advantage for epidemiological purposes of being a complete
series, at least in the sense that it is unselected for criminality. Denmark
provides excellent demographic facilities for such a study, with a small
population having low rates of emigration and immigration, a national
population register, and centralized police and psychiatric registers.

INITIAL STUDY OF 1145 MALE ADOPTEES

For purposes of comparison the 1145 adoptees were matched individually with a group of nonadoptees for sex, age, occupational status of their fathers, and residence. The nonadopted controls were drawn from census lists.

The police records for Denmark are housed centrally in the National Police Register (*Rigsregistraturen*). A chronological index by birth date gives access to the alphabetically arranged main files on all persons "known to the police" (*Hovedkartotek*). In itself, this file is unsuitable for criminological research because, in addition to criminal offenses, it includes very minor offenses and some things that are not offenses at all. Traffic offenses are included, although parking infringements, cycling without lights, and jaywalking are not. In addition, certain administrative matters are registered, such as hospitalization with concussion and self-discharge of psychiatric patients from the hospital. Inclusion in this file cannot by itself be taken as an indication of antisocial behavior.

A separate criminal record (*Personalia Blad*) is kept on all persons who have at any time been convicted of offenses treated as *statsadvokatsager*. These correspond very closely to indictable offenses in British justice and can be contrasted with *politisager* (summary offenses). Generally speaking, indictable offenses are those against the Danish penal code (*Straffeloven*) plus a few of the special laws (*Sœrlove*) such as narcotics offenses, cruelty to animals, and serious customs and excise offenses. On the other hand, some offenses against the penal code, such as begging and disorderly conduct, are normally dealt with as summary offenses. The distinction corresponds very roughly to the difference between felonies and misdemeanors in the United States.

Table 1

Distribution of the Initial Sample of Adoptees and Their Matched Nonadopted Controls in the Police Files

	% Adoptees	% Nonadoptees
With Criminal Record	16.2	8.9
Unidentifiable	0	0
Not Known to the Police	49.4	63.0
Minor Offenses Only	34.4	28.1

The criminal record is used as the primary source of information for this study. The lifetime risk for registration of a male in Denmark for criminality so defined is 8.9%.

The 1145 adoptees and their matched nonadopted controls were checked for registration in the police files. The distribution of these two groups in the files is shown in Table 1.

Table 2

Distribution in the Police Files of the Adoptive and Biological Fathers on the Initial Sample of Adoptees and of the Fathers of the Matched Nonadopted Controls

	% Biological Fathers	% Adoptive Fathers	% Fathers of Nonadopted Controls
With Criminal Record	30.8	12.6	11.1
Unknown or Unidentifiable	15.2	2.3	2.4
Not Known to the Police	40.5	65.9	68.0
Minor Offenses Only	13.5	19.2	18.5

It should be remembered that in this and succeeding tables the category "minor offenders" also includes some nonoffenders who are known to the police for one reason or another. As can be seen, 185 (16.2%) of the adoptees have criminal records, markedly more than either the controls (8.9%) or the corresponding population figure.

Table 3

Distribution of Adopted Danish Males Aged 30–44 Years by Registered Offenses and by Criminality of Their Adoptive Fathers

	CRIMINAL RECORD OF ADOPTEE		
Adoptive Father	Not Registered	Minor Offenses Only	Criminal Offenses
Criminal	9.2%	14.0%	21.7%
Noncriminal	90.8%	86.0%	78.3%
N	554	385	180

The adoptive and biological fathers of the adoptees and the fathers of the nonadopted controls were now checked through the police files. The distribution of the fathers is given in Table 2. The rates of criminality of the adoptive fathers and the fathers of the nonadopted controls are very similar. The biological fathers of the adoptees, however, evidence almost 3 times these rates of criminality.

The association between the registered criminality in the adoptees and their adoptive fathers is given in Table 3. The percentage of adoptees with a criminal adoptive father increases from 9.2% of the unregistered adoptees to 21.7% of the criminal adoptees. (χ^2 (2) = 19.25, $p < .001$).

The criminal status of the 971 adoptees whose biological fathers could be identified is tabulated in Table 4 in relation to their biological fathers' criminality. Taking into account the increased criminality among the biological fathers themselves, the same pattern can be seen as with the adoptive fathers (χ^2 (2) = 16.91, $p < .001$).

Table 4

Distribution of Adopted Danish Males Aged 30–44 Years by Registered Offenses and by Criminality of Their Biological Fathers

Biological Father	CRIMINAL RECORD OF ADOPTEE		
	Not Registered	Minor Offenses Only	Criminal Offenses
Criminal	31.1%	37.7%	48.8%
Noncriminal	68.9%	62.3%	51.2%
N	473	334	164

The results shown in Table 5 for the nonadopted controls are very similar to those of the adoptees and their adoptive fathers when expressed as percentages.

These results indicate an association between the criminality of the sons and their fathers. This association appears to approximately the same degree among both adoptees and nonadoptees. With the adoptees it appears on both the biological and adoptive fathers' side. Table 6 gives the distribution for the 965 adoptees and their fathers for whom all the necessary identifying information was available.

Table 5

Distribution of Non-Adopted Danish Males Aged 30–34 Years by Registered Offenses and by Criminality of Their Fathers

Father of Nonadopted Controls	CRIMINAL RECORD OF NONADOPTED CONTROLS		
	Not Registered	Minor Offenses Only	Criminal Offenses
Criminal	9.5%	12.4%	21.0%
Noncriminal	90.5%	87.6%	79.0%
N	706	314	100

It should be noted that the category "minor offender" is very unreliable in the older records (i.e., in the fathers' generation), in that old records for minor offenses may not always be found in the National Police Register. Nevertheless, a clear, rising tendency can be seen from 10.5% criminal adoptees when neither father is known to the police to 36.2% when both fathers are criminals. It is also apparent that the adoptive fathers' criminality appears to have little effect when the biological father has a clean record (11.5% criminal adoptees), whereas the effect of the criminality of the biological father when the adoptive father has a clean record remains considerable (22.0% criminal adoptees).

Table 6

Distribution of the Criminality of the Adoptees According to the Criminality of the Adoptive and Biological Fathers (N = 965)

Biological Father	Adoptive Father	Percent Adoptees Criminal	N
Not Registered	Not registered	10.5	333
	Minor offender only	13.3	83
	Criminal offense	11.5	52
Minor Offender Only	Not registered	16.5	103
	Minor offender only	10.0	30
	Criminal offense	41.1	17
Criminal Offense	Not registered	22.0	219
	Minor offender only	18.6	70
	Criminal offense	36.2	58

Note: As noted in the text, the information for the "minor offense only" category for the fathers is relatively unreliable. It also includes contacts with the police unrelated to asocial acts.

PROBAND STUDY OF 143 CRIMINAL ADOPTEES AND MATCHED NONCRIMINAL CONTROLS

The proband study was made in order to make a closer examination of the relatives of a criminal group and to compare them with the relatives of a matched noncriminal group, The design is discussed in Rosenthal (1970) and has been used by Kety et al. (1968) in their adoption study of schizophrenia and Schulsinger (1972) in his adoption study of psychopathy.

A group was selected from the 185 criminal adoptees to include all those cases in which the biological fathers were identifiable and whose adoptive and biological fathers were born from 1890 onwards. This latter criterion was included to maximize the reliability of the police records. These 143 criminal adoptees became the index probands. They were matched individually with 143 adoptees who were not known to the police and who became the control probands. Matching was made on the basis of age and occupational status of the adoptive father. Table 7

Table 7

Mean Characteristics of Index Adoptees (Criminal Probands) and Their Matched Control Adoptees (Noncriminal Probands)

	Index Adoptees (Criminal Probands) (N = 143)	Control Adoptees (Noncriminal Probands) (N = 143)
Occupational Status of Adoptive Father	2.3	2.4
Occupational Status of Biological Father	1.7	2.1
Age on 1 January 1971	35.3 yr	35.3 yr
Age at Birth of Child of		
Adoptive Mother	30.8 yr	31.6 yr
Adoptive Father	32.5 yr	33.6 yr
Biological Mother	23.3 yr	23.6 yr
Biological Father	26.1 yr	27.9 yr
Age at 1st Transfer to Adoptive Home (Median)	6 months	7 months
Age at Legal Adoption (Median)	19 months	16 months
Income of Adoptive Father	DKr. 4290	DKr. 4387
Fortune of Adoptive Father	DKr. 2065	DKr. 1848

presents identifying information on these two groups. As can be seen from the ages of first transfer to the adoptive homes, the amount of possible contact between the adoptee and his biological father was minimal. Actually, in almost all cases it was nonexistent, since the transfer to the adoptive home took place from a children's home rather than from the biological home.

Thirty-three (23%) of the adoptive fathers of the criminal probands had received criminal records as against only 14 (9.8%) of the control adoptive fathers. (χ^2 (1) = 8.25, $p < .01$). This difference was also reflected in various indices of criminality, such as number of recorded cases and total length of sentence.

Among the biological fathers of the index cases there are 70 (49%) who have criminal records as against 40 (28%) of the biological fathers of the noncriminal adoptees (χ^2 (1) = 12.42, $p < .001$). Again, the difference was found with all measures of criminality considered. Not only were the index biological fathers more often criminal than the controls, but they were worse criminals, with an average of 7.1 cases recorded against each of the criminals among the index fathers, compared with 4.7 cases against the control fathers who were criminals. On both the adoptive and biological sides the differences were more marked with respect to property offenses than to crimes of violence, but because of the overwhelmingly greater incidence of property offenses and the difficulty of classifying individuals according to dominant offenses it is difficult to draw a firm conclusion here.

When the criminal adoptees were graded in terms of the severity of their criminality by classifying them as recidivists, prisoners, and the like, there was some tendency for concordance rates to be positively associated with increasing severity. These differences were not statistically significant, but were more marked on the adoptive side.

Although there are relatively fewer adoptive or biological mothers registered as criminals, their data are, proportionately, in agreement with those of the fathers. Of the biological mothers of the index probands, 26 were criminal, as against 10 of the controls. In 18 of the former and 5 of the latter cases, the biological father was also a criminal.

There was considerably more mental illness recorded for the index probands than for the controls, with 56 of the former being known to the National Psychiatric Register, as against only 7 of the latter. Psychopathy was predominant, but it should be remembered that the presenting symptom is often the criminal act. More interesting in this context are the psychiatric records of the parents on the adoptive and biological sides. Here there was no difference between the psychiatric histories of the index and control adoptive parents. The adoptive parents had been quite thoroughly screened for mental illness, and there was a notable absence of psychosis. Forty-seven of the index probands and thirty-two of the control probands had at least one *biological* parent who was recorded in the Psychiatric Register. This difference was statistically significant at a low level (χ^2 (1) = 3.97, $p < .05$). The differences were mainly on the side of the mothers and were due to increased psychopathy and neurosis (especially depressive neurosis) rather than psychosis.

Midwives' reports were obtained on 92 of the index cases and 93 controls. The two groups did not differ in respect to the course of the pregnancy or delivery nor to the nature and extent of the ensuing complications. The slight differences that were noticed were in the direction of the index cases having slightly more favorable obstetric histories!

Up to this point a number of variables thought to be of relevance in the determination of criminal behavior have been examined independently. Two questions stimulated the analyses reported in the following section: (1) What is the *combined* effect of the several predictors believed to be of relevance? (2) Are different aspects of criminality differently determined?

The traditional way of attacking the first of these questions would be to combine several variables in "*n*-way" contingency tables. This is somewhat unsatisfactory. In the first place, examination of more than two or three predictors in such a manner requires prohibitive numbers of cases, certainly more than are available in the present design. But, basically, the problem is that of spuriousness. To what extent does the effect of A on X disappear when the effect of B on X is taken into consideration? This, of course, can be extended to variables not being examined, when it becomes a question of how much of the variance we are explaining. Such questions are best answered by the use of linear statistical techniques, in particular, multiple regression. These analyses enable one to measure the relation of the various predictors *inter se* and to avoid the risk of explaining the same variance several times and of giving an exaggerated impression of relationships that can arise from tabular analyses.

The independent variables were coded as contrasts, with a value of 1 signifying the presence of a particular factor, such as criminal or psychiatric diagnosis, and 0 as its absence. The following variables were included to predict the criminality of the adoptees: criminal record and psychiatric hospitalization in biological or adoptive mother or father, social class, severe birth complications, and several of the more promising interactions.

The data for the 143 noncriminal probands and 143 criminal probands were subjected to a stepwise multiple regression analysis. The three factors that contributed significantly to the regression analysis were (and chosen in this order):

1. Criminality in at least one *biological* parent
   $F = 16.31$ with d.f. $= 1/284 \, p < .001$
2. Criminality in at least one *adoptive* parent
   $F = 8.04$ with d.f. $= 1/283 \, p < .01$
3. Psychiatric diagnosis for the biological mother
   $F = 5.88$ with d.f. $= 1/282 \, p < .05$

It is realized that there are problems with stepwise procedures, and one cannot conclude from such an analysis that any one predictor is more important than another, or compare their relative importance. What one can do is to conclude that the predictors that make significant contributions to the regression equation do exert their effects independently of each other. In the present analysis the conclusion can be stated that the criminality of the biological parents and of the adoptive parents, together with the mental illness of the biological mother, make contributions to the criminality of the child, even when the partial correlations of these variables among themselves have been taken into consideration. Taken together, these three predictors reach a multiple r of 0.315, with the criminality of the adoptee indicating that altogether about 10% of the variance has been accounted for. When interpreting this figure, one should recall that variables were coded as values of either 1 or 0, which would tend to underestimate the multiple r, but also that the independent variable (criminality in the adoptee) represents two extreme groups from the population, namely, criminals and persons not known to the police, which would tend to overestimate the r.

When 12 indices of criminality among the criminal probands (such as type of crime and severity of sentence) were subjected to a factor analysis, two factors were extracted, which together accounted for about 70% of the variance. Factor 1, which is much the larger, is loaded heavily on theft, property damage, multiple offenses, number of offenses, and a relatively early start in criminal career. It would seem to be a fairly general factor describing typical nonviolent criminality. Factor 2 is clearly a factor correlated with offenses against the person. The high loading on injuries to the victim contrasts with the low loading on thefts and property damage. The high positive loadings on ages at first and last offenses indicate that these are crimes occurring fairly late in life.

When the regression analysis and the factor analysis were subjected to a split-half replication they both turned out to be reasonably stable.

The two factors obtained in the factor analysis were each separately regressed on the predictors of the regression analysis in order to pose the question of whether the different aspects of criminality were differently determined. This latter analysis was unclear in result and proved totally unstable when subjected to a split-half replication.

CROSS-FOSTERING ANALYSIS

The cross-fostering method, well known in genetic studies with animals, has been described in the context of studies such as the present, by Rosenthal (1970).

Returning to the total sample of 1145 adoptees, we find that the sample is just large enough to examine the cross-fostering situation. Fifty-two adoptees were born to biological fathers who were not known to the police but had criminal adoptive fathers. A larger group of 219 adoptees had biological criminal fathers but were adopted by fathers who were not known to the police. The distribution of these 271 adoptees in the police files is shown in Table 8. In this Table minor offenses are omitted. (Note that these figures may also be extracted from Table 6). When the adoptive father is not criminal but the biological father is criminal, 22% of the adoptees become criminal. When the biological father is not criminal but the adoptive father is criminal, 11.5% of the adoptees become criminal. This difference falls short of statistical significance, but the direction of the difference favors the strength of the influence of the biological fathers' criminality.

Table 8

"Cross Fostering" Analysis:
% of Adoptive Sons Who Are Registered Criminals

| | | IS BIOLOGICAL FATHER CRIMINAL? | |
		Yes	No
Is Adoptive	Yes	36.2% (of 58)	11.5% (of 52)
Father Criminal?	No	22% (of 219)	10.5% (of 333)

DISCUSSION

Within the boundaries of the adoption methodology there appears to be a correlation between criminality in adoptees and criminality in their biological parents. The most important limitation of the adoption method is the possibility that the adoption procedure results in selective placement, promoting correspondence between the adoptive home and the characteristics of the biological parents. Indeed, in this study a significant correspondence was noted in the social classes of the biological and adoptive fathers ($r = 0.22$; d.f. $= 880$; $p < .001$). The Danish organization which arranged many of the adoptions examined in this study states clearly that they do aim at matching in certain respects. Because the purpose of the adoptive method is the separation of genetic and environmental influences, this matching is a limitation of the method.

The analyses presented in Table 9 attempt to overcome this limitation in a group of 538 adoptees who were either "criminal" or "not known to the police" and whose fathers were identifiable and of determinable social class. Four predictors are combined in a multiple regression (MR). These are criminality and social class of the biological and adoptive fathers. In the first MR of the adoptive fathers' criminality and social class are considered as causally prior to the effect of the biological fathers. Two things are apparent. The social class and the criminality have independent effects, and the criminality of the biological father has an effect even when the effects from the adoptive father have been removed.

In the upper part of Table 9 the social class of the adoptive father is shown to have a predictive value with respect to criminality of the adoptee, even when the effect of the adoptive fathers' criminality has been partialled out. Furthermore, the criminality of the biological father has an effect, even when the criminality and social class of the adoptive father has been considered. Thus it can be concluded that the effects of the criminality of the biological and adoptive fathers are at least partially independent. In the lower part of Table 9 the effects of the biological father are considered prior to the adoptive father. A similar picture appears. Thus a causal network could handle either the adoptive or the biological influences as primary. The analysis of variance given at the bottom of Table 9 is, of course, the same for both analyses. Interactions were not significant.

A second limitation is that screening takes place both with regard to the children who are put up for adoption and of the prospective parents.

Table 9

Prediction of Criminality in Adoptees from Biological and Adoptive Fathers' Criminality and Social Class ($N = 538$)

	d.f.	F	P	R
1. Adoptive Father Criminal	1,536	5.70	< 0.025	0.103
2. Adoptive Father Social Class	1,535	13.00	< 0.001	0.184
3. Biological Father Criminal	1,534	16.88	< 0.001	0.252
4. Biological Father Social Class	1,533	3.13	NS	0.263
1. Biological Father Criminal	1,536	19.56	< 0.001	0.187
2. Biological Father Social Class	1,535	5.04	< 0.025	0.210
3. Adoptive Father Criminal	1,534	4.14	< 0.050	0.227
4. Adoptive Father Social Class	1,533	10.00	< 0.010	0.263

Analysis of variance

	d.f.	sum of squares	mean square	F ratio	P
Regression	4	28.208	7.052	9.886	< 0.001
Residual	533	380.221	0.713		

It is difficult to discover the procedures of 40 years ago, but it is conceivable that they were influenced by principles of psychiatric genetics. Screening can take place in several ways. First, precisely which children are put up for adoption can be a result of professional decision based on the background of the case, including information regarding the biological parents. Second, the adoptive parents become such both as a result of decisions they themselves have taken and after administrative screening. All three groups are thus highly selected.

With the adoptees whose biological fathers were criminal, the criminal adoptees were distinguished from the noncriminal adoptees to some extent by the criminality of the adoptive fathers, but they were also different with regard to the severity of the criminality of the biological fathers. That is to say, the criminal biological fathers were more criminal when the adoptees themselves were criminal than when the adoptees were not criminal. A similar picture appeared by comparing the criminal and noncriminal adoptees who have criminal adoptive fathers. There was no difference in the age at first transfer to the adoptive home in the criminals and the rest, but because this transfer takes place at the earliest at 4 months, we may be outside of the range of a critical period.

Although it is not intended here to postulate a simple genetic model for criminality, it can be pointed out that graded and even multifactorial phenotypic characters are no longer considered by modern genetics to be necessarily incapable of reflecting quite simple genotypic activity. Recourse to such mechanisms as incomplete penetrance are common in the genetics of mental illness. A more conservative answer would be to postulate a cumulative genetic disadvantage. Some individuals, because of their genetic endowment, find themselves physically and psychologically in a position in society in which they are more likely than their more fortunate fellow members to succumb to crime.

It is worth restating that the operational definition of criminal behavior used here is that of detected, apprehended, and registered acts defined by the Danish society as worthy of police and judicial action. It is thus primarily an administrative definition. The extent to which it is also a sociological definition is debatable; the extent to which it is a biological definition is even more doubtful.

FURTHER EXTENSION OF THE STUDY

The authors, in collaboration with Professor I. I. Gottesman and Professor K. O. Christiansen, are presently extending this study to include all the extrafamilial adoptions in Denmark from 1921 to 1947 with the support of the U. S. Public Health Service. The sample will involve 14,330 adoptions of both sexes. The extended sample will, in addition to an increased size, make a number of additional comparisons possible, including studies of criminality in rural and suburban areas and also female criminality. The pilot study utilized the National Police Register; the extended study is using the local penal registers, which are more complete and contain more accurate information on sentencing.

Using the model illustrated in this chapter we propose to study factors of etiological significance to criminality and their interaction. Some of the comparisons to be made are

1. Comparison of adoptees from lowest social class who do and do not become criminal, thereby identifying factors that precipitate or prevent criminality in a socially defined risk group.
2. Comparison of adoptees with criminal rearing background who do and do not become criminal.
3. Comparison of adoptees with and without criminal biological background.
4. Comparison of adoptees with and without psychiatric history on the biological side.
5. Comparison of adoptees with history of obstetric complications.
6. Comparison of adoptees coming from "criminogenic" geographical areas (high-density urban).

Because of the size of the total sample, we shall be able to study these factors in isolation by appropriate matching of the groups and their combined and interactive manifestation by the use of appropriate multivariate techniques.

We intend, by using the facilities of the *Folkeregister*, to obtain additional biographic information on the subjects, such as: residential changes during childhood and adolescence; divorce, separation, remarriage of adoptive parents; information (including criminality) on the half-siblings of the adoptees (which will appear partly as other adopted children and partly as later or earlier children of one of the biological parents who do not become adopted); information on the natural children of the adoptive parents who will thus form "nonnatural" siblings to the adoptees.

Our best estimate is that we can identify approximately 1300 male criminals among the adoptees and 150 female criminals. With these numbers we should be able to study specific kinds of criminality: recidivists, psychopathic criminals, white-collar criminals, violent offenders, sex offenders, criminality in association with alcohol misuse, and the like.

Chapter 8

Family and adoption studies of alcoholism*

Donald W. Goodwin

Alcoholism is a familial disorder; studies have repeatedly shown a high prevalence of alcoholism among the relatives of alcoholics. In studying a familial disorder, it is important to determine whether the illness is influenced by heredity. Separating "nature" from "nurture" is a difficult (some say impossible) task; nevertheless, through the years, there have been a number of studies and much speculation concerning a possible role of heredity in alcoholism.

Reviewed here are some of these studies—particularly those confirming a familial predisposition to alcoholism and recent studies of adopted and nonadopted children of alcoholics conducted by the author and collaborators in the United States and Denmark.

*The material presented in this paper has appeared in modified, more detailed form in the following publications: Goodwin, 1971; Goodwin, Schulsinger, Hermansen, Guze and Winokur, 1973; Goodwin, Schulsinger, Möller, Hermansen, Winokur and Guze, 1974.

The cohort of adoptees from which the Danish sample was drawn was originally identified for a study of schizophrenia sponsored by the National Institute of Mental Health and carried out under the auspices of the Psykologisk Institut at the Kommunehospitalet in Copenhagen. The investigators in this study were Drs. David Rosenthal, Seymour Kety, Paul H. Wender, and Fini Schulsinger. Their cooperation made this material available for our study.

FAMILY STUDIES

Early investigators, including Rybakow (1906), Kraepelin (1910), and Binswanger (1928), noted the high frequency of alcoholism and other psychopathology among the relatives of alcoholics and assumed it was higher than the occurrence of these disorders in the general population. More recently, investigators have recognized the need for suitable control groups and data about expectancy rates in the general population before making such assumptions.

By various sampling means, including studies of the relatives of nonalcoholics and one large-scale household survey, information has been obtained about expectancy rates of alcoholism in several countries. These studies, performed by Luxenburger (1928) in Germany, Bleuler (1932) in Switzerland, Sjögren (1948) in Sweden, Fremming (1947) in Denmark, and Slater (1935) in England, produced roughly equivalent findings. The lifelong expectancy rate for alcoholism among males appears to be about 3-5%; the rate for females ranges from 0.1 to 1%.

Without known exception, every family study of alcoholism, irrespective of country of origin, has shown much higher rates of alcoholism among the relatives of alcoholics than apparently occurs in the general population. These studies include the following.

Boss (1929), examining the siblings and parents of 909 male and 166 female alcoholics, found that alcoholism occurred in 53% of the fathers, 6% of the mothers, 30% of the brothers, and 3% of the sisters. Pohlisch (1933) compared the siblings and parents of chronic alcoholics with the siblings and parents of opiate addicts with respect to alcoholism and morphinism. Alcoholism was found in 22% of the brothers of alcoholics and 6% of the brothers of opiate addicts. Alcoholism occurred in 47% of the fathers of alcoholics and 6% of the fathers of opiate addicts. Conversely, among the parents and siblings of opiate addicts, opiate addiction occurred more frequently than did alcoholism. Studying a large sample of alcoholics and their relatives, Brugger (1934) found that about 25% of the fathers were alcoholic. Other authors reporting similar figures are Amark (1951), Gregory (1960), and Winokur and Clayton (1968). Viewing the situation from another aspect, Dahlberg and Stenberg (1934) reported that 25% of hospitalized alcoholics come from families in which one of the parents abused alcohol.

A more recent study by Winokur et al. (1970) showed a particularly high prevalence of alcoholism among the full siblings of alcoholics. Among the full siblings of male alcoholics there was a lifetime expectancy of excessive drinking in 46% of the brothers and 5% of the sisters; the lifetime expectancy of alcoholism among the full siblings of female alcoholics was 50% in the brothers and 8% in the sisters. These expectancy rates are higher than those reported in most other studies, possibly because the investigators studied family members rather than relying solely on information from alcoholic probands. A study by Rimmer and Chambers (1969) has shown that "family studies," in which family members are interviewed, show higher rates of alcoholism than occur in "family history studies," in which only alcoholic probands are interviewed.

Aware that "familial" does not necessarily mean "hereditary," several of the foregoing authors have attempted to analyze their data so as to control for environmental factors. Dahlberg and Stenberg (1934) established that one of the parents of their alcoholics was in 25% of the cases an alcoholic, and that both parents were abstainers in 12% of the cases. The severity of alcoholism was the same if the parents were alcoholics or abstainers. The authors interpreted this finding as indicating a hereditary influence in alcoholism. Amark (1951) reported that "periodic" and "compulsive" alcoholics more frequently had alcoholic children than did alcoholics whose illnesses, presumably, were less severe. Home environments were found to be equally "good" or "bad" in both groups, again suggesting that alcoholism had a hereditary component. Utilizing a pedigree approach to an investigation of a single large family, Kroon (1924) concluded that alcoholism was influenced by a sex-linked hereditary trait.

Alcoholism also has been studied with regard to its possible association with other psychiatric illnesses. On the basis of studies by Brugger, Amark (1951), Bleuler (1932), Winokur et al. (1970), and Guze et al. (1967), it appears there is an excess of depression, criminality, sociopathy, and "abnormal personality" in the families of alcoholics. Typically, depression occurs most often in the female relatives and alcoholism or sociopathy in the male relatives. Relatives of alcoholics apparently are no more often schizophrenic, mentally defective, manic, or epileptic than are relatives of nonalcoholics.

ADOPTION STUDIES

As noted, familial is not synonymous with genetic. Usually the biological parents of individuals are also important persons in their environment. One approach to separating nature from nurture is to study individuals separated from their biological relatives soon after birth and raised by unrelated foster parents.

With a number of American and Danish colleagues, the author has conducted such a study. It is described in some detail because it provides the strongest evidence available that alcoholism may not result entirely from life experiences, that a genetic factor may be present. For the reader to form his own opinion of the study, he needs to know how it was done and what was found.

The Danish Study: Part I

Adoption studies pose many problems. Obtaining access to adoption agency records may be difficult. Most agencies have little information about the parents whose children are placed for adoption. Among highly mobile people such as Americans, locating subjects is difficult.

For these reasons a collaborative adoption study was done in Denmark, a country in which few of these difficulties exist. There is little population movement in or out of the country, and centralized national registries are available for scientific purposes.

The study had two goals: (1) to determine whether men raised apart from their biological parents were more likely to have drinking problems or other psychiatric difficulties if one of their biological parents was alcoholic than if there was no recorded alcoholism among their biological parents; (2) to determine whether sons of alcoholics *raised* by their alcoholic parents were more likely to develop alcoholism than were their brothers who had been adopted in early infancy and raised by foster parents who were not alcoholic.

The subjects for the study were obtained from a pool of 5483 nonfamily adoption cases, all of which took place in the city and county of Copenhagen from 1924 through 1947. This pool of adoption cases was originally established as part of a family study of schizophrenia. As part of the same study, hospital records were screened to identify those adoptees and their biological and adoptive parents who had been psychiatrically hospitalized. Selected for our study were adopted men (hereafter referred to as probands) who had had a biological parent hospitalized for alcoholism. All had been separated from their biological parents in early infancy, had been adopted by nonrelatives, and had no known subsequent contact with their biological relatives. Only male adoptees were studied, because more men become alcoholic than women. Eighty-five percent of the alcoholic parents were fathers.

Another group of adoptees, the control group, was also studied. It differed from the proband group in one regard: the men had not had a biological parent hospitalized for alcoholism. The two groups had the same age composition, and the men in both groups had been adopted at the same age by nonrelatives.

A Danish psychiatrist interviewed the two groups without knowing whether they were probands or controls. The interviews were made in Danish but recorded in English. They lasted 2-4 hours and had a detailed format eliciting information about social and economic factors, the adoptive parents, psychiatric illness in the adoptees, drinking practices and problems, and a wide range of other life experiences. The study was not identified as an adoption study, and subjects rarely volunteered information about their biological parents; no subject mentioned that he had a biological parent with a drinking problem. Law-enforcement rec-

Table 1

Characteristics of Adoptees

	% Probands[a] (N = 55)	% Controls[b] (N = 78)
Age 20–24	9[c]	10
25–29	51	53
30–34	14	19
35–39	14	10
> 40	11	8
Marital History		
Ever Married (Never Divorced)	62	74
Ever Divorced	27	9
Never Married	11	17
Academic Education		
< 9 yr	67	69
9–11 yr	24	23
12–15 yr	7	8
> 15 yr	2	0
Socioeconomic Class		
Low	53	46
High	47	54
Served in Military	67	72

[a]Refers in this and other tables to adoptees of alcoholic percentage.
[b]Refers to adoptees of nonalcoholic percentage.
[c]Figures rounded off to nearest whole number for ease of perusal. Sums may therefore not equal 100%.

Table 2

Foster Home Experience

Adoptive Home Characteristics	% Probands (N = 55)	% Controls (N = 78)
Home Intact	87	86
Parental Economic Status		
Below Average	15	19
Average	58	55
Above Average	27	26
Parental Psychopathology, any	42	50
Father "Depressed"[a]		
Possible	2	8
Definite	7	4
Father "Alcoholic"		
Possible	5	10
Definite	7	12
Father "Antisocial"		
Possible	0	3
Definite	0	0
Father, any Psychopathology	24	36
Mother "Depressed"		
Possible	4	5
Definite	16	9
Mother, any Psychopathology	29	28

[a] "Diagnoses" are based on the adoptees' descriptions and do not represent first-hand psychiatric observations.

ords also were reviewed for information about the adoptees and their biological parents.

The interviews and records were sent to Washington University in St. Louis where computer analysis was performed, again without knowledge of the subjects' category. The study was blind from beginning to end.

A total of 133 subjects was located and cooperated in the study. They consisted of 55 adoptees with an alcoholic biological parent (the probands) and 78 adoptees (controls) with no known alcoholism in their biological parents.

Table 1 compares the proband and control groups. The mean age in both groups was 30 with a range of 23-45 years at the time of interview. The socioeconomic status and educational experience of the men in both groups was quite similar. Divorce was the only factor in Table 1 that "significantly" distinguished the two groups; the probands had a divorce rate 3 times greater than that of the control group.

Table 2 presents information about the adoptive parents. The home was "intact" when the subject lived with both adoptive parents from adoption until at least age 16. Estimates of psychiatric illness in the adoptive parents were based on information provided by their adopted children. The parents were considered depressed, alcoholic, or suffering from some form of psychiatric illness when they sought treatment for the condition.

In general, the two groups of adoptive parents were similar. The adoptive parents of the probands tended to have somewhat more depression than did the adoptive parents of the controls, but the differ-

Table 3

Psychiatric Disorders in Adoptees

	% Probands (N = 55)	% Controls (N = 78)
Anxiety Neurosis		
Possible	16	18
Definite	2	10
Depression		
Possible	13	17
Definite	2	3
Criminality		
Possible	0	3
Definite	5	3
Drug Abuse		
Possible	4	1
Definite	5	1
Personality Disturbances[a]	51	53
Psychopathology, any (Excluding Alcoholism)	56	53

[a]Refers to a variety of character diagnoses commonly used in Denmark, eg, anti-aggressive personality, compulsive personality, sensitive-insecure personality. Most of these are not synonymous with "psychiatric illness" as the term is commonly used.

ences were small. The alcoholism rate actually was higher in the adoptive parents of the control group, another presumably chance occurrence.

Table 3 compares psychiatric illness in the adoptees. Again, the differences were small. Total illness rates, exclusive of alcoholism, were almost identical.

Table 4 concerns the subjects' drinking behavior. Almost without exception, the proband group had more drinking problems than did the control group. With regard to five variables, the differences between the two groups were statistically significant.

"Hallucinations" in Table 4 refers to auditory or visual perceptual distortions associated with withdrawal from alcohol. "Lost control" refers to the experience of wanting to stop drinking on a particular drink-

Table 4

**Drinking Problems and Patterns
in Two Adoptive Groups**

	% Probands (N = 55)	% Controls (N = 78)
Hallucinations[a]	6	0
Lost Control[a]	35	17
Amnesia	53	41
Tremor	24	22
Morning Drinking[a]	29	11
Delirium Tremens	6	1
Rum Fits	2	0
Social Disapproval	6	8
Marital Trouble	18	9
Job Trouble	7	3
Drunken Driving Arrests	7	4
Police Trouble, Other	15	8
Treated for drinking, any[a]	9	1
Hospitalized for Drinking	7	0
Drinking Pattern		
Moderate Drinker	51	45
Heavy Drinker, ever	22	36
Problem Drinker, ever	9	14
Alcoholic, ever[b]	18	5

[a]$P < .05$
[b]$P < .02$

ing occasion but being unable to do so. "Morning drinking" refers to repeated morning drinking, not just one or two before-breakfast drinking experiences.

The men in the proband group had an average of 2.05 alcohol-related problems. Those in the control group had an average of 1.23 alcohol-related problems. The difference was significant.

Table 4 also compares the two groups with regard to how many had been treated for alcoholism. Nine probands had been treated, compared to one control. Six probands had been hospitalized and no controls.

The last items in Table 4 present a composite picture of drinking patterns based on quantity and frequency of drinking as well as problems associated with drinking. Criteria for the four drinking categories

Table 5

Criteria for Drinking Categories

Moderate Drinker	Neither a teetotaler nor heavy drinker.
Heavy Drinker	For at least 1 year drank daily and had six or more drinks at least two or three times a month; or drank six or more drinks at least one time a week for over 1 year, but reported no problems.
Problem Drinker	(a) Meets criteria for heavy drinker. (b) Had problems from drinking but insufficient in number to meet alcoholism criteria.
Alcoholic	(a) Meets criteria for heavy drinker. (b) Must have had alcohol problems in at least three of the following four groups: Group 1: Social disapproval of drinking by friends, parents Marital problems from drinking Group 2: Job trouble from drinking Traffic arrests from drinking Other police trouble from drinking Group 3: Frequent blackouts Tremor Withdrawal hallucinations Withdrawal convulsions Delirium tremens Group 4: Loss of control Morning drinking

are given in Table 5. Using these criteria, 10 of the 55 probands were "alcoholic" as compared to 4 controls. In other words, the probands had 3.55 times the alcoholism rate of the control group. Heavy and problem drinking occurred somewhat more frequently in the control group, but *only alcoholism significantly distinguished the two groups.*

In short, the study indicated that children of alcoholics are more likely to have alcohol problems than children of nonalcoholics, despite being separated from their alcoholic parents in early life. All individuals in the study were separated from their biological parents in early infancy and raised by nonrelatives without subsequent contact with their natural parents. Nevertheless, by their late 20s or earlier, the offspring of alcoholics had nearly 2 times the number of alcohol problems and 3.55 times the rate of alcoholism as children whose parents had no record of hospitalization for alcoholism.

Alcoholism is a term that lends itself to so many definitions that whichever is chosen can be challenged by those who disagree with it. It should be emphasized, therefore, that use of the term in this study was based on arbitrary criteria; a certain minimum number of problems was required before the diagnosis was made, and no single problem was considered indispensable to the diagnosis.

Perhaps the most objective measure of increased alcohol problems in the proband group was the extent of psychiatric treatment in the group. Eight of the fifty-five probands had been psychiatrically hospitalized as compared to two of the seventy-eight controls. Moreover, six of the eight probands hospitalized were diagnosed as alcoholic by criteria in Table 5. None of the four controls with a diagnosis of alcoholism had been hospitalized. Nine of the ten alcoholic probands had received psychiatric treatment, compared to one of the four alcoholic controls.

Apart from alcoholism, the two groups were virtually indistinguishable with regard to other types of psychiatric illnes and life experiences, with one exception: divorce. The probands were 3 times more likely to be divorced than the controls. Drinking did not appear to be related to the higher divorce rate. Moderate drinkers in the proband group were as likely to be divorced as heavy drinkers and alcoholics. Divorce and alcoholism have often been associated, but the former usually is attributed to disruptive effects of the latter. The explanation may be more complicated.

Concerning both alcoholism and divorce, it is important to note that most of the subjects have by no means transversed the age of risk for either of these problems. More than 60% of the subjects were still in their 20s at the time of interview. Studies indicate that the age of risk for alcoholism is roughly 20 through 45 (Amark, 1951). Therefore, the alcoholism and divorce rates may continue to increase over the next two decades, although whether the difference between the proband and control groups will continue to widen cannot be predicted.

The finding that, apart from divorce, *only* alcoholism significantly distinguished the two groups suggests there may be a specificity in the transmission of the disorder heretofore underestimated. The rates of diagnosable depression, anxiety neurosis, criminality, and drug addiction were fairly low in both groups, and neither group had a significantly higher rate of one of these conditions than did the other. Also, it is interesting that heavy and even problem drinking, as defined in this study, failed to distinguish the two groups. If anything, there was somewhat more heavy and problem drinking in the control group than in the proband group. *This suggests that severe forms of alcohol abuse may have a genetic predisposition but that heavy drinking itself, even when responsible for occasional problems, reflects predominantly nongenetic factors.* It should be emphasized that genetic predisposition remains more probable than proven, and certainly may not apply to all alcoholics.

Another nongenetic factor that may have biased the results is selectivity in the process of adoption. Possibly those infants having a known alcoholic parent at the time of adoption may have been matched with less "desirable" parents than children of nonalcoholic parents. Adoption practices in Denmark 20-50 years ago are difficult to assess. From an adoption study of criminality also conducted in Denmark, it appears that a bias did occur in the adoption process, but only at the extreme ends of the social spectrum. In other words, upper-class adoptive parents tended to receive upper-class biological children, and lower-class adoptive parents received lower-class adoptive children. However, in the very large middle-class group there was no evidence of bias. Moreover, because the adoptive parents of the two groups did not differ with respect to educational or economic status, it would appear that a selective bias in adoption was minimal at most (see Chapter 9).

The Danish Study: Part II

In some instances, the adopted sons of the alcoholics had biological siblings *raised* by the alcoholic parent. In the second phase of the Danish study we compared the drinking problems and psychiatric disorders of children of alcoholics raised by their biological parents with those of their brothers who had been adopted early in life and raised in a different environment.

Twenty adopted sons of alcoholics had brothers raised by their alcoholic parent and available for interview. Thirty of these brothers were interviewed by a Danish psychiatrist, using the interviewing method employed in the first phase of the study. To avoid bias, interviews also were conducted with 50 nonadopted control subjects selected from census records. All interviews were blind, the interviewer having no knowledge whether he was dealing with sons of alcoholics or controls.

As a group, the nonadopted sons of alcoholics differed from their adopted brothers in the following ways:

1. They were older by an average of 3 years.
2. They were less likely to have been married.
3. As adults, they belonged to a lower social class, and their parents-of-upbringing also were of a lower social class.
4. Their parents-of-upbringing had higher rates of alcoholism and were more often "antisocial." The former was predictable, because it was known from hospital records that *all* the parents of the nonadopted children had received a diagnosis of alcoholism at one time.

Table 6 shows problems associated with drinking. In general, the nonadopted sons had no more problems than the adopted sons. The last four items represent a composite picture of drinking patterns, based on the criteria given in Table 5. Using these criteria, five men in each group were considered alcoholic, resulting in a higher rate of alcoholism in the adoptees, but not a statistically significant difference. There was some evidence that as the severity of the parents' alcoholism increased (as measured by number of hospitalizations), tendency toward alcohol problems in the sons increased.

The main finding of the study was that sons of alcoholics were no more likely to become alcoholic if they were reared by their alcoholic parent than if they were separated from their alcoholic parent soon after birth and reared by nonrelatives. This was true despite the fact that, as a group, the nonadopted sons were older than their adopted brothers and, therefore, further advanced into the age of risk for alcoholism.

Compared to the adoptees, there was also evidence that the children exposed to their alcoholic parent were raised in environments associated in other studies with increased risk of alcoholism. Their parents-of-upbringing were of a relatively low social class, and the subjects themselves were of lower socioeconomic status than their adopted brothers (it has been found that there is an increased risk of alcoholism among the lower classes). Furthermore, the nonadopted children appeared to have had a more disruptive childhood than their adopted brothers. More of them received welfare help as children; more did poorly in school; more had a parental history of psychiatric illness; all these factors are in other studies associated with an increased risk of alcoholism.

It is interesting how little environment appeared to contribute to the

Table 6

Comparison of Drinking Problems and Patterns

	% Adopted Sons, (N = 20)	% Nonadopted Sons, (N = 30)
Hallucinations	10	10
Lost Control	25	10
Amnesia	40	13
Tremor	10	14
Morning Drinking	30	21
Delirium Tremens	10	3
Rum Fits	0	0
Social Disapproval	10	20
Marital Trouble	0	7
Job Trouble	10	10
Drunken Driving Arrests	0	3
Police Trouble, other	5	10
Treated for Drinking, any	15	13
Hospitalized for Drinking	10	10
Drinking Pattern		
Moderate Drinker	60	77
Heavy Drinker, ever	15	3
Problem Drinker, ever	0	3
Alcoholic, ever	25	17

development of alcoholism among the sons of alcoholics in this sample. Our findings tend to contradict the oft-repeated assertion that alcoholism results from the interaction of multiple causes—social, psychological, biological. This may be true of milder forms of alcoholism, but, conceivably, severe alcoholism could be relatively uninfluenced by environment, given free access to alcohol. The "father's sins" may be visited on the sons even in the father's absence.

Other Adoption Studies

In the early 1940s Anne Roe and her associates at Yale obtained information about 49 foster children (both sexes) in the 20-40 year age group, 22 of normal parentage and 27 with a biological parent described as a heavy drinker (1945). Among children with heavy-drinking parents, 70% used alcohol, compared to 64% in the control parentage group. In adolescence, two children of "alcoholic-parentage" got into trouble because of drinking too much, compared to one in the "normal-parentage" group.

The authors found that adopted children of heavy drinkers had more adjustment problems in adolescence and adulthood than did adopted children of nonalcoholics, but the differences were small, and neither group had adult drinking problems. They concluded that there was no evidence of hereditary influences on drinking.

This conclusion, however, can be questioned on several grounds. First, the sample was small. There were only 21 male children of heavy drinkers and 11 of normal parents. Because women at the time of the study were at very low risk for alcoholism, discovering that they had no problem with alcohol was not unexpected. Also, the probands in the Roe study differed from the controls in other, possibly important regards. They were older at the time of placement, and a much higher percentage were placed in rural areas or small towns where alcoholism rates were considerably lower than in urban areas.

Another factor, however, may be more germane in explaining the difference between the results of the Danish and Roe studies. Although the biological parents of the proband group in the Roe study were described as heavy drinkers, it is not clear that they were alcoholic. Most had a history of antisocial behavior, but none apparently had been treated for a drinking problem. By contrast, all the biological parents of the proband group in the Danish study received a hospital diagnosis of alcoholism at a time when this diagnosis was rarely employed in Denmark, which suggests that only severe alcoholics received the diagnosis.

That severity is an important dimension is further suggested by the finding that *only* alcoholism, not heavy drinking, differentiated the adopted sons of alcoholics from the adopted sons of nonalcoholics in the Danish study. In short, severe or "classic" forms of alcoholism may have mainly a genetic basis, whereas heavy drinking may have mainly psychosocial origins.

A Danish psychiatrist, Christian Amark (1951), came to a similar conclusion. In a well-known study of alcoholism in the early 1950s, he reported that periodic and compulsive alcoholics more frequently had alcoholic children than did alcoholics whose illness presumably was less severe. Home environments were found to be equally "good" or "bad" in both groups. A recent study compared severe alcoholics with milder alcoholics and found that severe alcoholics more often had a family history of alcoholism. Through the years there have been many attempts to subclassify alcoholism into various types. Based on these observations, it would appear that a classification based on severity and family history might be a useful one.

More recently, a group of investigators at Washington University in St. Louis (including the author) has studied a group of individuals reared apart from one of their biological parents where either the biological parent or a stepparent had a drinking problem (Schuckit et al., 1972). Strictly speaking, this was not an adoption study, because most of the subjects were raised by at least one biological parent. At any rate, the subjects were more likely to have a drinking problem if their biological parent was alcoholic than if they had a stepparent who was alcoholic. Studying 32 alcoholics and 132 nonalcoholics, most of whom came from broken homes, it was found that 62% of the alcoholics had an alcoholic biological parent compared to 20% of the nonalcoholics. Simply living with an alcoholic parent appeared to have no relationship to the development of alcoholism.

CONCLUSION

In the late nineteenth and early twentieth centuries, much attention was given to the problem of how much was inherited in human behavior, as opposed to how much was learned. As Popham (1967) has noted, concern with the so-called nature-nurture problem began to decline in the 1930s and had all but disappeared by the beginning of World War II. Until recent years, there was a virtual absence of research interest in heredity as a determinant of alcohol use and alcoholism. In part, this came from an increasing awareness of the complex interrelationships of genetic and environmental factors, convincing many scientists that nature and nurture could never be unraveled. Hebb (1958), for example, writing about intelligence, warned against regarding intelligence as due *either* to heredity *or* to environment, or partly to one, partly to the other. "Each is *fully* necessary . . . To ask how much heredity contributes to intelligence is like asking how much the width of a field contributes to its area."

Nevertheless, the fact remains that alcoholism, like many illnesses, runs in families. Any attempt to understand the development of alcoholism must account for this, by now, unchallengeable fact. Why does alcoholism run in families? It is almost impossible to approach these questions without asking: What is "given"? What "comes later"? Nature has provided only a few ways to even begin to distinguish the two. These ways have been discussed in this chapter and the attempts to study them reviewed.

Chapter 9

Some considerations in the interpretation of the Danish adoption studies in relation to asocial behavior*

Sarnoff A. Mednick

and

Barry Hutchings

The adoption files at the Psykologisk Institut in Copenhagen were established by Kety, Rosenthal, Wender, and Schulsinger (1968) in order to study the genetics of schizophrenia. Since that initial study, psychopathy (Schulsinger, Chapter 6), alcoholism (Goodwin, Chapter 8) and registered criminality (Hutchings and Mednick, Chapter 7) have been studied utilizing the adoption files in similar research designs.

The adoption studies argue for the consideration of the role of genetic factors in the etiology of deviant behavior. Because of their apparently excellent separation of genetic and environmental influences, they have a rather compelling face validity. If an adopted son never has seen his deviant biological father, but nevertheless succumbs to the same form of deviance, this seems to defy any interpretation that does not include some role for genetic factors. The *direct* role of the biological father in shaping his son clearly ended at conception or soon after delivery. The scientific importance of the findings to date and their convincing nature argue for careful consideration of possible *indirect*, environ-

*The authors wish to thank Drs. Donald Goodwin, Seymour Kety, Fini Schulsinger, and Paul Wender for their extremely useful comments and suggestions made to a first draft of this paper.

mental influences on the adoptee related to the deviance of his biological parents. Such *indirect*, nongene-mediated relationships between the biological parents' deviant characteristics and the adoptee's life experiences must be ruled out before sound interpretations of the findings are possible. In addition, responsible interpretation must consider the extent to which we can justify generalization of results on Danish adoptees to non-Danish, nonadoptees.

Some reservations regarding the adoption studies have been expressed in the three preceding chapters. This note recapitulates some of these reservations and considers some additional questions.

NONGENETIC LINKS BETWEEN BIOLOGICAL PARENTS' DEVIANCE AND ADOPTEES' LIVES

If we were to find any factor that produces a correlation between characteristics of the biological parents and the life *experiences* of the adoptees, the effects of this factor on research results would have to be carefully evaluated. As a matter of fact, at the time of these adoptions, adoptive agencies in Denmark had a policy of attempting to match the biological and adoptive parents for physical characteristics (e.g., eye and hair color) and vaguely defined social characteristics. That they succeeded is attested to by the significant correlation between the social class of the biological and adoptive fathers [r (880) = .22, p < .001]. Note that although this accounts for less than 5% of the variance it is a quantitative indication that matching for certain characteristics is the result of the adoption procedure. One would not postulate that the adoption agencies match specifically for social class, but rather that they match for more general characteristics, such as intelligence or educational background, which are themselves correlated with social class. With respect to schizophrenia the problem has been discussed by Wender et al. (1973)

Thus the social class levels of the biological and adoptive parents are not independent of each other. Social class is a variable that is not independent of the diagnoses of schizophrenia, psychopathy, alcoholism, and criminality; thus, it is conceivable that the correlation between the biological parents and the index cases observed in these studies might be partly mediated by social class.

In the adoption study on criminality (Chapter 7), it was observed that there was a distinctive relationship between the biological father's criminality and the criminality of the adopted son. To what extent does this correlation between the biological father's and son's social class of rearing explain the "genetic" relationship? By determining order of entry of adoptive and biological father's criminality and social class into a multiple regression analysis, it was determined that all three of these variables have significant and independent effects on the adopted son's criminality (Chapter 7, Table 9). In the case of criminality, the social class linkage apparently cannot explain away the "genetic" effect. This type of exercise is perhaps worth repeating in other adoption studies.

Potential labeling of the adoptee

Another potential problem with the adoption method is the possibility that the adoptive family is informed by the adoption agency of deviance in the biological family. This could conceivably result in the adoptee's behavior being interpreted in accordance with this information and the labeling of the adoptee resulting. This labeling might affect the probability of the adoptee's manifesting deviance. This again represents a form of correlation between the biological and adoptive parents that is unwanted in this research design. A social worker was sent to read some of the old adoption journals and formed the impression that serious deviance in the biological parents was routinely reported to the prospective adoptive parents unless they refused the information. When the full adoptee population has been assembled, we will be able to examine this question in some depth. Meanwhile, we have completed a simple examination of one hypothesis that could be provisionally tested with the information we already had from the adoptee pilot study on criminality.

It seems likely that if the biological father's criminal career *began* the year after the birth of the child, this criminality information could not have been transmitted to the adoptive parents. On the other hand, in cases in which the criminality of the biological father started *before* the birth of the adoptee, the information *could* have been communicated and could perhaps have affected the probability of criminality in the adoptee. Of the 347 criminal biological fathers in the adoptee pilot study, 67% had their first registration for criminality before the birth of the child and 33% began their criminal career after the birth of the adoptee. For all the 347 criminal biological fathers the probability of their biological son becoming a criminal is 23%. In the cases in which the biological father committed his first offense *before* the birth of the adoptee, 23% of the adoptees became criminal. In the cases in which the biological father committed his first offense after the birth of the adoptee, 23% of the adoptees became criminal. We can tentatively conclude from this simple analysis that the *possibility* of the adoptive family being informed of the biological father's criminality is not related to an altered likelihood that the adoptive son will become a criminal. Note that these results cannot be directly interpreted as negating any influence of labeling. It is conceivable that both positive (compensatory) parental behavior and negative (vindictive) parental behavior produced a zero-sum-total effect. This question needs further study. It is also conceivable that some age-related factor (e.g., seriousness of criminality) in the biological father's criminality is confounded with this "before-and-after-adoption" variable. This possibility will be examined in future analyses.

Rosenthal et al. (1971) in their studies of schizophrenia consider a related point. They indicate that 87% of their schizophrenic biological parents first were admitted for this disorder well after the adoptee was born (average 11 years). These data are cited to indicate the minimal influence of the possible environmental variables of perinatal disturbance or rearing by a schizophrenic parent. The data could as well be used to negate a labeling hypothesis.

GENERALIZATION FROM DANISH ADOPTION STUDIES

Adoption screening

The special circumstances of the adoptions and their location in Denmark must be evaluated before the results are generalized to nonadoptive, non-Danish populations. First let us consider the fact of adoption itself.

The biological and adoptive parents and the adoptees do not represent unselected populations. The biological fathers and mothers tend to have a high prevalence of criminality (see Chapter 7). The male adoptees are somewhat more criminal than the other males in their generation. Adoptees born in the early 1930s were reared during the Great Depression; the youngest adoptees were reared during the German Occupation of Denmark, World War II, and in the immediate postwar period. Adopted controls matched for age can control for most of these effects. We do not attempt to analyse the influence of these social upheavals on the interpretation of results from the Danish adoption studies. We wish only to urge their being taken into consideration in any generalization. These problems are probably more important in the case of social deviance than mental illness. The rates of schizophrenia do not differ between adoptees and nonadopted controls (Kety, personal communication), but the criminal rates are much higher for adoptees.

We must also recall that the adoptive process results in screening of the biological and adoptive parents and the adoptee by the adoptive agencies. This screening can produce skewed populations; this possibility must be checked and taken into account in application of findings to nonadopted populations. In the case of the schizophrenia adoption studies a nonadopted control population was gathered to examine precisely this question. It is difficult to determine the exact practices of 40 years ago. Even given the stated policies of administrative agencies, the day-to-day practice would vary from case to case as a function of individual and local factors. However, there were stated policies which were more or less uniformly administered. These appear in several sources, including the major organizations involved in adoption for the period 1924-1947. In the annual report for 1946-1947 the largest of these organizations states the following (authors' translation):

"Before a child is cleared for adoption, it is investigated with respect to health, and an attempt is made to obtain detailed information on the child's family background and to form an impression of its developmental potential. Not only for the adoptive parents, but also for the child itself, these investigations are of great importance for its correct placement. Information is obtained on the child's mother and father; on whether or not there is serious physical or mental illness in the family background; criminal records are obtained for the biological parents; and in many cases school reports are obtained. By means of personal interview with the mother an impression of her is formed. Where information is uncovered on convicted criminality or on mental retardation, mental illness, etc. in the family background, the case is referred to the Institute of Human Genetics of Copenhagen University, with whom there exists a valuable cooperation for advice on the advisability of adoption." (Mothers Aid Organization for Copenhagen, Copenhagen County and Frederiksborg County. Annual Report for 1946-47, page 13).

Danish site effects

We will now discuss the possible effect of the fact that the adoptions took place in Denmark. Denmark must rank among the more homogeneous (low variability) Western nations with respect to social, economic, or most other deviance-related environmental dimensions. This fact has implications for the interpretation of Danish genetic research findings.

The laboratory experimenter in behavior genetics reduces the variance ascribable to environmental influences when he wishes to explore behavioral differences between genetically differentiated strains. The less the environmental variance, the easier it is to interpret existing strain behavior differences as genetically inspired. As environmental variance increases, the strain difference effects will become more and more masked. The researcher in *human* behavior genetics operates with considerably reduced or, more often, no control over the variability of his subjects' environment. Nevertheless, the extent of variability of a natural human research milieu (in our case the Kingdom of Denmark) may markedly influence the extent to which existent genetic factors will be masked or observed. As mentioned above, the amount of variability in Denmark for most known deviance-related environmental dimensions is less than that of most Western countries. Consider what this might mean for twin research. If a pair of identical twins lives in an homogenous society, then, even if they are separated temporarily or for long periods, their surrounds will most likely remain relatively similar. As a consequence, their genetic and environmental similarity will tend to result in concordance for deviant behavior. On the other hand, consider a pair of identical twins living in a society characterized by high variability. During temporary or extended separations, the twins may be exposed to environments with dramatically divergent crime-inducing properties (e.g., a small town versus a ghetto area in a metropolis). If crime-related genetic predispositions exist, and if these twins have inherited such predispositions, then observed discordance for criminality in these monozygotic twins may actually mask an existing genetic factor. An analogous argument could be made for the adoptee and his biological parents. Note that these arguments are especially relevant for asocial behaviors, because these are more sensitive to social inequalities.

Thus the extent to which existing genetic predispositions to deviance are observed in any given empirical investigation depends on the study site's variability on critical dimensions. In a high variability site, existing genetic predispositions tend to be masked; in a low variability site, existing genetic predispositions are more readily expressed.

Denmark is a relatively good environment for observation of the expression of existing genetic factors. Extrapolation of the findings of the Danish adoption studies to other national circumstances must take these considerations into account.

Chapter 10

XYY and XXY Men:
Criminality and Aggression*

Herman A. Witkin

Sarnoff A. Mednick

Fini Schulsinger

Eskild Bakkestrom

Karl O. Christiansen

Donald R. Goodenough

Kurt Hirschhorn

Claes Lundsteen

David R. Owen

John Philip

Donald B. Rubin

Martha Stocking

*For advice, in various ways at different points in the conception and conduct of the study, in analyses of the data, and in the preparation of this report we are grateful to L. L. Cavalli-Sforza, P. Holland, J. Lederberg, R. Schiavi, S. A. Shah, and A. Theilgaard. We are indebted to the Danish Ministry of Justice for making available the criminal records used in this report. This paper is reprinted with the kind permission of *Science*, 1976, 193, 547-555.

Few issues in behavior genetics have received more public and scientific attention than that given to the possible role of an extra Y chromosome in human aggression. Soon after the literature began to suggest an elevated frequency of the XYY genotype among inmates of institutions for criminals and delinquents, interest in this issue had a meteoric rise; and it has been sustained ever since. This happened for several reasons. Stories about a few men who had or were presumed to have an extra Y chromosome and who had committed serious crimes were given prominent attention in the press, suggesting the intriguing idea that the single Y chromosome normally found in males contributes to "aggressive tendencies" in that sex and that an extra Y carries these tendencies beyond their usual bounds. Reports of antisocial behavior in XYY men, often based on a single case, soon began to appear in the scientific literature. (Forssman, 1967; Goodman, Smith, and Migeon, 1967; Kelly, Almy, and Bernard, 1967; Persson, 1967; Richards and Stewart, 1966) and were taken as evidence of an XYY-aggression linkage. The serious moral and legal implications of such a linkage attracted the interest of social scientists and legal groups to the XYY phenomenon (Shah, 1970) and students of genetics and psychology saw in it, as Lederberg, (1973) has said, "one of the most tangible leads for connecting genetic constitution with behavior in man."

A number of studies have supported the earlier finding of an elevated frequency of cases with an XYY complement among men in institutions, particularly in penal-mental institutions. In view of institutional variations in admissions policies, not always clearly specified in the published reports, it is difficult to judge whether the tendency of XYY men to appear more frequently in penal-mental than in straight penal institutions reflects the involvement of a mental aspect as well as a penal aspect. No clear tendency toward higher representation of XYY's in mental institutions has been found; however, studies of such institutions have been few (Jarvik et al., 1973; Borgaonkar and Shah, 1974; Hook, 1973; and Owen, 1972). At the same time, these studies have not provided clear evidence of whether or not there exists an "XYY syndrome" of which antisocial behavior is a prominent component. Neither have they provided a definitive answer to the question of why men with an extra Y chromosome are at higher risk for institutionalization than XY men. For the sake of identifying the kind of research that is needed to clarify these issues, it is worth reviewing the main limitations of the studies on which our present information about XYY men is based, and also the lacunae in our knowledge.

First, the search for XYY men has often been conducted in selected groups presumed to be likely to contain them, such as institutionalized men and tall men. Second, a number of reports now in the literature are based on observations of a single case or just a few cases. Third, many studies of XYY's have not included control XY's; and in those that did, comparisons were often made with knowledge of the genotype of the individuals being evaluated (Borgaonkar and Shah, 1974). The control groups used have varied in nature, and comparison of results from different studies has therefore been difficult. There has been a dearth of psychological, somatic, and social data obtained for the same individual XYY men. Finally, there do not yet exist adequate prevalence data for the XYY genotype in the general adult population with which the XYY yield of any particular study may be compared. Though incidence data on neonates are available for a fairly large number of subjects, incidence studies of neonates are still few, and there are potential problems in the practice of pooling highly variable incidence findings from studies with populations that are quite different from each other or whose characteristics have not been adequately specified.

With the evidence in its present state, it is not surprising to find divergent views about the support it provides for a link between XYY and aggression, as for example in the contradictory conclusions reached in recent reviews of the XYY literature (Jarvik, et al. 1973; Borgaonkar and Shah, 1974; Hook, 1973; and Owen, 1972). Whatever the interpretation of the available evidence, however, most investigators concerned with the XYY problem are agreed on the research that is now required to determine whether the XYY complement has any behavioral or social consequences. What is needed, ideally, is an ascertainment study of a large population unselected with regard to institutionalization or height, and a comparison of the XYY cases identified with control XY's in psychological, somatic, social, and developmental characteristics, the evaluation of these characteristics in the two groups being made according to a double-blind procedure.

The study we undertook, done in Denmark because of the excellent social records kept there, was designed to meet as many of these specifications as our financial resources allowed. It was already evident at the time we undertook the study that XYY's tend to be very tall. This has been shown both by height data from XYY ascertainment studies of unselected male populations (Bartlett, Hurley, Brand, and Poole, 1968; Crandall, Carrell, and Sparkes, 1972; DeBault, Johnston, and Loeffelholz, 1972; Hook and Kim, 1971; Jacobs, Price, Richmond, and Ratcliff, 1971; Nielsen, 1971; Vianna, Frota-Pessoa, Lion, and Decourt, 1972) and by studies that compared XYY's in height to their siblings and parents (Owen, 1972). As a way of maximizing the chances of obtaining a sufficient sample of XYY's for intensive individual study, we decided to do chromosomal determinations of all men in the top 15 percent of the height distribution of our Danish male population. A sampling of men in the bottom 85 percent would also have been desirable, but the probability of finding XYY's among shorter men is so small as to make an effective study of shorter XYY's too expensive to conduct.

A first aim of this research project was to determine whether XYY's from the total general population have an elevated crime rate. A second aim, if an elevated crime rate appeared, was to identify intervening variables that may mediate the relation between an extra Y chromosome and increased antisocial behavior. Three variables of particular interest are aggressiveness, intelligence, and height.

A common interpretation of the finding that XYY's tend to be over-represented in criminal institutions is that aggressiveness is an intervening variable. In this view, an extra Y chromosome increases aggressive tendencies and these, in turn, lead to increased criminal behavior. If this interpretation is correct, we may expect crimes committed by XYY men to be aggressive in nature, involving assultive actions against other persons. We designate this the aggression hypothesis.

Concerning intelligence the reasoning is as follows: In common with most genetic aberrations, an extra Y in the male chromosomal complement is likely to have an adverse effect on development. Among possible dysfunctions, of particular interest for the XYY question is dysfunction in the intellectual domain. There is some evidence, although it is hardly consistent, of an intellectual impairment in XYY men (Owen, 1972; Baughman, Jr., and Mann, 1972; Finley, et al., 1973; McKerracher, 1971; Nielsen and Christensen, 1974 and Noël et al., 1974). Intellectual impairment may contribute to antisocial behavior. It seems plausible also that when individuals with impaired intellectual functioning commit crimes, they are more likely to be apprehended than are criminals of normal intelligence. This conception of intelligence as an intervening variable, mediating the relation between the presence of an extra Y chromosome and antisocial behavior, may be designated the intellectual-dysfunction hypothesis.

The extreme height of XYY's may facilitate aggressive acts on their part. In addition, it may cause them to be perceived by others as dangerous, with the possible consequence that they are more likely than shorter men to be suspected of crimes, to be pursued and apprehended, and, when tried, to be convicted. The view that tallness may serve as an intervening variable we designate the height hypothesis.

Because XYY's (Klinefelter males) also tend to be tall, we could expect our case-finding effort in the top 15 percent height group to identify a number of XXY's as well as XYY's. Most studies of XXY's have suffered from essentially the same limitations as those mentioned earlier for studies of XYY's; a study of XXY's is therefore of value in its own right. In addition, there is some evidence that XXY's also appear in institutions with disproportionate frequency. This raises the possibility that any sex chromosome aberration in males, and not particularly an extra Y, may be associated with increased risk of institutionalization (Borgaonkar and Shah, 1974). Comparison of XYY's and XXY's may help to assess this possibility.

This Chapter deals with the results of the case-finding study among tall men and with the evidence obtained to this point from the social records available for the XYY and XXY men who were found. An intensive individual study is now being conducted with these men and their controls.*

CASE-FINDING PROCEDURE

The population from which we sampled consisted of all male Danish citizens born to women who were residents of the municipality of Copenhagen, Denmark, between 1 January 1944 and 31 December 1947, inclusive. Not only did Copenhagen afford a very large source population, but available demographic data indicated that most men born in the city at that time would still be living there. The parish records, in which all births are registered, were used to identify the males born there in the chosen period. They numbered 31,436. The *folkeregister* (the Danish national register) provided current addresses and other information.

Information about the height of these men was obtained from draft board records where possible. The use of the four-year period between 1944 and 1947 to define the target population provided us with a group of men who were at least 26 years old, the age by which Danish men are required to report to their draft boards for a physical examination, at which time their heights are recorded. For the small group of men who for some reason had never visited their draft boards, height data were obtained from other sources, such as institutions and the civil defense. In the very few cases where such sources were not available, cards were addressed directly to the men themselves requesting that they send us their heights.

---

*Subjects in the individual case study are the XYY's and XXY's identified in the case-finding study described below, and two XY controls for each. Both controls are matched to the proband in height, age, and parental social class, and one is matched as well in intellectual level, as judged from scores on an army-selection test. The tests given these subjects include a battery, approximately 16 hours in duration, of cognitive tests, personality tests, an interview, and physical, neurological, and neurophysiological examinations.

By these methods, a group was composed consisting of 28,884 men who were still alive when the study began and for whom height information could be obtained. This group numbered 2552 fewer cases than the target population of 31,436 Copenhagen-born men. Of these 2552 cases 1791 were dead; 37 could not be traced for height determination; 21 could not be located at all in the *folkeregister* (probably for such reasons as name changes, death at birth, address change at birth), and 703 had emigrated and no record of their height was available. Of the 644 emigrants for whom we were able to determine age at emigration, 85.2 percent had emigrated before age 18, so that it is probable that in many of those cases the decisions about emigration were made by parents.

A cutoff point of 184 cm was used in composing the tall group in which the search for sex chromosome anomalies was to be conducted. The resulting group consisted of 4591 men, the top 15.9 percent of the height distribution in the total group of the 28,884. Deaths reduced the tall group by 33 during the case-finding period, leaving a total of 4558 men to be searched for sex-chromosome anomalies. An attempt was made to visit the homes of all 4558 for the purpose of obtaining blood samples and buccal smears to be used in determining chromosomal constitution.

Before home visiting began, members of the study staff were interviewed by the news media. These interviews provided an opportunity to publicize the purpose and nature of the study, with the result that most of the men who were asked to participate in the study had already heard of it when first approached. The initial individual contact was made by a letter, which mentioned the nature of the study and indicated that someone from the study staff would visit at a specified time. If the subject expected not to be at home at that time, he was asked to return a card on which he could suggest an alternative time. Men not found at home, and who had not asked for an alternative date were subsequently revisited, up to a total of 14 times in the most extreme instance.

When the subject was seen, he was shown a newspaper clipping reporting the interview with our staff members and any questions he had were answered. The subject was also assured that his anonymity would be maintained. He was then asked whether he would be willing to give a buccal smear and, if he agreed, whether he would be willing to give a few drops of blood from an earlobe as well. The home visitor also asked the subject to fill out a questionnaire, and told him that at a later time he might be asked to participate further in the study. As the case-finding effort progressed, various methods were adopted to facilitate and encourage participation, such as setting up a station at one of the centrally located hospitals in Copenhagen to which the men were invited to come during a wide range of daytime and evening hours, and offering small financial inducements.

The 4139 men for whom sex chromosome determinations were made constituted 90.8 percent of the starting group of 4558 living tall men. The identity of two of the sampled cases found to be XY's was lost to us in our records and could not be considered in the data analysis. Of the 419 unexamined cases, 174 men declined to participate; 138 men emigrated in the course of the study or were sailors and away from Denmark; 25 were destitute men without identifiable homes; and 82 men, on repeated visits, were not found at the official addresses listed for them in the *folkeregister*. It is likely that many of these 82 men had moved in with friends and did not register this move as an official change of residence. Some characteristics of these cases, and of the 174 men who declined to take part are given below.

The buccal smears and blood samples were taken to the Chromosomal Laboratory of Rigshospitalet, in Copenhagen, for analysis. The buccal smears were stained with hematoxylin for the detection of X chromatin (Barr and Bertram, 1949) and with quinacrine dihydrochloride for the detection of Y chromatin (Pearson and Bobrow, 1970). The peripheral blood was treated by a micromethod modification (Hirschhorn, 1965) of the method of Moorhead et al., (1960). Chromosome preparations were stained conventionally with orcein and by the method of Seabright (1971) for G-banding and Caspersson et al. (1970) for Q-banding and identification of the Y chromosome (Philip et al., in press).

DOCUMENTARY DATA

A variety of records was available for almost all the men in the study. The present report is limited to data from these records for five variables: height, convictions for criminal offenses, level of intellectual functioning as indicated by scores on an army selction test and by educational attainment, and parental social class at the time of the subject's birth.

The sources of information about height have already been described.

The source of data on convictions for criminal offenses was penal certificates (*straffeattest*) obtained from penal registers (*strafferegistrene*) maintained in the offices of local police chiefs. These certificates are

extracts of court records of trials and cover all violations of the penal
code that resulted in convictions. Offenses in the Danish penal code
include such acts as these, among others: forgery, intentional arson,
sexual offenses, premeditated homicide, attempted homicide, man-
slaughter, assault and battery, housebreaking, larceny, receiving stolen
goods, and damage to property belonging to others. The penal certificates contain highly reliable information concerning the section of the
penal law violated and the penalty imposed. A subject was considered
to have a criminal record if he was convited of one or more criminal
offenses.

For evaluation of level of intellectual functioning, two kinds of measures were used. One was scores from the test employed in screening
army recruits for intelligence, the Børge Priens Prøver (BPP), available
from the draft-board records. Because the BPP was constructed as a
screening device, it covers only a limited number of cognitive dimensions. The BPP scores are accordingly only rough indicators of intellectual level. The scores could not be obtained for some men; most frequent
in this group were men who had never taken the test and men whose
records were not available because they were in the army.

The second measure of intellectual functioning was educational level
achieved. In Denmark examinations are given at the end of the 9th, 10th,
and 13th years of schooling. From the available social records it was
possible to determine which, if any, of these examinations was passed.
For our "educational index" subjects who passed no examination were
given a score of 0, and those who passed the first-, second-, and third-
level examinations were given scores of 1, 2, and 3, respectively. It
should be noted that the maximum rating assigned was 3 regardless of
how many additional years of education the individual may have had.
Not a single one of the XYY's or XXY's reached the 13-year examination,
but a number of the XY controls did and may have gone on for
additional education. In a very small number of cases information
needed for determining the educational index could not be obtained.

Parental socioeconomic status (SES) was classified primarily according to father's occupation at the time of the subject's birth. In a small
number of cases the father or his occupation was not known; in some of
these instances mother's occupation was known and was used instead.
A seven-point SES classification was used, modified from a nine-point
classification devised by Svalastoga (1959).

Table 1

Crime Rates and Means for Background Variables for XY's, XYY's and XXY's

Group	CRIMINALITY		ARMY SELECTION TEST BPP			EDUCATIONAL INDEX			PARENTAL SES			HEIGHT		
	Rate	N	Mean	SD	N	Mean	SD	N	Mean	SD	N	Mean	SD	N
XY	9.3%	4096	43.7	11.4	3759	1.55	1.18	4084	3.7	1.7	4058	187.1	3.0	4096
XYY	41.7[b]	12	29.7[c]	8.2	12	.58[b]	0.86	12	3.2	1.5	12	190.8[c]	4.6	12
XXY	18.8	16	28.4[c]	14.1	16	.81[a]	0.88	16	4.2	1.8	16	189.8[c]	3.6	16

[a] $p < .05$
[b] $p < .01$
[c] $p < .001$

Note: Significance level next to any value refers to difference between that value and corresponding value for control group, using a two-sided test. For criminality rate, an exact binomial test was used; for all other variables a *t* test was used.

FREQUENCY OF XYY's AND XXY's
AND OF CRIMINALS AMONG THEM

Among the 4139 men for whom sex chromosome determinations were made, 12 XYY's and 16 XXY's were identified. These frequencies represent prevalence rates of 2.9/1000 and 3.9/1000 respectively. Thirteen men were identified as XY's with other chromosomal anomalies. The remainder, all identified as having the normal XY complement, constituted the control group. (The identity of two of the sampled cases found to be XY's was lost to us in our records and could not be considered in the data analysis).

A search in the penal registers showed that 41.7 percent of the XYY's (5 of 12 cases), 18.8 percent of the XXY's (3 of 16 cases), and 9.3 percent of the XY controls had been convicted of one or more criminal offenses (Table 1). The difference between the percentages for the XYY's and the XY controls is statistically significant ($p < .01$, exact binomial test). The rate for the XXY's is somewhat higher than the rate for the XY controls, but that difference is not significant; neither is the difference in rates between the XYY's and XXY's.

A first approach to evaluation of the aggression hypothesis was to examine the nature of the crimes of which the five XXY's had been convicted (Table 2). Their offenses were not particularly acts of aggression against people. Only in case 2 do we find an instance of such an act. The difference between the XYY's and XY's in percentage of cases with one or more convictions for crimes of violence against another person— 8.4 percent (1 man out of the 12) versus 1.8 percent (71 out of 4096)—is not statistically significant (one-tailed exact binomial test). If we compare only those who had criminal convictions, the XYY's and XY's are again very similar in percentage of convictions that involved crimes of violence against a person (20.0 and 19.4 percent respectively). These data provide no evidence that XYY's are more likely to commit crimes of violence than XY's. Of the 149 offenses of which the five XYY's were convicted (most of them attributable to two of these men), 145 were against property, many of them thefts of a motor vehicle, a motor-assisted cycle, or a bicycle. The four exceptional offenses include the one instance of aggression already cited, one case of procuring for prostitution, one case of a false alarm to the police, and one case of calling the fire department after setting a small fire.

The generally mild penalties imposed on the convicted XYY's (Table 2) indicate that their crimes were not extremely serious. By far the most severe sentence was imprisonment for somewhat less than a year (case 2). As an aid to maintaining anonymity of the cases and yet conveying

Table 2

Nature of Offenses of XYYs Convicted on One or More Criminal Charges

Case #2

This man is a chronic criminal who, since early adolescence, has spent 9 of 15 years in youth prisons and regular prisons. By far his most frequent criminal offense, especially in his youth, has been theft, or attempted theft of a motor vehicle. Other charges included burglary, embezzlement, and procuring for prostitution. On a single occasion he committed a mild form of violence against an unoffending person; for this together with one case of burglary he received a sentence of around three quarters of a year. This aggressive act was an isolated incident in a long period of chronic criminality. Except for this act, and the charge of procuring, all his nearly 50 offenses were against property, predominantly larceny and burglary. His single most severe penalty was somewhat less than a year in prison. Most of his crimes were committed in the company of other persons. (BPP, 27)

Case #3

This man committed two thefts, one in late adolescence, the second in his early twenties. The penalties for both were mild; a small fine for the first, and less than 3 months in prison for the second. He has been crime-free for the past 7 years. (BPP, 37)

Case #5

This man committed two petty offenses as a young adult, within a short time of each other (one the theft of a motor-assisted cycle, the other a petty civil offense) for which the penalties were detentions of approximately 2 weeks and less than 2 weeks, respectively. He has been crime-free for the past 10 years. (BPP, 28)

Case #7

This man committed his only criminal offenses in his twenties, within a short period of time: falsely reporting a traffic accident to the police and causing a small fire. On both occasions he was intoxicated. The penalty was probation. He has been crime-free for the last 5 years. (BPP, 25)

Case #12

This man was under welfare care as a child and has spent only 3 to 4 years of the last 20 years outside of institutions for the retarded. He is an episodic criminal who, when very young, committed arson. Later, his crimes included theft of motor vehicles, burglary, larceny and embezzlement. His more than 90 registered offenses were all against property, mostly theft and burglary.

Table 2 (Continued)

For crimes committed while he was out of an institution, the penalty imposed was placement in an institution for the mentally retarded. For crimes committed while he was in this kind of institution—once theft of a bicycle, another time theft of a quantity of beverage—he was continued in the institution. (BPP, 18) (Since this man was mentally retarded and spent many years in an institution for the retarded, he was not given a BPP at the draft board. The BPP of 18 was estimated by a stepwise linear regression, using a double cross-validity design, from the correlation between BPP scores and scores for the WAIS for the men in the individual case study.)

Table 3

Nature of Offenses of XXYs Convicted on One or More Criminal Charges

Case #17

This man's only criminal offense, committed when he was well into his 20s, was that he attacked his wife in an exceptionally brutal way, though she did not provoke him. This happened twice, within a very short interval, while he was under the influence of liquor. For this he was imprisoned for somewhat more than a year. (BPP, 26)

Case #25

The criminal career of this man consisted of two offenses: the first, in late adolescence, a theft of edibles from a food store, for which he was placed on probation, the second, the theft of a motor vehicle, for which he was given less than 3 weeks of simple detention. Both crimes were committed in company with others. He has been crime-free for the last 7 years. (BPP, 11)

Case #27

This man had a short period of juvenile delinquency. His offenses included attempted theft and theft of a motor vehicle and a bicycle, burglary, and theft from a vending machine. On his first offense, in early adolescence, the charge was withdrawn and he was put under the care of child welfare authorities. His two other penalties consisted of withdrawal of charge on payment of a fine. Several of his offenses were committed in company with another person. For the last 10 years he has been crime-free. (BPP, 16) the essence of their criminal records, approximate, rather than actual, values of penalties (as in this instance) and ages are given in the text and in Table 2. Also suggesting that the XYY's with records of criminal convictions are not serious criminals is the fact that for one (case 5) the last conviction was ten years ago, for another (case 3) five years ago, and for a third (case 7) five years ago. Of the remaining two XYY's, both of whom had extensive criminal records, one (case 12) is mentally retarded. In fact, all five of these XYY's have BPP's below the average of 43.7 (Table 1) of the XY controls, all but one of them well below that average.

There is a suggestion in our data that several of the crimes of XYY's were committed under circumstances which made detection of the crime and apprehension of the perpetrator particularly likely. Thus, one man sent in a false alarm directly to the police about a presumably serious traffic accident. Another man committed many burglaries of homes while the owners were on the premises.

Turning to the three XXY's with criminal records (Table 3), we find that one, in the single crime he committed, assaulted his wife in an extremely brutal way, while under the influence of alcohol. The other two had short periods of juvenile delinquency, and the penalties imposed on them were slight. The last conviction of one was seven years ago, of the other ten years ago. All three have BPP scores well below the XY average. Finally, in percentage of cases with one or more convictions for crimes of violence against another person, the difference between the XXY's and the XY controls (6.2 percent versus 1.8 percent) was not statistically significant (one-tailed exact binomial test).

Our case-finding procedures provided an opportunity to obtain some additional evidence on real-life social behavior of XYY's and XXY's. As noted, when necessary, repeated visits were paid to the homes of men from whom we were seeking buccal smears and blood samples. It is reasonable to speculate that men who required many visits before contact was made with them, under circumstances where the visit was expected and the opportunity given to propose an alternative time, were thereby showing a lack of cooperativeness. The mean number of home visits required to obtain a specimen was not significantly different between the XY controls and the XYY's or XXY's. Being at home or not seems related to marital status. A comparison of randomly selected samples of 150 men found at home on the first visit and 150 men not at home showed that in the first group 35 percent were single and 65 percent were married, whereas in the second group 60 percent were single and 40 percent married.

In the individual case study, the XYY's and XXY's were again not significantly different from their controls in frequency of refusals to participate on the first invitation.

As a first step toward evaluating the intellectual-dysfunction hypothesis, the intellectual level of each of the two proband groups was compared to that of the XY controls, scores on the army selection test (BPP) and the educational index being used for this purpose. For both kinds of measures the mean for the control group (Table 1) is significantly higher than the means for either the XYY or the XXY group ($p < .05$ in each instance, t test). The means for the two proband groups are not significantly different from each other. (It should be noted that the two indicators of intellectual level we used are highly related, for the control group the correlation between BPP scores and educational index is .59 [$p < .00005$, t test].)

Having established that the proband groups are significantly lower than the XY controls on both measures of intellectual level, we next examine the relation of these measures to criminality. Our data show, first, that BPP scores are significantly related to frequency of occurrence of registered crimes leading to convictions. In the control group, men with no record of such crimes had a mean BPP of 44.5, whereas those with one or more such crimes had a mean BPP of 35.5 ($p < .0001$, t test). The educational index showed a similar relation to criminality (means of 1.62 for noncriminals and 0.74 for criminals [$p < .00001$, t test]).

Overall, then, the pattern of results on intellectual functioning provides support for the intellectual-dysfunction hypothesis.

Both proband groups are significantly taller than the XY control groups (Table 1). Within the restricted height range of the XY's, however, noncriminals (mean height 187.1 cm) were slightly taller ($p = .0013$, t test) than criminals (mean height, 186.7 cm), a finding contrary to the hypothesis that tallness may include the relation between the extra Y chromosome and the likelihood of criminal convictions.

In neither proband group is parental SES significantly different from that of the XY control group (Table 1). As expected, parental SES was significantly higher ($p < .0001$, t test) for noncriminals (mean = 3.71) than for criminals (mean = 3.02).

CRIMINAL RATES AFTER ADJUSTMENT FOR BACKGROUND VARIABLES

We next compare the criminal rates of XYY's and XXY's with those of XY's equivalent to them in level of intellectual functioning, height, and parental SES. Only subjects for whom complete data were available are included (all 12 XYY's, all 16 XXY's, and 3738 XY's). The analysis consists of three stages: the first step establishes the probability that an XY, with a particular set of values for the background variables is a criminal; the second step establishes for each XYY or XXY the probability that he would be a criminal if he were an XY with his background-variable values; the third step compares the observed frequency of criminals in the proband group with the frequency predicted in the second step.

To permit use of existing programs for the log-linear analysis we employed, it was necessary to make the two continuous variables, BPP and height, categorical. Past work (Cochran, 1968) with simpler problems suggests that five or six categories often provide a very good representation of a continuous variable. Because height showed a very low relation to criminality in our sample of tall men, we used only five categories for height. The finding that BPP is strongly related to criminality, particularly within the restricted range of low BPP scores, made it advisable to use more categories for BPP. Accordingly, seven categories were employed for this variable.

In the 980-cell contingency table representing all combinations of the $3 \times 7 \times 4 \times 7$ categories for height, BPP, educational index, and parental SES, respectively, let us consider a particular cell. If $n_1 + n_2$ of the 3738 XY's (n_1 being criminals and n_2 noncriminals) fall in that cell, the proportion $n_1/n_1 + n_2$ gives a good estimate of the probability that a new XY in that cell will be a criminal, provided the value of $n_1 + n_2$ is large. In many of the 980 cells, however, both n_1 and n_2 are small; in fact in 376 cells both n_1 and n_2 are zero. But it is not necessary to consider each cell independently. Instead, a model may be built for these probabilities which lets us "borrow strength" from similar cells. Critical in building such a model is the definition of similarity. The method we used in constructing a model for our contingency table has been described by Bishop, Fienberg, and Holland (1975). This method is based on log-linear models that are analogous to the usual linear models (that is, regression and analysis of variance). The difference between them is that log-linear models are appropriate for categorical dependent variables (such as criminal/noncriminal), whereas linear models are appropriate for continuous dependent variables. For those familiar with linear models, it is appropriate to think of the analyses performed here as if they were regressions, with criminality taken as the dependent variable and BPP, height, parental SES, and educational index as independent variables, even though in fact the computations required for the log-linear analyses are quite different. We present here only the final results of our analyses.

For the 3738 tall XY's used in the analyses, the proportion of criminals in each of the 980 cells of the contingency table can be very accurately predicted from a model with only six parameters; a grand mean parameter, reflecting the overall level of criminality in the population; one regression parameter reflecting the tendency of criminality to increase as parental SES decreases; two regression parameters (for linear and quadratic components) reflecting the tendency of criminality to increase more and more rapidly as educational index decreases; and two regression parameters (for linear and·quadratic components) reflecting the tendency of criminality to increase more and more rapidly as BPP decreases. The absence of two kinds of parameters should be noted. There are no parameters relating criminality to height; because in the presence of the components for parental SES, BPP, and educational index there is no additional effect attributable to height. Also, there are no parameters reflecting interactions among these variables, because their effects on criminality are independent.

The fit of this six-parameter model to the full contingency table is extremely good. Globally, the adequacy of the fit is indicated by the log-likelihood ratio criterion divided by its degrees of freedom. (In fact,

Table 4

Individual XYY's: Values of background variables, observed criminality (1 = record of one or more convictions, 0 = no record), and probability of criminality predicted from the XY model.

Case No.	Educa-tional Index	Parental SES	BPP	Height (cm)	Observed	PREDICTED Proba-bility	Standard Error
1	0	2	41	201	0	.14	.013
2	0	1	27	188	1	.21	.018
3	2	6	37	194	1	.05	.008
4	1	3	23	100	0	.22	.026
5	0	3	28	191	1	.18	.012
6	0	3	19	191	0	.27	.022
7	0	4	25	193	1	.16	.013
8	2	4	44	192	0	.05	.005
9	0	4	24	187	0	.25	.024
10	2	2	37	184	0	.07	.009
11	0	5	33	196	0	.15	.016
12	0	1	18[a]	185	1	.31	.027
					$n = 5$	$n = 2.06$	

[a]Estimated (see Table 2, footnote).

this corresponds to an F test in the analysis of variance or multiple regression. Under the null hypothesis that the model reflects the true state of nature the ratio should be about unity, and it should be larger than unity if the model does not fit). This criterion for the six-parameter model and our four-way table is 491.65/(980-376-6) or 0.82. The significance test of the adequacy of the model follows from the fact that under the six-parameter model the log-likelihood criterion is distributed as χ^2 with 598 degrees of freedom. Hence, the significance level for the text of the adequacy of the six-parameter model, as opposed to the alternative one-parameter-per-cell model, is $p > 0.99$. The six-parameter model thus cannot be rejected.

Locally, the fit of the six-parameter model is also very good. In individual cells with reasonably large $n_1 + n_2$ values, the estimated probability is close to the observed proportion; and in collections of cells in which the total $n_1 + n_2$ is large, the estimated probability is also close to the observed proportion.

We now apply this model to the XYY and XXY probands. Table 4 and 5 show the educational index, parental SES, BPP, and height of each proband and whether or not he had a criminal record. Also shown is the probability, predicted from the six-parameter model, that he would be a criminal if he were an XY. The last column gives the estimated standard errors of the estimated proportions. Since the sample size for the model (3738) is very large compared to the number of parameters used, these estimated standard errors are probably very accurate. It should be noted that for both XYY's and XXY's, the standard error is less than 16 percent of the estimated proportion except in one case (an XXY), in which it is 19 percent. Hence, the predicted probabilities are very accurate, particularly for the XYY's and may be considered exact for our purposes.

The number of criminals to be expected in each of the proband groups if their crime rate was the same as that of XY's equivalent in parental SES, educational index, BPP, and height is given by the sum of the predicted probabilities (column 7 of each table); the observed number of criminals is given by the sum of the 0 and 1 values (column 6).

The result of adjustments for BPP, parental SES, and educational index indicates that these variables account for some of the raw differences in criminality between the XXY and SES groups. However, an elevation in crime rate among the XYY's remains ($p = .037$; one-sided exact binomial test) even after these adjustments are made, the observed and the predicted number of criminals in the XYY group being 5 and 2.06, respectively. The XXY's are not significantly different in criminality from the XY group ($p = .41$) after the adjustment for background variables is made, as is shown by the agreement between observed and predicted number of criminals (3 versus 3.16).

Table 5

Individual XXY's: Values of background variables, observed criminality (1 = record of one or more convictions, 0 = no record), and probability of criminality predicted from the XY model.

| | | | | | CRIMINALITY | PREDICTED | |
Case No.	Educa-tional Index	Parental SES	BPP	Height (cm)	Observed	Proba-bility	Standard Error
13	1	4	27	188	0	.13	.014
14	2	5	47	185	0	.04	.005
15	0	4	35	191	0	.16	.013
16	0	3	23	184	0	.27	.022
17	1	3	26	187	1	.14	.014
18	2	4	50	195	0	.05	.005
19	0	5	14	192	0	.37	.058
20	2	7	49	186	0	.04	.006
21	0	3	14	188	0	.41	.054
22	0	5	9	197	0	.37	.057
23	1	1	39	191	0	.12	.015
24	2	7	33	188	0	.07	.013
25	0	4	11	190	1	.39	.055
26	0	1	15	195	0	.31	.027
27	0	4	16	190	1	.25	.024
28	2	7	46	189	0	.04	.006
					$n = 3$	$n = 3.16$	

DISCUSSION AND CONCLUSIONS

A first question to consider is the validity of the ascertainment data of 2.9/1000 XYY's and 3.9/1000 XXY's among the tall men sampled in the study.

For XYY's other prevalence data are available from two recent large-scale studies of tall men, but, comparison with ours is made difficult by differences in source populations and in the heights taken as cut-off points. In one of these studies (Zeuthen and Nielsen, 1973) the prevalence rate for the tall normal men sampled appears to be a good deal higher than our own, whereas in the other (Noël, et al, 1974) it seems not very different.

Studies of the incidence of XYY in neonates are still few in number and their results variable. Two recent reviews have tentatively suggested an incidence rate of about 1/1000 live-born males (Hook, 1973; Owen, 1972) another (Borgaonkar & Shah, 1974) rate in the range of 1/1500 to 1/3000. On the basis of these values the expected number of XYY's in our total population at birth would be about 9 to about 29. For several reasons it is difficult to determine the proportion of these who would be likely to present in the tall segment we sampled in adulthood. There are uncertainties about the rate of attrition through death among XYY's.* There are also uncertainties about how many XYY's there might be among the unexamined tall men in our study (those who refused to participate, who emigrated, or who could not be located) and among the shorter men we did not examine.* Though our obtained frequency falls well within the range estimated from neonatal studies, given all the limitations and uncertainties involved in generating those estimates the correspondence must be interpreted with caution. At the same time, there seem to be no grounds in these figures for suspecting a bias in our prevalence findings.

Evaluation of our XXY prevalence figure of 3.9/1000 presents the

---

*There is some suggestion in our data on reasons for draft-board rejection, that XYY's may be vulnerable to somatic disorders, so that a correction factor derived from attrition data for the general population may not be appropriate for XYY's. The draft-board rejection data are not considered in detail here because of some ambiguities in the rejection classification used. Even if somatic difficulties are more common among XYY's, however, this in itself is probably not a contributing factor to their elevated frequency of criminal offenses. In our XY's a χ^2 test showed that the difference in frequency of criminal offenses between men rejected by their draft boards for health reasons (9.8 percent) and men not rejected on such grounds (12.4 percent) was not significant.

*This question deserves particular attention because some of the subgroups in the unexamined sample have unusually high crime rates, as might be expected. The rates were 17.2 percent for men who declined to participate in the study, 17.4 percent for those who emigrated or were away at sea; 44.0 percent for the destitute men; and 31.7 percent for those who were not living at their address of record. The differences between these values and the 9.3 percent rate of the tall XY men examined are all statistically significant (χ^2, $p < .003$). If XYY's do tend to have higher crime rates, then according to these data XYY prevalence rates may be higher in the unexamined group than in the examined group. The number of unexamined tall men is relatively small, however. Further, if we apply to the unexamined group the finding for the examined group of a 1.3 percent XYY rate among all tall men with criminal convictions, then the probability is that among the 97 men with one or more criminal convictions in the unexamined tall group there is only one XYY. Because the crime rate of the unexamined group may understate the case, and because of uncertainties about some of the extrapolations made, this pattern of results cannot of course be taken as definitive.

same problems as our XYY data; there are no satisfactory prevalence data for comparison, and incidence data are not yet adequate.

As to the rate of criminality, our finding is consistent with past findings from studies of institutionalized populations, in that the XYY's we identified had a higher mean rate of criminal convictions than the XY controls.

With regard to the possible correlates of the elevated XYY crime rate, the hypothesis we considered that height may be an intervening variable was not confirmed. In fact, within our tall XY group height showed a small but statistically significant negative relation to criminality.

On the other hand, the evidence from this study is consistent with a second hypothesis we considered, the intellectual-dysfunction hypothesis. The XYY's had an appreciably lower mean on the BPP, the army selection intelligence test, than did the XY's, and they also had a substantially lower mean on the related index of educational level attained, although some of the XYY's were within or not far out of the normal range on these variables. Moreover, in our XY sample criminality showed a substantial relation to both measures of level of intellectual functioning.

While intellectual functioning is thus clearly implicated as an important mediating variable, we cannot at this time say whether it is the only factor involved. When the two intelligence indicators were controlled, along with parental SES and height, in order to determine how these variables account for other observed XYY-XY differences in crime rate, an elevation in the XYY crime rate remained, though the difference was reduced. However, the BPP is not a comprehensive test of intelligence. It is possible that there are areas of cognitive dysfunction in XYY's that it does not tap and that a more comprehensive battery of cognitive tests would increase the explanatory power of the intellectual-dysfunction hypothesis. In fact, in our individual case study, we do have data from a wider assortment of cognitive tests for the probands and their matched XY controls, which indicate that this may be true. These data suggest that more of the difference in rate of criminality between the XYY's and XY's might have been accounted for had they been tested for an additional cognitive factor, figure fluency (FF) (Ekström, French, and Harman, 1975). A test of the FF factor was included in the battery used in the individual case study, but this factor is not well represented in the BPP, as shown by a low, nonsignificant correlation of .28 between scores from the test of this factor and BPP scores. After adjusting for BPP and other background variables by the analysis of covariance, we find FF means of 32.5, 24.0, and 26.0 for XY's, XYY's, and XXY's, respectively. The F test for difference of means is significant at the .05 level. Especially significant (p = .02, two-tailed) is the t test for the difference between the XYY adjusted mean and the XY adjusted mean, indicating that the average scores of the XYY's on FF are lower even after controlling for BPP and the other background variables. Furthermore, among the 49 XY controls the 8 men with records of convictions for one or more criminal offenses had a mean FF score of 29.0, whereas the mean for the 41 noncriminal XY's was 36.0 (p = .05, one-tailed t test).

In evaluating that hypothesis it is important to recall that the crime data we used were derived from records of individuals who were actually apprehended. People of lower intelligence may be less adept at escaping detection and so be likely to have a higher representation in a classificatory system based on registered crimes. The elevated crime rate found in our XYY group may therefore reflect a higher detection rate rather than simply a higher rate of commission of crimes.

It should be stressed that finding a relation between the presence of an extra Y chromosome and impaired intellectual functioning does not mean that the Y chromosome is ordinarily implicated in intellectual functioning and that a specific genetic basis for intelligence has thereby been established. That is no more true than would be the conclusion that, because trisomy 21 is associated with the markedly impaired intellectual functioning found in Down's syndrome, autosome 21 must make a direct genetic contribution to ordinary intellectual development. Chromosomes and genes exert their influence on development in concert; altering any one of them may accordingly affect the overall organization of the individual's genetic material, with consequences beyond the specific contribution each component may make individually. The potentially serious consequences of altering the organization of genetic material is reflected in the finding that chromosomal abnormalities are evident in about half of all spontaneous abortions in the first trimester of pregnancy, the period when such abortions are most frequent (Bove, Bove, and Lazar, 1975). In the case of the XYY complement, as in the case of Down's syndrome, it seems more plausible that the intellectual deficit found is one manifestation of altered ontogenetic development, resulting from a change in overall organization of genetic material, than that the particular chromosome involved (the Y chromosome or autosome 21) is directly implicated in ordinary intellectual functioning. A finding that has already emerged from the individual case studies we are conducting of the XYY's and the XY controls seems consistent with the view that the aberrant XYY complement may have broad adverse developmental consequences. In waking electroencephalograms the XYY's showed a significantly lower average frequency of alpha rhythm than matched XY controls (see Chapter 11, this volume)). Slower EEG frequencies are normally predominant at an earlier age (Lindsley, 1939; Matousek and Petersen, 1973); our finding can therefore be viewed as suggesting a developmental lag.

The third hypothesis we examined, the aggression hypothesis, received little support in an examination of the criminal records of the XYY's. Among all offenses committed by XYY's there was only a single instance of an aggressive act against another person; and in that case the aggression was not severe. Thus the frequency of crimes of violence against another person was not statistically significantly higher in the XYY's than in the XY's. The elevated crime rate in our XYY sample reflects an elevated rate of property offenses. This picture is in keeping with results of previous studies, most of which have also found the XYY's are not more likely to commit crimes against people than are XY's (Borgaonkar and Shah, 1974). The infrequency of violent criminal acts among our XYY's is in line as well with the observation that XYY's show less aggressive behavior while in prison than do XY prisoners (Price and Whatmore, 1967; Street and Watson, 1969). Also consistent is our finding that XYY's were no more likely to decline to participate in this study than XY's. The aggression hypothesis cannot be ruled out by the analyses done thus far, but the evidence from the personality evaluations and the social-developmental histories in the individual case studies now being analyzed will allow a further and more direct assessment of that hypothesis.

We did not examine shorter XYY's in this study, but such men appear to be uncommon in institutions, even when ascertainment has been done with men unselected for height. Further, a recent study by Owen (in preparation), based on the entire group of approximately 28,000 men who served as the source population for this study, has shown a slight inverse relation between height and criminal offenses. Thus height differences would not explain why short XYY's should appear less frequently in institutions than tall ones. Whether they do not appear because they are uncommon or because they do not commit detectable crimes, with regard to aggression shorter XYY's need be of no greater concern to society than the general run of men.

In addition to the variables on height, intellectual functioning, and aggression thus far examined as possible mediators in the relation between the XYY complement and an elevated crime rate, other variables are being considered in the individual case studies. These include characteristics of endocrine, neurological, and neuropsychological functioning.

The picture of the XXY's that has emerged to this point is in most ways similar to that of the XYY's. The XXY's showed a somewhat elevated crime rate compared to the XY's, but below that of the XYY's. The difference in crime rate between the XXY's and XYY's was not statistically significant. Though the XXY crime rate was slightly higher than that of the XY's, the difference was not statistically significant and the elevation disappeared when background variables were controlled. As to aggression, only one of the XXY's was convicted for an act of aggression, which was severe in nature. The XXY's were not significantly different from the XY's in frequency of crimes of violence against other persons. The XXY evidence thus does not provide any more impressive support for the aggression hypothesis than the XYY evidence does. With regard to intelligence, the XXY's, like the XYY's, had a substantially lower mean BPP and mean intellectual index than XY's did. The similarities between the XYY's and the XXY's suggest that, with regard to the characteristics considered thus far, the consequences of an extra Y chromosome may not be specific to that chromosomal aberration but may result from an extra X chromosome as well.

The data from the documentary records we have examined speak on society's legitimate concern about aggression among XYY and XXY men. No evidence has been found that men with either of these sex chromosome complements are especially aggressive. Because such men do not appear to contribute particularly to society's problem with aggressive crimes, their identification would not serve to ameliorate this problem.

Chapter 11

EEGs of XYY and XXY men found in a large birth cohort*

*Jan Volavka, Sarnoff A. Mednick, Joseph Sergeant,
and Leif Rasmussen*

The most publicized studies of XYY (YY) individuals have centered on the question of whether they evidence excessive quantities of asocial behavior, particularly of a violent nature (see Witkin et al., 1976, Chapter 10). If such deviant behavior were demonstrated, it would be possible to hypothesize that the extra Y chromosome, directly or indirectly, causes an alteration in brain function that manifests itself in deviant behavior. This chromosomal anomaly presents an exceptional opportunity to link a reliably detectable genetic factor with human functioning. Is there a measurable aspect of brain functioning that is related to the presence of the extra chromosome? This question has been investigated by studying the EEG of XYY men located in prisons, institutions for the criminally insane, and other psychiatric establishments. The EEG of the institutionalized XYY men showed a generalized slowing of background activity (Poole et al., 1970; Fenton et al., 1971). However, results of examinations of such samples are not ideal for the purposes of generalization to noninstitutionalized YY men.

*This chapter is reprinted with the kind permission of the *British Journal of Psychiatry*, 1977, *130*, 43-47. More recent computer scoring has confirmed the hand-scoring results.

A group of investigators in Denmark began, in 1971, a two-phase project aimed at karyotyping an entire, well-defined birth cohort of men so as to identify all those with chromosome anomalies. In phase 1 the asocial behavior of the YY men was examined (Witkin et al., 1976, Chapter 10). They were found to have more often been convicted of criminal offenses, but these offenses were not of an especially violent nature. In addition, a good deal of the asocial behavior could be related to their low intelligence. In the course of this study, men with XXY chromosome aberrations were also found. In phase 2, the men with YY and XXY (XX) chromosome anomalies and their controls were brought in for extensive examination. Part of this examination involved EEG and evoked potentials procedures. This paper is a report of the initial visual analysis of a part of the EEG records.

PROCEDURE

The general plan of the study was to identify a large, total birth cohort of males currently in their middle twenties, then to find the tallest of these men and make sex chromosome determinations from buccal smears and peripheral blood.

Delineation of the population.   The birth cohort was defined as consisting of all men born to residents of Copenhagen municipality from January 1, 1944 to December 31, 1947, a total of 31,438 men. Because of losses due mainly to death and emigration, this total was reduced to 28,885 cases. Their height was ascertained from draft-board records. Because YY and XX cases apparently tend to be more frequent among tall men (Baker et al., 1970), the target population was reduced to the 4559 living men over 184 cm in height.

Sex chromosome ascertainment.   The addresses of these 4558 men were obtained from the Danish *Folkeregister.* A team visited them in their homes and took buccal smears and blood samples from which karyotypes were prepared. To date, chromosome determinations have been made for 4139 men. The remaining 419 cases have either refused or are temporarily unavailable. Twelve YY and sixteen XX men were identified. Details of the above-described procedures may be found in Witkin et al., Chapter 10.

Selection of controls.   One group of controls (Control 1) was matched individually to the sex chromosome anomaly cases for age and social class. The *Børge Prien Prøve* (BPP), a Danish group intelligence test, (Rasch, 1960) was given to draftees, and the test scores were available to us at the draft board. The BPP scores for the XX and YY subjects were observed to be rather low. For this reason a second control group (Intelligence Control) was matched individually to the XX and YY subjects for age, social class, and the group intelligence test score (BPP). These procedures resulted in six groups, the YYs and their two controls and the XXs and their two controls (a total of 77 subjects), who underwent an EEG examination. Three XX and five controls have not yet been examined.

Methods of EEG recording

The international 10-20 system was used for electrode placement. A Beckman R Dynograph was employed for amplification and paper recording. In addition to the paper record, an analog magnetic tape record was made. The EEG was recorded under four conditions: (1) resting EEG awake, (2) hyperventilation, (3) photic and auditory stimulation, and (4) sleep. The subjects were placed in a semi-reclining position with their eyes closed during conditions 1, 2, and 4 and open in condition 3. The ambient light in the recording room was dim during conditions 1-3; the room was almost completely darkened for condition 4. The resting awake EEG was recorded for 20 minutes. Four montages (5 minutes each) were used. Bipolar and common reference derivations were employed. In each montage, six EEG derivations and an electrooculogram were recorded. After the 20-minute resting EEG, 3 minutes of hyperventilation followed by 2 minutes of resting EEG were recorded. In condition 3, sequences of visual and auditory stimuli were presented at rates between 1 and 18 per second. A detailed description of the stimulation will be published elsewhere.

After stimulation, the subjects were told to relax as much as they could, and to go to sleep if possible. The recording was continued until the EEG signs of stage I or II sleep appeared, or until 2 hours elapsed.

Study of possible drug influence

Various substances can affect the EEG. On the day of the EEG examination, all subjects were interviewed by a physician regarding such substances they may have taken. In addition, a urine sample from each subject was subjected to thin-layer chromatography and investigated for the presence of nitrazepam, chlordiazepoxide, diazepam, morphine, codeine, methadone, and amphetamine. In one subject's urine aprobarbital was found. Two subjects had taken aspirin. Two subjects had taken hashish the day before the EEG examination; one of these along with valium and alcohol. Both were YY subjects whose alpha frequencies were 11.15 and 8.75 (an average of 9.95). Because the total YY group average was 9.15, it is clear that these two individual's drug intake was not responsible for the low YY group alpha frequency average reported below. We wish to thank Dr. John Christiansen of Rigshospitalet, Copenhagen for the TLC investigation.

METHODS OF EEG EVALUATION

Conventional visual assessment of paper records

Visual assessment of the paper records was done by J.V., who was unaware of the subjects' group membership. The visual evaluation yielded nine variables for each record.

1. *Adequate amount of regular alpha activity.*
This item indicated whether or not a rhythm between 7 and 12 Hz was the dominant activity in the waking part of the record.
2. *Low voltage or fast background.*
Most of the activity exceeding the amplitude of 5 microvolts was high frequency rhythm (15 Hz or more).
3. *Activity below 7 Hz.*
This feature was rated as being present or absent during the waking period.
4. *Focus (waking, resting EEG).*
This characteristic was rated present if a limited scalp region showed an activity distinctly different from other regions. In our samples, theta activity and/or sharp waves were the typical focal activities.
5. *Burst (waking, resting EEG).*
A group of transients, standing out against the background activity, starting and ending abruptly, yielded a present rating.

6. *Hyperventilation.*
Slowing of the background activity below 3 Hz, bursts of sharp waves, or asymmetrical response was rated as abnormal.
7. *Photic and auditory stimulation.*
Bursts of asymmetrical activity were rated as abnormal. At this time, no attempt was made to assess the amount of driving.
8. *Sleep record.*
The presence or absence of any abnormality was rated.
9. *Overall assessment.*
The records were classified into three groups: normal, borderline, and abnormal.

A total of 77 EEGs were recorded. For technical reasons, six of these could not be evaluated and were dropped from the visual assessment.

Manual scoring of alpha frequency

During the conventional visual assessment of the paper records, an unusual abundance of 7-9 Hz activity was noted in some EEGs. This type of slowing had been reported for XX records by Hambert and Frey (1964); we decided to adopt their method of manual scoring. The alpha frequency was measured in the right and left parietooccipital derivation between the fifth and tenth minute after the start of the record. Three 1-second measurements were taken in each derivation. The average of these six measurements was used as an estimate of the alpha frequency. The interscorer reliability of these measurements was tested in a randomly selected subset of 15 records containing scorable alpha activity. The Pearson correlation coefficient between two independent scorers measuring the alpha frequency in identical epochs was .97. The scorers were "blind" as to the subjects' group membership.

In eight records, no alpha activity was present between the fifth and the tenth minute. Four of these records exhibited EEG signs of drowsiness or light sleep in that period; the alpha frequency for these subjects was, therefore, measured in the first 5 minutes while the subjects were fully awake. Occipitotemporal derivations were used for alpha measurement in these four subjects. The other four subjects exhibited low-voltage, fast records, and no scorable alpha was detected anywhere in their resting record. It was afterward noted that two of these individuals were XX subjects and two were controls. This left a total of 73 subjects for the evaluation of alpha frequency.

Table 1

**Number of Subjects Evidencing Slow
Activity in the Waking EEG**

Groups	SLOW ACTIVITY (BELOW 7 Hz)		
	Present	Absent	Total
YY	9	3	12
Control 1	4	6	10
Intelligence Control	5	5	10
XX	7	6	13
Control 1	3	11	14
Intelligence Control	4	8	12
Pooled XX and YY	16	9	25
Pooled Control 1	7	17	24
Pooled Intelligence Control	9	13	22

RESULTS

Conventional visual assessment

Of the nine variables of the conventional visual assessment, only one differentiated the XX and/or YY groups from controls. That variable was activity below 7 Hz. The numbers of subjects in each group evidencing slow activity (below 7 Hz) is presented in Table 1. Slow activity is more common in the sex chromosome anomaly groups. Although neither the XX nor YY groups are significantly slower than their respective controls, the pooled XX + YY groups have significantly more subjects evidencing slow activity than the pooled controls (χ^2 (1) = 4.47, $p < .03$). The slow activity was usually 5-7 Hz, occurring diffusely and mixed with alpha activity with a local maximum over the temporal areas.

The result of the overall EEG assessment is presented in Table 2 for purposes of comparison with other reports. As mentioned, the groups did not differ significantly on this variable.

Table 2

Overall EEG Assessment

	NUMBER OF SUBJECTS EVIDENCING ABNORMALITY			
Groups	Abnormal	Borderline	Normal	Totals
YY	3	3	6	12
Control 1	2	2	6	10
Intelligence Control	0	5	5	10
XX	1	3	9	13
Control 1	0	2	12	14
Intelligence Control	2	2	8	12
Pooled XX and YY	4	6	15	25
Pooled Control 1	2	4	18	24
Pooled Intelligence Control	2	7	13	22

Alpha frequency

The mean alpha frequencies for the six groups are presented in Table 3. Except for two of the YY subjects, all subjects had mean alpha frequencies above 8 Hz. The pooled YY and XX mean alpha frequencies are significantly slower than that of the pooled Control 1 groups (t (23) = 3.62, $p < 0.01$), and than that of the pooled Intelligence Control groups (t (20) = 2.11, $p < 0.05$). The YY group is significantly slower than its Control 1 (t (11) = 4.31, $p < .001$) and significantly slower than its Intelligence Control (t (9) = 2.29, $p < .05$). No significant differences were detected between the XX group and either of its two control groups. The mean alpha frequencies in the YY and XX groups were not significantly different from one another.

DISCUSSION

The principal finding is that the YY subjects have a slower EEG than the controls, and the XX show a similar tendency. This slowing was ascertained by two independent procedures: an electroencephalographer's rating of theta activity and other observers' measurement of the alpha frequency. Conspicuous theta activity in the YY subjects has been reported by Fenton et al. (1971). Nine of their twelve YY probands showed such activity, which is exactly the number we found among our twelve YY subjects. Fenton's measurement of dominant activity was used to classify records into two groups (below or above 8 Hz). This measure is probably similar to our determination of the alpha frequency. Fenton reported that significantly more probands with chromosome aberrations than controls had the dominant frequency below 8 Hz. These data were presented after pooling twelve YY, six XX and four XXYY probands. Eight of these twenty-two probands had a dominant frequency below 8 Hz; only two of our twelve YY subjects and no XX subjects or controls had an alpha frequency between 7 and 8 Hz. It would seem that the slowing in Fenton's sample was more pronounced than in our subjects. His probands were inmates of a special hospital "for the treatment of patients of dangerous, violent or criminal propensities." This selection limits the generalizability of his findings. However, patients with a history of brain damage or epilepsy were excluded from Fenton's sample, as were patients who had received any psychotropic drugs for at least a month before the EEG examination.

Poole et al. (1970) have reported a generalized EEG slowing in a sample consisting of five YY and seven XX or mosaic probands. An EEG slowing in XX subjects was reported by Hambert and Frey (1964). Their measurement method was almost identical to ours; they found considerably slower alpha activity than we did. Nine of their thirty XX probands (nonpsychotic, nonepileptic) had alpha activity at 7 or 8 HZ; all of

Table 3

Mean Alpha Frequency

Groups	Mean Frequency (Hz)	Standard Error of the Mean	N
YY	9.15	.30	12
Control 1	10.57	.19	12
Intelligence Control	9.91	.19	10
XX	9.70	.23	12
Control 1	10.03	.16	14
Intelligence Control	9.74	.25	13
Pooled YY and XX	9.43	.19	24
Pooled Control 1	10.27	.13	26
Pooled Intelligence Control	9.82	.16	23

our XX subjects had a mean frequency above 8 Hz. Almost all their probands were detected in mental hospitals and similar institutions. Various EEG changes (including diffuse slowing) are commonly found in these populations (e.g., Hill, 1963). Furthermore, it is not clear whether any of their subjects were receiving psychoactive drugs (many of which would tend to slow the EEG) at the time of EEG recording. The amount of theta activity in XX subjects was reported to be somewhat less than in YY subjects (Fenton et al., 1971).

Numerous reports have described EEG abnormalities in YY subjects (Fenton et al., 1971; Nielsen et al., 1973; Forssman and Hambert, 1966, 1967, etc.). These abnormalities include the generalized slowing of the background activity, focal spikes and slow waves, generalized paroxysmal features, and other striking changes usually encountered in patients with structural or metabolic brain pathology. Other authors have reported normal EEG in YY subjects (Borgankoar et al., 1968; Falek et al., 1970; Leff and Scott, 1968, etc.). In the XX individual there is, again, an array of studies reporting diverse EEG abnormalities (Hambert and Frey, 1964; Dummermuth, 1961; Zuppinger et al., 1967); however, Pasqualini et al. (1957) did not find any abnormality in 11 XX cases. In our sample, neither the XX nor the YY pattern was associated with overall EEG abnormality. The amount of theta and slow alpha activity was greater in the chromosomal aberrations (particularly YY) than in the controls, but it was largely within normal limits. The difference between our results and those who have found distinct abnormalities may be due to the sampling biases discussed above.

Our results indicate that the YY probands differ in a measurable aspect of their brain functioning from persons without such chromosomal aberration. In contradistinction to all previous research, the difference *cannot* be explained as an effect of sampling biases. The functional difference is manifested by an EEG slowing. A similar EEG change (although larger in size) has been reported by many other authors studying the XX and YY probands located in hospitals and prisons. The mechanism that produces the slowing is unclear. In view of the overlap between the probands and controls on all EEG measures, an interaction between the sex chromosome pattern and other factors must play a part in any explanatory model. These other factors might be genetic or environmental. For example, the effects of subtle perinatal brain injuries might interact with a brain cell anomaly caused by an extra sex chromosome (Volavka and Matousek, 1969).

It is possible that the YY chromosome aberration retards the development of brain function; slower EEG frequencies normally predominate at an earlier age. Developmental trajectories of the occipital alpha frequency have been published by Lindsley (1939). In his data the average occipital alpha frequency at 7 years was 9.0 Hz; at 8 years it was

9.30 Hz. The value we obtained in our adult YY probands was 9.15. In other words, the EEG slowing in our YY probands could be viewed as a sign of developmental immaturity. Our controls matched with the probands for intelligence have an intermediate alpha frequency between the controls and the proband groups. Slowing of alpha activity and excess of theta has been reported to occur frequently in personality disorders by Hill (1952), who has interpreted these findings as maturational defects of cerebral organization.

The observed slowing of alpha activity in this study was partly related to intelligence. Statistical analyses indicate that the relation between the slowing and the YY pattern remains significant even if the intelligence is accounted for.

Chapter 12

Electrodermal Activity and Psychopathy*

David A. T. Siddle

Studies within both criminality and psychopathology have focused considerable attention on psychopathy, and numerous clinical descriptions of the disorder have been reported. According to Cleckley (1964), the main characteristics of psychopathy are at least average intelligence, lack of neurotic or psychotic symptomatology, irresponsibility, untruthfulness, lack of guilt associated with antisocial behavior, inability to learn from experience, poverty of affect, lack of insight, lack of responsiveness in personal relationships, poorly integrated and impersonal sex life, and failure to follow any life plan. Similar characteristics have been noted by other authors. Arieti (1963), for example, has emphasized the psychopath's inability to delay gratification, and McCord and McCord (1964) and Craft (1965) have suggested that the main feature of psychopathy is an inability to form affectionate relationships. These clinical features appear to describe the American Psychiatric Association's (1968) classification of "personality disorder: antisocial personality." According to this classification, the term antisocial personality refers to individuals who "are basically unsocialized and whose behavior pattern

*The author wishes to thank Professors G. B. Trasler and P. H. Venables for their comments on an earlier draft of this paper.

brings them repeatedly into conflict with society. They are incapable of significant loyalty to individuals, groups or social values. They are grossly selfish, callous, irresponsible, impulsive and unable to feel guilt or to learn from experience and punishment" (p. 43).

Some authors (Arieti, 1963; Hare, 1968) have distinguished between primary and secondary psychopathy. It is argued (Hare, 1968) that the former group represents the "true" psychopath, whereas in the latter, psychopathic behavior "is assumed to be merely symptomatic of some underlying psychoneurotic (and in some cases psychotic or organic) condition" (p. 2). Hare (1970a) has also suggested a distinction between primary and dysocial psychopathy. He argues that although individuals in the latter group display deviant behavior, they also exhibit strong loyalties and warm relationships within their peer group. Hare maintains that a more appropriate classification of this disorder might be subcultural delinquency.

Some authors (e.g., Hare, 1968, 1970b) have urged the adoption of Cleckley's (1964) criteria of psychopathy so that the results of experimental studies will be more comparable. However, this procedure presents several difficulties. First, all Cleckley's criteria involve subjective, clinical ratings of a qualitative nature (Trasler, 1973), and some of the attributes (e.g., lack of guilt) are difficult to assess (Robins, 1966). Second, although it may be possible to isolate secondary psychopathy conceptually, in practice, secondary psychopathic groups frequently contain subjects about whose classification the experimenter has some doubt as well as those who display both psychopathic and neurotic symptomatology (e.g., Lykken, 1957; Hare, 1968). A third difficulty is that the use of clinical criteria implicitly assumes that psychopathy constitutes a discontinuous disease entity. It is possible, however, to conceptualize psychopathy as a dimension, and factor analytic studies of data from delinquent samples have isolated dimensions that appear to be similar to clinical descriptions. Quay and his colleagues (Quay, 1964; Peterson, Quay, and Tiffany, 1961) have reported three consistent factors from delinquent samples, namely psychopathic delinquency, neurotic delinquency, and subcultural delinquency. The first factor seems to reflect amoral, rebellious, and impulsive behavior and may correspond to primary psychopathy in adulthood. Neurotic delinquency reflects the same behavior, but in this case it is associated with guilt and depression. The third factor, subcultural delinquency, appears to be similar to dysocial delinquency described earlier (see also Chapter 6).

Despite the difficulties associated with identification of psychopathic individuals, a number of authors have recently reported studies aimed at testing the validity of some of the clinical descriptions of psychopathy. In view of the role of autonomic activity in emotional behavior, it seems reasonable to argue that a number of the psychopath's characteristics such as apparent lack of guilt, general poverty of affect, and inability to learn from experience will be manifest by abnormalities of autonomic functioning. Accordingly, many of the recent studies have been concerned with psychophysiological correlates of psychopathy in general, and with electrodermal measures in particular. It is with the electrodermal correlates of psychopathy that this chapter is concerned.

TONIC ELECTRODERMAL ACTIVITY DURING "REST"

Skin conductance level

A variety of studies have examined skin conductance level (SCL) in psychopathic and nonpsychopathic individuals under conditions of "rest," usually preceding a stimulation or task period. Fox and Lippert (1963) reported no significant difference between groups of male delinquents diagnosed as sociopathic personality disturbance: antisocial reaction, and personality pattern disturbance: inadequate personality, respectively. The criteria on which diagnosis was made were not reported. Similar results were obtained from a subsequent study which utilized a double-blind design and essentially the same diagnostic procedures (Lippert and Senter, 1966). Goldstein (1965) also reported no SCL differences between subjects clinically diagnosed as suffering from character disorders and noninstitutionalized controls. Again, the diagnostic criteria were not reported, and the author merely states that "all the patients with character disorders were of the type commonly labelled psychopathic or sociopathic" (p. 41). Although none of these studies reported psychopathic/nonpsychopathic differences in tonic SCL, the paucity of diagnostic details prevents a clear-cut interpretation of the results. It is likely that the psychopathic groups in all three studies contained a mixture of primary and secondary psychopaths.

However, negative results were also reported by Schmauk (1970), Borkovec (1970), Sutker (1970), Siddle, Nicol, and Foggitt (1973) and Schalling, Lidberg, Levander, and Dahlin (1973). In Schmauk's (1970) study, groups of primary and secondary psychopaths were selected on the basis of MMPI profiles. It was also reported that the primary psychopathic group differed significantly from the normal control group in terms of the Pd (psychopathic deviate) subscale of the MMPI, the Taylor Manifest Anxiety scale and the Welsh Anxiety scale. The male juvenile subjects in Borkovec's (1970) study were selected on the basis of scores on the Behavior Problem Checklist (Quay, 1964) and divided into groups of primary and secondary psychopaths and subcultural delinquents. Although the data were collected under blind conditions, it is not clear whether such a procedure was adopted for data reduction and analysis. Sutker's (1970) report is somewhat unusual, in that the psychopathic subjects (males) were recruited through mental health agencies and were not institutionalized at the time of testing. Subjects were selected on the basis of a previous diagnosis of sociopathic personality disorder (criteria not reported) and an elevated score on the Pd scale of the MMPI. Unfortunately, the control group consisted of male undergraduates. Although Sutker reports no significant differences between the groups in terms of mean age and years of education, such analyses are difficult to assess in the absence of measures of variability. In Siddle et al.'s (1973) study, which also reported negative results, the subjects were male juvenile offenders from a borstal institution. They were divided into high, medium, and low antisocial groups on the basis of criteria derived from Robins (1966), and a double-blind design was employed. Although the selection procedure allowed quantification of deviant behavior outside the institution, it is likely that all three groups contained a large proportion of subcultural delinquents rather than psychopaths. Nonsignificant differences in SCL were also reported by Schalling et al. (1973), who employed offenders who scored high and low on the Gough Delinquency Scale (Stein, Gough, and Sarbin, 1966).

Hare and his colleagues (Hare, 1965, 1968; Hare and Quinn, 1971; Hare and Craigen, 1974) have generally reported that primary psychopaths display significantly lower SCL than do nonpsychopaths. In his 1965 study Hare employed groups of institutionalized primary psychopaths and nonpsychopaths and noninstitutionalized control subjects. Subject selection was made by a staff psychologist at the institution on the basis of 12 criteria provided by Cleckley, and groups were similar in terms of age and years of education. Psychopathic subjects were found to display lower SCL than did either the institutionalized nonpsychopathic subjects or the control group. In subsequent studies (Hare, 1968; Hare and Quinn, 1971), the Cleckley criteria were employed, both by the institution staff and two research psychologists from outside the institution. In the Hare and Quinn (1971) study the research psychologists made global ratings of psychopathy on a seven-point scale; they agreed exactly in 70% of cases and were one scale point apart in 26%. Both Hare (1968) and Hare and Quinn (1971) tested groups of primary and secondary psychopaths and a nonpsychopathic control group (all institutionalized). Hare (1968) reported that the primary psychopathic group displayed significantly lower SCL than did the nonpsychopathic group, whereas in the Hare and Quinn (1971) study, this difference was not significant. More recently, Hare and Craigen (1974), using the same selection procedures, reported no significant SCL difference between groups of psychopaths and nonpsychopaths during a 1-minute rest period prior to participation in a mixed-motive game.

The data concerning resting SCL and psychopathy present a confusing picture, and it would appear that no firm conclusions can be drawn. On balance, however, there seems to be little evidence that psychopaths differ from nonpsychopaths in terms of SCL. Even if only the results of those studies that have employed consistent selection criteria are considered, the data are contradictory. Thus, although Hare (1965, 1968) has reported significantly lower SCL in primary psychopaths, these results were not replicated by Hare and Quinn (1971) or Hare and Craigen (1974).

Spontaneous electrodermal activity

Only one study (Fox and Lippert, 1963) has indicated that psychopaths display significantly fewer spontaneous fluctuations (SFs) in SCL than do nonpsychopaths. Schalling et al. (1973) did report such a difference during a rest period *following* 21 presentations of a tone, but not during a prestimulation period at the beginning of the testing session. Other studies have failed to report significant differences. Lippert and Senter (1966) found no differences between their clinically diagnosed groups, and similar results were reported by Siddle et al. (1973), who tested groups of high, medium, and low antisocial borstal inmates. Both Hare (1968) and Hare and Quinn (1971) reported that primary psychopaths displayed fewer SFs than did nonpsychopaths, but in neither case was the difference significant. In general, there seems to be little evidence to indicate that psychopaths differ from nonpsychopaths in terms of frequency of SFs, at least during resting conditions.

TONIC ELECTRODERMAL ACTIVITY DURING STIMULATION

The data concerning changes in SCL and SFs during stimulation are more consistent than those from rest periods. During relatively monotonous stimulation, the SCL of primary psychopaths decreases more than that of nonpsychopaths. For example, both Hare (1968) and

Hare and Quinn (1971) reported that SCL declined significantly more for psychopathic than for nonpsychopathic groups during tone presentation and a conditioning procedure, respectively. Similar results were reported by Schalling et al. (1973), but not by Borkovec (1970). With regard to spontaneous electrodermal activity, Hare and Quinn (1971) reported that the frequency of SFs increased throughout a conditioning session in nonpsychopaths, but decreased in psychopaths. Schalling et al. obtained similar results from a tone stimulation period.

In situations involving the threat of noxious stimulation, psychopaths display smaller increases in SCL and frequency of SFs than do nonpsychopaths. Hare (1965) measured SCL while groups of psychopaths and nonpsychopaths viewed serially presented numbers in the window of a memory drum. Subjects had previously been informed that a strong electric shock would follow the number 8. Hare reported that psychopaths, unlike the nonpsychopathic group, displayed little increase in SCL prior to presentation of the number 8. More recently, Hare (1972) has reported that the imminence of injections produced a large increase in the SCL of nonpsychopaths, but only small changes in psychopaths. In Lippert and Senter's (1966) experiment, threat of shock resulted in a larger increase in the frequency of SFs in nonpsychopaths than in psychopaths. No differences were reported for tonic SCL.

Both Schmauk (1970) and Sutker (1970) employed the amplitude of spontaneously occurring SCRs as a measure of anticipatory arousal prior to noxious stimulation. Both authors reported that the nonpsychopathic group displayed less anticipatory arousal to impending shock than did the psychopathic group. An interesting aspect of Schmauk's (1970) study was that the psychopathic group only displayed less anticipatory activity under conditions of threatened shock or social disapproval; when the punishment consisted of loss of money, no group differences were evident. More recently, Dengerink and Bertilson (1975) have reported that in a situation in which subjects were required to deliver shocks to others, psychopaths (selected on the basis of the Cleckley criteria) displayed significantly smaller increases in SCL across trials than did nonpsychopaths.

PHASIC ELECTRODERMAL ACTIVITY

Skin conductance responses to nonsignal stimuli

Several authors (Eysenck, 1963; Quay, 1965; Hare, 1970b) have suggested that psychopathy is characterized by extreme stimulation-seeking behavior. Quay (1965) has argued further that this behavior is a manifestation of the psychopath's inability to tolerate routine and boredom, and he has hypothesized that it is related to autonomic hyporeactivity.

Clear differences in SCR amplitude were obtained by Borkovec (1970) and Siddle et al. (1973). Both studies employed pure tones of 1000 Hz; the stimulus intensity was described as moderate in Borkovec's study, whereas the intensity employed by Siddle et al was 75 dB (re: 0.0002 dyne/cm²). Borkovec reported that the psychopathic group displayed significantly smaller SCRs to the first tone stimulus than did a neurotic or subcultural delinquent group, and Siddle et al. found that the high antisocial group displayed significantly smaller SCRs than did the low antisocial group. On the other hand, Hare (1968) reported no differences in SCR amplitude to an 80-dB tone on either trial 1 or on a trial involving a change in tone intensity and pitch. Subsequently, however, Hare (1975) has reported that correction of response amplitude in terms of the range of responsiveness displayed by each subject (Lykken and Venables, 1971) revealed that the psychopathic group displayed smaller SCRs than did the nonpsychopathic group on both trial 1 and the change trial.

Psychopaths also appear to be less responsive when noxious stimuli are employed. Hare and Quinn (1971), Lykken (1957), and Hare and Craigen (1974) have all reported that primary psychopaths display significantly smaller SCRs to shock stimuli than do nonpsychopaths. However, these data should be interpreted with caution. As Hare (1975) has pointed out, all these studies employed shock in the context of a conditioning paradigm, and there is evidence that in this situation the conditional stimulus may exert an inhibitory influence on response to the unconditioned stimulus (Kimmel, 1966).

Negative results have also been obtained. Goldstein (1965) reported no difference between character disorder and normal groups in terms of skin conductance changes produced by 1 minute of white noise. Similar results were reported by Lippert and Senter (1966) in relation to SCR amplitude to visual and auditory stimuli. The stimulus intensity was not reported in either study.

Recovery limb of the SCR

Recently, a number of investigators have focused on the possibility of psychopathic/nonpsychopathic differences in the recovery limb of the SCR. Although, in general, this refers to the time between peak SCR amplitude and a defined fall in response amplitude (Venables, 1974), a number of specific measures have been proposed. Because the recovery limb appears to be exponential in form (Edelberg, 1970), it has been argued that recovery measurements based on this exponential form should reflect the theoretical independence of recovery rate and the response peak (Venables, 1974). The three measures proposed, rate constant, time constant, and half-recovery time, have been described by Venables (1974), who has also discussed the central and peripheral factors thought to be involved in SCR recovery. A fourth measure, half-recovery rate (which is not theoretically independent of response amplitude), has also been proposed (Mednick and Schulsinger, 1964).

Interest in the relationship between antisocial behavior and SCR recovery stems from Mednick's (1970, 1974) examination of the application of Mowrer's (1960) two-factor learning theory to the development of deviant behavior. A number of authors (e.g., Trasler, 1973) have suggested that Mowrer's passive avoidance learning paradigm provides an appropriate laboratory analogue of some aspects of the socialization process, and a number of studies (e.g., Lykken, 1957; Schmauk, 1970) have indicated that psychopaths are inferior to nonpsychopaths in terms of passive avoidance learning. Mednick has argued that if dissipation of anticipatory fear serves as a reinforcer for the inhibition of an antisocial act, then the rate at which fear dissipates might be a critical variable. Relatively rapid dissipation of fear should result in more immediate and greater reinforcement of response inhibition and lead to more effective avoidance learning. This conceptualization predicts that those who commit antisocial acts will be characterized by slow autonomic nervous system (ANS) fear dissipation, and Mednick has suggested that the recovery rate of the SCR provides a measure of such dissipation (see also Chapter 1).

Some data have been reported that are consistent with this hypothesis. Mednick and his colleagues (Mednick, 1974) have reported a relationship between criminality (but not necessarily psychopathy) and slow SCR recovery in "high-risk" subjects. Similarly, Siddle, Mednick, Nicol, and Foggitt (Chapter 13) have reported that the high antisocial group from their 1973 study displayed significantly longer half-recovery times than did the low antisocial group and significantly slower recovery rates. In a reanalysis of his 1968 data, Hare (1975) has reported that although psychopaths and nonpsychopaths did not differ in terms of mean half-recovery time during 15 tone presentations, the psychopaths displayed significantly slower recovery times on a trial involving stimulus change. Of particular interest is Loeb and Mednick's report in Chapter 17 that delinquent subjects (at least two court convictions) tested during adolescence and *prior* to committing any antisocial acts displayed significantly slower SCR recovery than did matched controls with no history of deviant behavior.

The results concerning SCR recovery and antisocial behavior appear to be quite consistent. Subjects who display antisocial behavior (psychopaths, adult criminals, and adolescent delinquents) also display significantly slower SCR recovery than do matched controls.

DISCUSSION

The psychophysiological data on psychopathy have generally been interpreted in terms of cortical arousal, where it has been argued (Hare, 1970b; Schalling et al. 1973) that psychopaths are cortically under-aroused. This interpretation has been formulated on the basis of EEG studies purporting to show a predominance of slow wave activity in psychopaths and on the basis of the hypothesized relationship between autonomic lability and cortical arousal (Lacey and Lacey, 1958). In terms of resting electrodermal activity at least, there seems to be little evidence to support such a conclusion. It could be argued, of course, that EEG studies provide a more direct test of the hypothesis. However, in his excellent review of this area, Gale (in press) has concluded that the view that psychopaths are characterized by an abnormal EEG is a "psychophysiological myth" (p. 1).

The data do seem to indicate, however, that psychopaths and nonpsychopaths differ in terms of electrodermal arousability; psychopaths display a greater decrease in tonic electrodermal activity under conditions of monotonous environmental stimulation than do nonpsychopaths, and smaller increases in electrodermal activity when threatened with noxious stimulation. If Claridge's (1967) conceptualization of arousal processes is applied, it would appear that there are no psychopathic/nonpsychopathic differences in terms of tonic arousal, but that the groups differ in terms of arousal modulation.

The data concerning electrodermal responsivity are relatively consistent and are of some importance in that the SCR is one component of the orienting response (OR). According to Sokolov (1963), an important property of the OR is that it facilitates both stimulus reception and conditioning; that is, elicitation of an OR by a stimulus facilitates its ability to acquire signal value. Some researchers (Maltzman and Raskin, 1965; Maltzman 1967) have emphasized the importance of individual differences in the OR for learning. Maltzman and Raskin (1965), for example, have reported that high orienters (relatively large responses to a novel stimulus) display superior semantic conditioning of autonomic responses and paired-associated learning than do low orienters (relatively small responses to a novel stimulus). Moreover, they report that in a classical conditioning paradigm, in which awareness of stimulus relations seems to be necessary for conditioning (Dawson and Furedy, 1976), high orienters are better able to verbalize the experimental contingencies. On this basis, the SCR findings reviewed in this chapter suggest that psychopaths might be less attentive to some aspects of their environment and less aware of the relationship between stimulus events. Although the data concerning the relatively poor passive avoidance learning (Lykken, 1957; Schmauk, 1970) and classical conditioning (Lykken, 1957; Hare and Quinn, 1971) of psychopaths are consistent, the role of attentional factors in these situations has not been investigated in relation to psychopathy. In this connection, it is interesting to note that in his study of passive avoidance learning in psychopaths, Schmauk (1970) reported that under physical and social punishment conditions, psychopaths were not able to verbalize the experimental contingencies as well as were nonpsychopaths. However, generalizations about attentive processes in psychopaths are probably not appropriate, as it is possible to imagine a number of situations in which psychopaths are perhaps more attentive than nonpsychopaths to environmental cues. Indeed, Schmauk (1970) has reported that psychopaths were more aware of the experimental contingencies when punishment constituted loss of money than when the punishment was shock, and that there was no difference between psychopaths and nonpsychopaths in the loss-of-money condition.

This interpretation of diminished orienting activity in psychopaths is consistent with some interpretations in the SCR recovery limb. It has already been noted that Mednick (1974) regards SCR recovery as a measure of ANS fear dissipation. An alternative interpretation can be made in terms of the attentional significance of the recovery limb. For example, Edelberg (1972) has shown that SCR recovery is situationally determined and has suggested that fast recovery times indicate a preparation for goal-directed behavior. This notion has been extended by Venables (1974) who, on the basis of studies of SCR recovery in schizophrenic patients (Venables, 1973a) and consideration of Lacey's views concerning the functional significance of heart deceleration and acceleration (Lacey, Kagan, Lacey and Moss, 1963), has speculated that SCR recovery might reflect a dimension of "openness-closedness" to the environment. This idea is similar to that advanced above in terms of SCR amplitude, and it may be, therefore, that attentional stance or openness-closedness is indexed by both SCR amplitude and SCR recovery. One difficulty with this suggestion is that SCR amplitude and recovery are theoretically independent. However, Edelberg's (1970) data indicate that independence of the two measures is not shown by all

subjects. Similarly, Lockhart (1972) has reported significant positive correlations (between subjects) for SCR amplitude and half-recovery time
on disparity trials, that is, trials on which an unexpected stimulus occurred. These results have not been replicated by Rippon (personal
communication), and Gruzelier (1973) has reported significant *negative*
correlations between SCR amplitude and half-recovery time in schizophrenic patients but not in normal controls. Clearly, SCR recovery and
its relationship with response amplitude depends on the situation employed, the type of subject tested, and, perhaps, the interaction between
them. A working hypothesis might be that psychopaths represent extreme closedness to the environment (or at least some aspects of it) as
indexed by both small SCR amplitudes and long recovery times, and
they they are less attentive to environmental cues and less aware of the
relationships between stimulus events. An alternative view is that although SCR recovery may indicate attentional stance, SCR amplitude
reflects stimulus "registration" (Venables, 1973b; Pribram and McGuinness, 1975). That is, occurrence of an SCR indicates that a stimulus has
been registered neurally. Clearly, this view is conceptually similar to
that outlined earlier, and it is not inconsistent with an interpretation of
psychopathic behavior in terms of attentional deficit.

CONCLUSION

It seems appropriate to conclude this chapter with an examination of
sources of error that might be present in psychophysiological studies of
psychopathy, and to suggest directions in which future research might
move.

Although subject selection is of fundamental importance, there
seems to be little agreement concerning this issue. Some authors have
employed psychiatric diagnosis (usually with the criteria unstated);
others have used scores on a variety of inventories such as the MMPI,
the Gough Delinquency scale, and the Behavior Problem Checklist.
Hare and his colleagues have consistently employed clearly stated
criteria and have made some attempt (Hare & Quinn, 1971) to assess
interrater reliability. It is likely that the primary psychopathic groups in
most of the studies which employed psychiatric diagnosis contained
some secondary psychopaths, as well as individuals more properly considered subcultural delinquents. In short, there is little reason to suppose that many of the samples tested actually consisted of homogeneous

groups of psychopaths. Moreover, the low reliability of psychiatric diagnosis is well attested (Zubin, 1967). A related problem concerns whether psychopathic behavior is viewed as a diagnostic category or merely an extreme form of antisocial behavior. Intuitively, it would seem that all individuals display antisocial behavior to a greater or lesser extent, and this orientation suggests that "psychopaths" do not display behavior that is qualitatively different from that displayed by the "normal" population, but merely exaggerated forms of such behavior (Gale, in press). A starting point for examination of this problem might be Schalling's (in press) review of personality measures and psychopathy.

Age of subjects is a variable that has not been treated in any systematic fashion. Age is frequently not stated (e.g., Fox and Lippert, 1963; Lippert and Senter , 1966; Borkovec, 1970), and although most studies have employed control groups comparable in age with the psychopathic group, age differences do pose a problem for comparisons between studies. Although the age differences are perhaps not large enough to involve the effects of age on central and peripheral determinants of electrodermal activity, the effects of age on the experimenter-subject interaction cannot be overlooked (Rosenthal, 1966). This is particularly important when the effects of experimenter-subject interaction on psychophysiological activity are considered (Christie and Todd, 1975).

The third area of concern is the measurement of electrodermal activity itself. Again, a wide variety of recording and scoring techniques are evident, and very little attention has been paid to important variables such as temperature, humidity, and time of day of testing (Venables and Christie, 1973). There is a growing awareness of the need for standardization of electrodermal measurement (Lykken and Venables, 1971), and perhaps this will result in more comparability between studies conducted in different laboratories or institutions. For example, Lykken and Venables (1971) have suggested that SCL and SCR amplitude should be expressed in specific conductance, that is, umhos/ cm². At present, direct comparisons across studies are frequently impossible, because apparently SCL and SCR amplitude are related to recording area, which is often not reported. Similarly, strong arguments have been advanced for range-correction procedures (Lykken, Rose, Luther, and Maley, 1966; Lykken and Venables, 1971) which are designed to remove the effects of peripheral factors not related to the psychological variables of interest. The adoption of such procedures might remove a large proportion of measurement error and hence increase the precision of electrodermal measures.

With regard to future research, the theoretical orientation adopted here suggests that the systematic study of attentional processes in psychopaths might be worthwhile. Such research could proceed by examining orienting and defensive behavior in psychopaths, by investigating SCR recovery, and by studying passive avoidance learning. The functional significance of the OR appears to involve the facilitation of selection, transmission, and analysis of environmental information (Sokolov, 1966; Spinks and Siddle, in press), whereas the defense response (DR) may serve to attenuate the effects of aversive stimulation. A good deal is known about the elicitation, habituation, and reelicitation of the OR (Graham, 1973; Siddle and Heron, 1975), as well as those situations in which ORs and DRs may be elicited in different groups of subjects (e.g., Klorman, Wiesenfeld and Austin, 1975). The employment of these paradigms, using a wide variety (e.g., verbal and social) of both signal and nonsignal stimuli, may help delineate those situations in which psychopaths display an attentional deficit.

The position with regard to SCR recovery is not as straightforward, in that less is known about its functional significance (Bundy and Fitzgerald, 1975). For example, Edelberg (1972) has linked fast recovery with goal orientation, whereas Mednick (1974) views recovery as an index of fear dissipation. An appropriate research strategy might involve investigations of the functional significance of SCR recovery, followed by examination of psychopathic/nonpsychopathic recovery differences in those situations thought to be important in the development of psychopathic behavior. Passive avoidance learning appears to be of particular interest in this regard (Trasler, in press), and the assessment of attentional stance or openness-closedness to environmental cues in this situation might provide insights into the development of deviant behavior.

Chapter 13

Skin conductance recovery in anti-social adolescents*

David A. T. Siddle, Sarnoff A. Mednick, A. R. Nicol,
and Roger H. Foggitt

Chapter 1 gives a theoretical account of how law–abiding behavior might be learned. This brief chapter reports an interesting test of a critical aspect of the theory.

Essentially, the theory argues that the young child must learn to curb his antisocial impulses. He must learn to inhibit aggressive and stealing responses in order to make civilized community-living possible. It is suggested that if the normal child is punished by the family for the commission of antisocial acts, anticipation of such acts will elicit anticipatory fear. If he inhibits the antisocial act, the anticipatory fear will be reduced. This fear reduction can serve as a reinforcement for the immediately preceding inhibition of the antisocial act. The rate at which the fear reduction takes place is a critical variable. Relatively rapid dissipation of fear should result in more immediate and greater reinforcement of response inhibition and lead to more effective avoidance learning. This orientation predicts that those who commit antisocial acts will be characterized by slow ANS-fear dissipation; the more serious and repetitive the antisocial acts, the slower will be the dissipation. Because

*We wish to thank the editors of the British Journal of Social and Clinical Psychology for their kind permission to use this article (1976, 15, 425–428).

the fear response is controlled chiefly by the ANS, Mednick has suggested that the recovery rate of the electrodermal response (EDR) provides a measure of rate of ANS-fear dissipation.

Siddle, Nicol, and Foggitt (1973) have reported that EDR magnitude varied inversely as a function of adolescent antisocial behavior. Through the good offices of Peter Venables, these authors were encouraged to rescore their data for recovery as a test of Mednick's proposals. This chapter reports the results of this reanalysis. It was hypothesized that EDR recovery rate would be slower and EDR half-recovery time longer as the degree of antisocial behavior increased.

Details of subject selection and test procedures have been reported elsewhere (Siddle et al., 1973). Briefly, a 10-item scale was employed to divide 68 male borstal inmates into high (Group H, $n = 15$), medium (Group M, $n = 33$), and low (Group L, $n = 20$) antisocial groups. Electrodermal activity was measured in response to a 1000-Hz, 75-dB tone of 2 seconds duration, presented at randomly ordered intervals of 15, 20, and 25 seconds. Half-recovery time was measured as the time taken from peak-response amplitude to half-response amplitude; recovery rate was measured by dividing one half of the response amplitude by the half-recovery time (Edelberg, 1970; Mednick and Schulsinger, 1964).

It is obvious that the EDR recovery limb can be measured only on those trials on which a measurable EDR, uncontaminated by multiple responding, occurs. Because of these restrictions, only trial 1 yielded

Table 1

Interrelationships of Electrodermal Variables

Variable	Tonic SCL (Log μmhos)	EDR Amplitude	Half-Recovery Time	Recovery Rate
EDR Amplitude (Δlog μmhos)	0.24			
Recovery Half- Time (sec.)	-0.38^a	0.12		
Recovery Rate (Δlog μmhos/sec.)	0.45^b	0.57^b	-0.51^b	
No. of Responses (First Four Trials)	0.38^a	0.21	-0.37^a	0.43^b

[a] $p < 0.05$
[b] $p < 0.01$

Table 2

Classification of Subjects Using Recovery Measures

	RECOVERY RATE Group		
	H	M	L
Greater than Median	2	10	11
Less than Median	9	7	5

Median ($\times$ 1000) = 3.95 log μmhos/sec
$\chi^2 = 7.16$; d.f. = 2; $P < 0.05$

	HALF-RECOVERY TIME Group		
	H	M	L
Greater than Median	9	8	5
Less than Median	2	9	11

Median = 3.66 sec
$\chi^2 = 6.762$; d.f. = 2; $P < 0.05$

recovery data on a large proportion of subjects (11 from group H, 17 from group M and 16 from group L). Table 1 reports intercorrelations for all 44 subjects of tonic skin conductance level (SCL) during the pre-stimulus period, EDR amplitude, half-recovery time and rate on trial 1 and number of responses displayed to the first four stimuli. Both recovery rate and half-time correlate significantly with number of responses on the first four trials. Subjects who stop responding quickly have slower EDR recovery than do those who continue to respond. It follows, therefore, that trial 1 yields data most representative of all groups.

Analyses of variance performed on the recovery data from trial 1 indicated significant effects for both half-recovery time ($F = 3.44$; d.f. = 2,41; $P < 0.05$) and recovery rate ($F = 6.51$; d.f. = 2,41; $P < 0.01$). Further analyses of the half-time data indicated that groups H and M displayed significantly slower recovery than did group L ($t = 3.39$; d.f. = 25; $P < 0.005$ and $t = 1.91$; d.f. = 31; $P < 0.05$, respectively). In the case of recovery rate, groups H and M again displayed significantly slower recovery than did group L ($t = 2.53$; d.f. = 25; $P < 0.01$ and $t = 1.84$; d.f. = 31; $P < 0.05$, respectively).

To determine how well the recovery measures classified subjects, each group was divided into those above and below the median of the pooled groups (Table 2). Both variables differentiated the groups at a statistically significant level, although the differentiation was best for Group H.

The ability of this ANS recovery index to differentiate the groups is impressive for the following reasons:

1. The controls for group H were other borstal inmates and not noninmates.

2. Because the subjects were 16-18 years of age at the time of testing, it is possible that some subjects in groups M and L may behave in such a manner as to make it more appropriate to classify them in group H.

3. The recovery measures were taken from a single trial with only one peripheral index of ANS functioning.

However, because EDR recovery has been shown to be situationally determined (Edelberg, 1970), further work must be aimed at replicating the present findings, using more noxious stimulation as punishment for inappropriate behavior.

Chapter 14

Electrodermal parameters in male twins

Brian Bell, Sarnoff A. Mednick, Irving I. Gottesman,
and Joseph Sergeant

A number of investigators have employed the classical twin method
in attempts to determine the genetic and environmental components of
autonomic nervous system functioning. Some measure of consistency
for a genetic factor has been reported in studies of EEG activity
(Dustman and Beck, 1965; Young and Fenton, 1971) where higher intraclass correlations were found for monozygotic (MZ) pairs than for dizygotic (DZ) twins and unrelated control subjects. However, findings
that suggest a significant genetic component in electrodermal parameters have been somewhat equivocal.

Early evidence that indicated a hereditary factor in electrodermal
activity was provided by Jost and Sontag (1944) who compared data
obtained from MZ twins, siblings, and unrelated controls; they found
that the mean difference scores for twin subjects were significantly less
than for their nontwin subjects. The reliability of this early report is
difficult to assess, because there exists some doubt over which electrodermal parameters were in fact employed. Apparently, the terms conductance and resistance are used interchangeably (Pp. 308 and 310).
Rachman (1960) failed to find significant correlations for a measure of
habituation rate, but the latency of the skin resistance response (SRR)
was highly correlated between members of a pair. This study employed

only a group of MZ twins as subjects, and no comparison is, therefore, available with DZ subjects. Nonsignificant within-pair variance ratios for SRR amplitude in five differing stimulus conditions were reported by Vandenberg, Clark, and Samuels (1965). In contrast to Rachman's (1960) report, Lader and Wing (1966) concluded that there was evidence for a genetic component in not only the frequency of response but also in the habituation of the skin conductance response (SCR).

Two recent studies have employed endosomatic measures of electrodermal functioning: Hume (1973) reports significantly higher MZ intraclass correlations for skin potential responses (SPR) to a cold pressor stimulus as well as for SPR habituation during orienting. Zvolský, Jirák, Drábková, Cerný, and Kubićková (1973) used four stimulus conditions which included a sound signal intermittently accompanied by an electric shock, an orienting task, and a startle stimulus. Tonic skin potential was also measured in their group of MZ and DZ twins. These authors conclude that a significant genetic component was evident only in response to the startle stimulus.

The extent to which a hereditary factor is implicated in electrodermal activity remains unclear. Undoubtedly, much of the discrepancy between results from various laboratories lies in the fact that widely disparate measurement systems, stimulus paradigms, and subject samples have been used. Failure to specify the characteristics of stimulus material is a hallmark of psychophysiological studies with twin subjects: stimuli have been used that range from a harsh buzzer sound (Rachman, 1960) to the falling hammer of Vandenberg, Clark, and Samuels (1965). It would seem appropriate in this respect to quote Hume's (1973, p. 88) statement: "Lamentably few of these studies can be regarded with any degree of credibility."

Mednick and Schulsinger (1973), studying children of schizophrenics, observed the relationship between a number of critical environmental variables and skin conductance parameters. Because recovery was unrelated to these environmental variables, they tentatively suggested that it "may be an important part of the genetic pattern passed onto the child" (p. 260) by the schizophrenic parent. Recovery is also an integral part of the theory of law abidingness presented in Chapter 1. Of all the electrodermal parameters that have been the subject of research, recovery has received the least attention: only one published report on twin psychophysiology has considered this variable. In no instance with either cardiovascular or skin potential measures did Hume (1973) find a significant genetic component for response recovery in the cold pressor test.

In view of the importance of recovery to the theory presented in Chapter 1 and the position adopted by Mednick and Schulsinger (1973), we considered it necessary to carry out a preliminary investigation using twin subjects to determine the extent to which skin conductance parameters evidence a genetic component. In this study a group of MZ and DZ twins were tested under controlled laboratory and test conditions. The twin sample was tested together with a larger group of subjects who were taking part in a large-scale study dealing with psychophysiological reactions in children. A standardized experimental procedure was adopted with all subjects who underwent a series of psychophysiological and psychological tests during an intensive one-day examination. Only data relating to skin conductance parameters are reported here.

METHOD

Subjects

The subjects were 46 male twins (10 MZ pairs and 13 DZ pairs) who were born at Rigshospitalet, Copenhagen, between 1959 and 1961. The mean age of the MZ group at the time of testing was 11 years and 7 months, and that of the DZs was 11.5 years. Zygosity of the subjects was determined by means of finger ridge counts, eye color, and facial characteristics as judged from color photographs.

Physiological Recording

A 12-channel Beckman R dynograph was used to monitor the various physiological parameters. Eight channels were employed for EEG, and four were devoted to cardiac and electrodermal recording. Skin conductance was measured bilaterally with two constant voltage couplers as described by Lykken and Venables (1972). Calibration was carried out on a daily basis, and all measures were recorded on FM precision instrument PI6200 eight-channel tape recorder. Analog recordings were monitored downstream via a Tektronix dual beam oscilloscope (R5031). A paper writeout was also obtained.

Beckman Biopotential skin electrodes (AgAC1) of 0.3 cm diameter were used to record SC parameters. The electrolyte used was 0.5% KCl in an agar 2 medium. The electrodes were attached to the medial phalangae of the index and middle fingers of each hand with standard Beckman electrode collars..

Stimulus Material

Each subject listened to a stimulus tape. The stimuli used in the experiment were a series of tones that comprised an orienting (OR) and a differential conditioning (COND) paradigm. The presentation of the OR and COND series was separated by a 10-minute recording of EEG activity.

There were 14 presentations of the OR stimulus, a 75-db tone of 1 second's duration. The interstimulus interval varied between 34 and 42 seconds. In the COND section of the tape there were 12 presentations of a conditioned stimulus (CS) paired with an unconditioned stimulus (UCS): the CS was a 1-KHz, 60-db tone of 10 seconds' duration, and the UCS was 4.5 seconds of noise presented at 96-db. The interstimulus interval was similar to that during orienting. Calibration of the volume control for stimulus output to the subject was made with a Brüel and Kjaer precision sound level meter 2203 with an artificial earpiece (type 4152).

Nonreinforced and generalization trials were also included on the tape; however, because of the low frequency of responding in these conditions a reliable analysis of these data cannot be made.

Procedure

The subjects were tested in the afternoon of their visit to the laboratory. An attempt was made to counterbalance the order of testing between the first- and second-born members of pairs. Each subject removed any articles from his hands and arms which were then washed with a proprietary brand of soft soap; the electrode sites were then cleansed with acetone. The subject sat in a reclining armchair, which was placed in a copper-shielded room immediately adjacent to the equipment area. After the physiological transducers had been applied together with the headphones (TDH-39 with 10 ohms resistance), calibration of the polygraph was carried out. The room temperature and humidity were then noted. The light above the subject was extinguished and he was told to relax. The experimenter told the subject over the headphones to listen to the prerecorded instructions and the series of tones which would follow.

Presentation of the stimulus tape was completed within 30 minutes, during which continuous recording of electrodermal and cardiac activity took place.

RESULTS

Data Quantification

Data reduction of the analog tapes was carried out with a special-purpose program developed for use with a Linc-8 computer. This procedure was carried out at the Department of Psychology, Birkbeck College, University of London.

For each presentation of the OR and COND stimulus the following response characteristics were measured: onset latency (seconds), rise time (seconds), peak amplitude (micromhos), and half-recovery time (seconds). For the purposes of the present analysis, the mean value for any parameter was derived from the number of observed responses for a given subject in the appropriate stimulus condition. For each condition various response categories were determined. For OR, a response which occurred in the period 0.5-5.0 seconds following tone onset was termed a *type-1 response* (R1). Two response categories were considered in the COND series. An R1 was obtained from the period 0.5-5.0 seconds following the onset of the CS. The second response category comprised those that took place between 0.5 and 5.0 seconds after the UCS onset, a type-3 response (R3)

Correlation Analysis

Intraclass correlations together with associated F-ratios were computed from the summary data, with the hands being considered separately in all instances. Results are given in Table 1.

a) Orienting: Only one response category was considered in the OR series. Data from the left hand for onset latency resulted in a zero correlation for MZ subjects and a correlation of $-.16$ for DZ twins. On the right hand the MZ r was .39, and again a negative r of $-.46$ was found for DZ subjects.

Rise time of the left-hand orienting response produced correlations

Table 1

Interclass Correlations and Within-pair Variance Ratios for SC Parameters

Parameter and Stimulus Condition	LEFT HAND			RIGHT HAND		
	rMZ	rDZ	F	rMZ	rDZ	F
Onset Latency						
Orienting (R1)	.00	−.16	< 1	.39	−.46	1.68
Conditioning (R1)	.55[a]	.16	1.18	.22	−.16	1.10
Conditioning (R3)	.46	.04	1.94	.15	.39	<1
Rise Time						
Orienting (R1)	.14	−.36	1.97	.06	.11	<1
Conditioning (R1)	.59[a]	.22	1.46	.19	.25	1.08
Conditioning (R3)	.75[b]	.33	3.87[a]	.67[a]	.87[c]	<1
Peak Amplitude						
Orienting (R1)	.42	.19	3.01	.66[a]	.68[a]	2.79
Conditioning (R1)	.18	.40	< 1	−.23	.21	<1
Conditioning (R3)	.08	.62[a]	< 1	.25	.65[a]	<1
Half-Recovery Time						
Orienting (R1)	.33	−.07	10.65[c]	.34	.39	<1
Conditioning (R1)	.25	.05	2.85	.54	.74[a]	1.33
Conditioning (R3)	.60[a]	.41	5.87[c]	.68[a]	.61	2.77

[a] $p < .05$
[b] $p < .01$
[c] $p < .001$

of .14 and −.36 for the MZ and DZ groups, respectively. A low MZr of .06 and a DZr of .11 were found for the right hand.

The intraclass correlation for the MZs' peak amplitude (left hand) was .42; the DZr was somewhat lower at .19. However, data from the right hand resulted in much higher correlations in both the MZ ($r = .66$) and DZ ($r = .68$) groups, indicating a high similarity in the responses produced by members of both MZ and DZ pairs. The corresponding F-ratio however was not significant.

A correlation of .33 was found for MZs with regard to half-recovery time on the left hand; a negative correlation occurred for the DZ group ($r = −.07$). A highly significant F-ratio was also found ($p < .001$). On the right hand, the MZr was relatively unchanged (.34), but the DZr was increased to .39.

b) Conditioning—type-1 response: The intraclass correlation for the MZ·twins for onset latency (left hand) was .55; the DZr was much smaller at .16. On the right hand the MZr reduced to .22, whereas the DZr reduced to −.16.

For rise time the MZr was .59 and the DZr was .22 for data derived from the left hand. The MZr on the right hand was reduced to .19, with the DZr showing a slight increase to .25.

The DZr for amplitude was higher (.40) than that for the MZ twins (.18) on the left hand. Data from the right hand showed a smaller DZr of .21, whereas a negative correlation was found for the MZ group (−.23).

Left-hand half-recovery time was correlated .25 in the MZ twins and only .05 in the DZs. On the right hand both MZ and DZ correlations were substantially higher, with the DZr (.74) again being greater than that found for MZs (.54).

c) Conditioning—type-3 response: For latency on the left hand, similarity was greater between MZ twins ($r = .46$) than for DZ pairs ($r = .04$). A right-hand reversal took place, with DZs producing a correlation of .39 and the MZs reducing to .15).

A significant *F*-ratio of 3.87 ($p < .05$) for rise time on the left hand was associated with an MZr of .75 and DZr of .33: the right hand MZr was again less (.66) than that found for DZ pairs (.87); the *F*-ratio was, however, not significant.

The intraclass correlation for MZ twins on peak amplitude of the left-hand response was close to zero (.08): in contrast, the DZr was .62; for the right hand, the MZr showed some increase to .25, and the DZr remained relatively unchanged at .65.

The ratio of the MZ and DZ within-pair variances for left-hand half-recovery time was significant at the 0.1% level ($F = 5.87$) and was associated with an MZr of .60 and a DZr of .41. For the right hand, the MZr was .68 and the DZr was .61; the *F*-ratio failed to reach significance.

In summary, in only three instances was there a significant *F*-ratio of the MZ and DZ within-pair variances; this was always derived from data relating to responding on the left hand. Two of the significant *F*-ratios were with half-recovery time measures, the other was for rise time of the response elicited by the UCS. For all time-related measures on the left hand, with the exception of orienting onset latency, the MZr was positive and ranged from .14 to .75. The DZ correlations ranged between −.36 and .41. MZ correlations were always higher than the corresponding DZ values. In contrast, the intraclass correlations for the MZ twins relating to right-hand responses showed less consistency, ranging from .06 to .68. The DZ correlations for right-hand time-related measures ranged between −.46 to .87, and in several stimulus conditions were substantially higher than the corresponding positive MZr. Except for the left hand R1 during OR, DZr was higher (positive) than the corresponding MZr for peak amplitude measures; the DZr ranged from .19 to .68 and MZr from −.23 to .66, across both hands. The *F*-ratio of the variances approached significance for R1 in the OR condition for both hands.

DISCUSSION

Two main points arise from the results presented. The first of these is concerned with the fact that significant genetic factors seem to be limited to measures that are time related, namely, rise time and half-recovery time. There is less indication that hereditary may be involved in latency measures. Second, there appears to be a laterality difference, such that where significant within-pair variance ratios occur, they are limited to data from the left hand.

When the half-recovery time correlations are employed to compute heritability indices [where $h^2 = (MZr-DZr)/0.5$] the following values are obtained: R1 orienting = .80, R1 conditioning = .40, and R3 conditioning = .38.

There would appear, then, to be some support for the hypothesis that recovery may be partly genetically determined. Furthermore, there is some indication that rise time also had a hereditary component. That a similar pattern should emerge for these two parameters of the SCR is not altogether surprising, for high positive correlations have been found between these measures by Lockhart (1973), Sergeant (1974) and in unpublished analyses in this laboratory.

However, the conclusion that genetic factors are involved in SC functioning must be tempered with the finding that such evidence was restricted to data obtained from the left hand. It is worthwhile to note at this point that the data on which Mednick and Schulsinger (1973) based their genetic pattern hypothesis were also obtained from unilateral recording on the left hand. It is difficult to envisage a satisfactory explanation as to why a genetic effect should be present unilaterally. Rachman (1960) concluded that the occurrence of a response was determined primarily by environmental influences and that the response characteristics were structurally (genetically) weighted. It may be, in these data at least, that some developmental process which involves a significantly increased dominance of the right hand in terms of its use in manipulative behavior results in electrodermal activity in that hand which reflects ongoing situational responding. On the left hand, activity is determined primarily by structural factors. Sergeant (1974) has found that responsivity on the right hand is consistently higher than the left. These comments are advanced in a purely speculative way; it is recognized that this study cannot be regarded other than an exploratory one. It is evident that a considerable amount of additional research needs to be carried out to expand and clarify the possible genetic components of electrodermal functioning.

Chapter 15

A prospective study of predictors of criminality:
1. Introduction

Sarnoff A. Mednick

In 1962, Mednick and Schulsinger in Copenhagen began a prospective longitudinal study that had as its objective the detection of characteristics which distinguish children who at some later point in their lives become schizophrenic. The project began with the intensive examination of 207 children with schizophrenic mothers and 104 control children. This examination resulted in a large pool of data collected at a time when the children had not yet evidenced abnormal behavior. In 1975 the children had a mean age of 28 years. Since the 1962 assessment, many of them had evidenced a variety of mental illnesses (Mednick, Schulsinger, and Schulsinger, 1975). The original examination materials have been used to attempt to detect early (predictive) characteristics of these children (Mednick, Schulsinger, Higgins, and Bell, 1974). These data can also be used to describe the premorbid characteristics of individuals who have evidenced forms of deviance other than mental illness. Since 1962, many of the 311 subjects have been convicted for having committed criminal acts. The four papers in this section ask what early, (premorbid) characteristics distinguish the individuals who later became criminal.

An advantage of this method is that it is prospective; the key predictive measures and observations were made before anyone (including the subject) knew that he or she would become a criminal. They are, consequently, not biased by this information.

Many studies in the literature utilize other prisoners, or patients designated as nonpsychopathic, as controls for psychopathic prisoners (or hospitalized patients). In addition to the problems of diagnosis inherent in this experimental design, it becomes difficult to evaluate the differences in response between legal offenders and the law-abiding population at large. Where noninstitutionalized controls have been included, one is confronted with the impossibility of controlling for the effects of institutionalization and other experiential *consequences* of pathological conditions, which may in themselves account for differential results on experimental measures (cf. Mednick and McNeil, 1968 for a full discussion of the advantages of the longitudinal method).

The exploitation of this longitudinal project also has disadvantages. Inasmuch as two thirds of the 311 subjects are children with schizophrenic mothers, it is possible that findings that differentiate criminals from noncriminals could be specific to individuals with this type of disturbed parental background. This problem is considered in each of the analyses below.

Descriptions of the sample and definitions of criminality are given in the first chapter and discussed in the other chapters only in the case of the forming of special control subgroups. The first chapter considers directly the relationship between schizophrenia and criminality in the sample. The subsequent chapters attempt to relate premorbid autonomic nervous system (ANS) functioning, school behavior, and intelligence to later criminal behavior.

The chapter on ANS functioning was the first in this series and uses a very mild criterion of early criminality, including traffic offenses. The subsequent chapters make use of a stricter definition; at least one court conviction for an offense against the criminal law.

Chapter 16

A prospective study of predictors of criminality:
2. A description of registered criminality
in the high-risk and low-risk families*

Lis Kirkegaard-Sørensen
and
Sarnoff A. Mednick

In 1966 Heston reported on the fate of 47 individuals born to schizophrenic women in an Oregon state hospital. These children were placed in orphanages from which they dispersed, to be interviewed by Heston an average of 37 years later. Heston also interviewed controls born to nonmentally ill women who had been placed in the same orphanage. Individuals in both groups had a variety of life outcomes. Of special interest to Heston was the fact that none of the controls and 16% (corrected) of the children of schizophrenics were diagnosed schizophrenic.

Some results of Heston's study have not received wide attention; eight of the experimental group (17%) and two of the controls were diagnosed psychopathic. Seven of the experimental and two of the control offspring were reported to have been criminal. These results recall Kallmann's findings (1938) that 17% of children of schizophrenics were diagnosed as psychopaths (5% criminal). What is common in both Kallman and Heston studies is the broad definition of psychopathy and the chronic hospitalized proband population studied.

*We wish to thank the Editors of *Journal of Abnormal Psychology* for permission to reprint this article (1975, 84, 197-204.)

In Israel, Landau et al. (1972) reported 7.6% delinquency in children whose parents evidenced a wide variety of psychopathology (63.5% schizophrenia); however, only 0.7% delinquency was reported among controls. These results suggest that offspring of a schizophrenic parent have an elevated risk for psychopathy and criminality. Kallmann suggested three possible explanations for these findings: (a) perhaps the environmental stress of having a schizophrenic parent increased the likelihood of psychopathy in the children; (b) perhaps schizophrenia and psychopathy are genetically linked; (c) perhaps schizophrenics tend to marry disturbed individuals such as psychopaths and criminals.

These hypotheses are not mutually exclusive. The first of the hypotheses seems contradicted by Heston's study, which found increased criminality in schizophrenic mothers' children despite the fact that these children were not raised by their mothers. Kallmann dismisses the second of these possibilities (genetic linkage), because he found "that the particularly high criminality rate in our probands and their children depends exclusively on the large number of schizophrenic psychoses among them" (p. 232). He assumes that if an individual is psychotic, his criminality is ascribable to his mental illness. The third hypothesis would explain the increased yield of psychopathy and criminality of the children as an expression of the genetic or familial environment transmissions of the psychopathic characteristics of the non-schizophrenic parent (see Chapters 7 and 8). We now attempt to evaluate these hypotheses in the light of the data of this study.

In our own initial 1962 longitudinal, high-risk study of Danish children with schizophrenic mothers (Mednick and Schulsinger, 1968) we noted that mental illness in the offspring was frequently accompanied by the commission of criminal acts. To understand better the factors relating to the onset of mental illness in these offspring, and to further illuminate the relation between schizophrenia and criminality, we determined in this chapter to describe the kinds and amounts of registered criminality in families with a schizophrenic mother. In view of the Kallmann, Heston, and Landau et al. results, it seems reasonable to hypothesize that the schizophrenic mothers, their mates, and children will evidence higher levels of registered criminality than comparison groups.

METHOD

The subjects were 311 children divided into two groups. The experimental (high-risk) group contains 207 children whose mothers were diagnosed as severely schizophrenic on the basis of the following diagnostic criteria:

1. The mother was in a psychiatric hospital for 5 years; *or*
2. The mother was hospitalized for at least three periods, each of at least 3 months duration. There was not complete recovery between hospitalizations; *or*
3. The mother has had a long-term hospitalization and has received an invalid pension based on her diagnosis of schizophrenia; *and*
4. No marked precipitating factors were observed, *and*
5. The mother must have had at least two serious symptoms of schizophrenia.

We tried to include as many siblings as possible. The number of schizophrenic mothers was 129. There were a few more high-risk fathers (139), inasmuch as not all of the siblings in a family have the same father.

The control (low-risk) group consisted of 104 children whose parents and grandparents had never been psychiatrically hospitalized. In this group there were 88 mothers and 88 fathers. Table 1 presents information on the matching (1962) of the experimental and control groups.

Definition of Registered Criminality

The National Police Register and the Penal Register. The criminality of the mothers, fathers, and children was obtained from two sources: The National Police Register (NPR) in Copenhagen and the Penal Register (PR) maintained in the birthplace of the subject. The NPR describes contacts of Danish citizens with the Danish police. It is a register including information for the entire country. If an individual has not been in contact with the police, he will not be listed in the NPR; if he has committed a minor offense (such as driving violation) he will have a record in the main catalog. If, on the other hand, the individual has been convicted of a violation of the criminal code (serious offense), he will have a record called a *Personalieblad* (P-blad). It should be pointed out that one can also be listed in the main catalog if he has been named a missing person or if he has been admitted to a psychiatric department. However, such listings have not been included in our tabulations.

Each time a resident of Denmark is convicted of a crime by a Danish court and each time the Danish authorities are informed of a conviction of a Dane in other lands, this event is recorded in a penal register (PR)

Table 1

**Characteristics of the Experimental
and Control Samples**

Characteristic	Control	Experimental
Number of Cases	104	207
Number of Boys	59	121
Number of Girls	45	86
Mean Age[a]	15.1	15.1
Mean Social Class[b]	2.3	2.2
Mean Years of Education	7.3	7.0
Percentage of Group in Children's Homes (5 Years or More)[c]	14	16
Mean Number of Years in Children's Homes (5 Years or More)[c]	8.5	9.4
Percentage of Group with Rural Residence[d]	22	26

[a]Defined as age to the nearest whole year in 1962.
[b]The scale runs from 0 (low) to 6 (high) and was adapted from Svalastoga (1959).
[c]We considered only experience in children's homes of 5 years or greater duration. Many of the children in the experimental sample had been in children's homes for a brief period while their mothers were hospitalized. Such experience was regarded as quite different from that of children who actually had to make a children's home their home until they could go out and earn their own living.
[d]"Rural residence" was defined as living in a town with a population of 2500 persons or fewer.

maintained in the police district in which he was born. Note that this penal register only contains information on convictions. Access to the PR requires definite information regarding birth place. Because this information was not as accurate for the mothers and fathers, these data are only reported for the children. (Additional details on these registers may be found in Chapters 5 and 7).

Comparable Danish Population Statistics

Inasmuch as the low-risk group was chosen to match the high-risk group for a number of different social characteristics, it cannot be seen as representative of the general population. In view of this, we wished to compare the frequency of criminality in our experimental and control groups with the frequency in the general population. To do this we had to prepare a definition of criminality that was in agreement with that used in official Danish criminal statistics. In these publications a violation against the criminal code is registered if it is accompanied by a sentence which is more severe than a fine (for example, a jail sentence). Thus in those tables below where we compare our samples with the general population, we make use of this definition of criminality.

We must emphasize that when the term criminality is used in this chapter, reference is being made only to *registered criminality*. The authors are quite conscious of the existence of hidden criminality and of the possibility that registered criminality may be unrepresentative of criminality in general.

Note that these data offer certain advantages over the Heston and Kallmann studies. We have registered the identity of the husbands or mates of the schizophrenic women. We can directly observe whether there is a differential mating of schizophrenic women with criminal men. Perhaps most important is the fact that we have the benefit of complete, centralized national registers for criminality.

RESULTS

The results are presented in three sections. These sections discuss criminality among the mothers, fathers, and children. As mentioned above, we hypothesize higher levels of criminality for the high-risk families. In view of this, one-tail tests of significance are utilized below.

Mothers' Criminality

Table 2 presents the listing in the National Police Register for the mothers in the experimental and control groups.

The experimental mothers exhibit more criminality, criminality of a more serious nature, for which they have received more convictions. In Table 3 we compare the experimental and control mothers with the percentage of criminality for women in the Danish population who reached their mean age at the same time. As mentioned, the definition of criminality, in this case, is a conviction with a sentence greater than a

Table 2

**Percentage of Mothers, Fathers, and
Children Registered in the National
Police Register (NPR)**

Registration	Experimental	Control	χ^2	df
MOTHERS (EXPERIMENTAL n = 129; CONTROL n = 88)				
Not Registered	64.3	95.4		
Registered	35.7	4.6	31.9[c]	1
Only Minor Offense	24.8	2.3		
Serious Offense	10.9	2.3	28.8[c]	2
Number of NPR Cases				
0	64.3	95.4		
1	21.1	2.3		
2 or more	14.6	2.3	28.7[c]	2
Convictions				
0	77.5	95.4		
1 or more	22.5	4.6	11.3[c]	1
FATHERS (EXPERIMENTAL n = 139; CONTROL n = 88)				
Not Registered	50.4	55.7		
Registered	49.6	44.3	ns	1
Only Minor Offense	24.4	27.3		
Serious Offense	25.2	17.0	ns	2
Number of NPR Cases				
0	50.4	55.7		
1	21.6	11.4		
2 or more	28.0	32.9	ns	2
Convictions				
0	60.4	58.0		
1 or more	39.6	42.0	ns	1
CHILDREN (EXPERIMENTAL n = 201; CONTROL n = 104)				
Not Registered	69.2	81.7		
Registered	30.8	18.3	5.53[b]	1
Only Minor Offense	24.4	16.4		
Serious Offense	6.4	1.9	6.40[a]	2
Number of NPR Cases				
0	69.2	81.7		
1	12.9	8.7		
2 or more	17.9	9.6	5.70[a]	2

Table 2 (Continued)

Convictions				
0	76.7	86.5		
1 or more	23.3	13.5	4.22[a]	1

Note. "Minor Offense" includes individuals who only are listed in the main catalog of the NPR. "Serious Offense" includes individuals who have a Personalieb-lad in the NPR.
[a] $p < .05$, one-tailed test.
[b] $p < .01$, one-tailed test.
[c] $p < .001$, one-tailed test.

fine. With this definition of criminality in mind, the experimental mothers again evidence the highest level of registered criminality. They are significantly more criminal than the controls (χ^2 (1) = 3.41, $p < .05$) and the female population (χ^2 (1) = 16.47, $p < .001$). The control mothers do not differ significantly from the female population. We should note that statistics are not available for criminality among Danish mothers as differentiated from Danish women. It is difficult to judge how this factor influences the comparisons in Table 3. We should also note that in order to evaluate the probability of the distribution of frequencies in Table 3 with the χ^2 test we converted the percentages for the Danish female population into frequencies by assuming a normal Danish female sample equal in size to the experimental plus control mothers groups ($N = 217$). Rounding up for decimals over .5 gave us a frequency of two registered criminals and 215 noncriminals in the Danish female population group. Similar procedures were followed for the fathers and children in Table 3.

Fathers' Criminality

Table 2 presents a comparison of the registration for criminality of the fathers. As can be seen, there are no significant differences in kind or amount of registration of the experimental and control fathers. Table 3 presents a comparison of the experimental and control fathers and Danish men of their age and generation for registration for criminality. It is important to note that both experimental and control fathers evidence over 3 times greater percentage criminal registration than comparable Danish males. In pairwise analyses both the experimental and control fathers evidence higher levels of criminality than the Danish male population (experimentals versus population: (χ^2 (1) = 22.18, $p < .0005$); control versus population: (χ^2 (1) = 16.00, $p < .0005$).

Table 3

Percentage of Registered Criminality in Mothers, Fathers, and Children in Comparison with Danish Population Rates

Group	EXPERIMENTAL		CONTROL		Danish Comparison Population	χ^2 $(df = 2)$
	n	%	n	%		
Mothers	129	10.6	88	3.4	.7	17.10[a]
Fathers	139	25.2	87	24.1	7.5	12.85[a]
Male Children	114	14.9	60	8.3	2.8	14.10[a]
Female Children	87	4.6	44	2.3	.3	ns

Note. The bases of the computations of the Danish comparison population may be found in Tables 1 and 2 in Christiansen and Pál (1965). We wish to thank Professor Karl O. Christiansen for his kindness in calculating these population estimates.
[a]$p < .001$, one-tailed test.

Control fathers' criminality.   The high level of criminality among the control fathers deserves some comment. The study was initiated to examine factors relating to schizophrenia and mental illness in general. In view of this, the high-risk group was selected, because their mothers were chronic schizophrenics. Except for the fact that these schizophrenic women must also have had children in a given age range, no other selection restriction was placed on this group. Information concerning the fathers and other relatives in the high-risk group was not even sought until a year after the completion of the 1962 testing. On the other hand, a determined effort was made to be certain that there was no trace of hospitalizable mental illness in the control children, mothers, fathers, and grandparents on both sides. Because of registers existing in Denmark, it was possible to carry this plan through rather effectively.

By careful matching, the researchers attempted to minimize the possibility that any differences observed between the high-risk and low-risk groups could be ascribed to factors other than the risk for schizophrenia. For example, the high-risk group (because of their mother's illness) has spent much time in child-care institutions (children's homes). The controls were carefully matched for this characteristic (see Table 1). When a potential children's-home control was located, his family was checked through the Demographic Institute to eliminate those with any hospitalization for mental illness in themselves, their parents, or grandparents. Many were rejected on this ground, this being a frequent reason for the child's institutionalization. Another common reason for a child's institutionalization was criminality in the family. This was not considered grounds for eliminating a potential control. Thirty-eight percent of children's-home controls have fathers with serious criminality. This compares with 11% of family-reared controls. This difference is significant (χ^2 (2) = 7.44, $p < .05$). This method of selecting the controls had the effect of artificially increasing the percentage of criminals in the fathers. Because the percentage of criminality in the fathers of controls was inflated in this manner, comparisons of level of criminality between the experimental and control fathers must be interpreted with considerable caution. Comparisons between the experimental father's criminality and that of the relevant Danish population are, on the other hand, probably more appropriate for purposes of generalization.

Children's Criminality

The age range of the "children" at the time we checked the NPR was between 21 and 31 years of age. In this age range we know that further registration for criminality may be expected. However, in view of the fact that the groups were equated for age and that most male criminal careers begin before an individual is 20 years of age, the results should not change in a way that will markedly alter interpretations. Table 2 presents information on registration in the NPR for the children. The experimental children exhibit more criminality and criminality of a more severe nature for which they have received more convictions. Table 4 presents data from the PR of the experimental and control children; 17.9% of the experimental children have had court convictions for crim-

Table 4

Number and Percentage of Male and Female Children with One or More Convictions in the Penal Register

Children	EXPERIMENTAL		CONTROL		χ^2 (df = 1)
	n	%	n	%	
Total	201	17.9	104	8.7	4.76[a]
Male	114	28.1	60	13.3	4.71[a]
Female	87	4.6	44	2.3	

[a]$p < .05$, one-tailed test.

inal behavior as opposed to 8.7% of the controls. This difference is significant (χ^2 (1) = 4.76, $p < .05$). Table 4 also gives the PR data separately for males and females. The experimental males have significantly more convictions than the control males. Although the experimental females evidence twice the rate of convictions of the control females, the numbers are too small for statistical comparison.

Table 5 presents the NPR data for the children by sex. Both male and female experimental subjects have elevated percentages of registration in the NPR. Table 3 compares the criminal registration data for the experimental and control male and female children and comparable Danish population figures. Both the experimental males and experimental females evidence more criminality than comparable sectors of the Danish population. The differences are significant for the experimental males [χ^2 (1) = 15.16, $p < .0005$] but not for the experimental females. The control rates do not differ significantly from the population rates.

Table 5

Registration of Experimental and Control Children by Sex in the National Police Register (NPR) (in Percentages)

Registration	Experimental	Control	χ^2	df
MALES (EXPERIMENTAL n = 114; CONTROL n = 60)				
Not Registered	56.1	70.0		
Registered	43.9	30.0	3.21[a]	1
Only Minor Offense	33.4	26.7		
Serious Offense	10.5	3.3	4.27[a]	2
FEMALES (EXPERIMENTAL n = 87; CONTROL n = 44)[b]				
Not Registered	86.2	97.7		
Registered	13.8	2.3		
Only Minor Offense	12.6	2.3		
Serious Offense	1.2	0.0		

Note. "Minor Offense" includes individuals who are listed in the main catalog of the NPR. "Serious Offense" includes individuals who have a Personalieblad in the NPR.

[a]$p < .05$.

[b]Expected number too small for chi-square. For registered versus not registered. Fisher exact test, $p = .015$.

Father's Criminality and Children's Criminality.

Table 6 presents data on the criminality of the high- and low-risk children as a function of the criminality of their fathers. In the case of the criminal fathers, the criminality of the children varies significantly as a function of risk [χ^2 (2) = 8.30, $p < .025$, two-tailed test]. If the fathers are not criminal, the relationship is not significant. Criminality in the children is highest where the fathers are criminal and the mothers are schizophrenic.

Table 6

Registration for Criminality of Experimental and Control Children as a Function of Their Fathers' Criminality (in Percentages)

Children	CRIMINAL FATHERS		NONCRIMINAL FATHERS	
	High Risk (n = 79)	Low Risk (n = 42)	High Risk (n = 128)	Low Risk (n = 62)
Criminal Law Conviction	20.2	4.8	15.6	11.3
Minor Offense	19.0	11.9	9.4	12.9
Not Registered	60.8	83.3	75.0	75.8

Note. "Criminal Law Conviction" includes only individuals with registration for a court conviction for a criminal offense in the National Police Register. "Minor Offense" includes individuals who are only listed in the main catalog of the National Police Register. A father is classified as criminal if he is registered for one or more convictions.

DISCUSSION

Danish families with a schizophrenic mother evidence higher rates of criminality than do matched controls or corresponding sectors of the Danish population. The schizophrenic women themselves are also registered for more criminal acts and more convictions than comparison groups. The mates of the schizophrenic women have higher rates of registered criminality than comparable Danish males (the control mates were judged to be unsuitable for comparison). Both male and female experimental children evidenced more criminality than their controls or corresponding sectors of the Danish population.

It is difficult to compare these results with those of previous studies. Landau et al. (1972) presents very little information identifying groups or defining criminality. However, Landau et al. report more delinquency among children of psychotics than controls. Kallmann (1938) also reports increased criminality for children of schizophrenics as well as for the schizophrenics themselves. Heston (1966) reports higher rates of criminality for children with a schizophrenic mother than for controls.

The general trend of the results of these three studies is in agreement with those of the present study. It would be of interest to be more precise in this comparison of results. For example, Heston reports that 14.9% of the male children of schizophrenic women evidenced criminality; Kallmann's rate for male children with one schizophrenic parent (mother or father) is 14.49%. The relevant figures for male high-risk children in the current study vary between 10.5%, 14.9%, 28.1%, and 43.9%, depending on the definition of criminality utilized. Comparisons of precise percentage across three different cultures, legal systems, and methods of obtaining information are not likely to be productive. However, the agreement in the direction of the results across the studies is clear; families with a schizophrenic member manifest relatively high levels of criminality.

Schizophrenic mother's criminality.   Kallmann (1938) attempted to assess whether the criminality among his schizophrenic probands was genuine; he concluded that it was not genuine, but rather a symptom of their illness. In the case of the schizophrenic mothers in this study, there is indirect evidence suggesting the same conclusion. For one thing, in Denmark an offender's serious mental illness is frequently grounds for dropping prosecution of a case. Of the schizophrenic mothers, 16.7% had charges against them that were dropped by the state attorney. None of the control mothers had charges dropped. If we disregard the dropped cases, however, we still see that the schizophrenic women have an excess of convictions for a wide variety of offenses: disturbance of the peace, property crimes, violence, and attempted murder. Of these 14 schizophrenic mothers with serious criminality, 11 committed their first offense after having already received a diagnosis of schizophrenia. This suggests that their criminality may be a symptom of or at least related to their mental illness. Perhaps the criminality is a reflection of their inability to cope with a difficult environment.

Experimental fathers' criminality.   In attempting to explain the relatively high rates of criminality among children with a schizophrenic parent, Kallmann suggests the possibility that schizophrenics may assortatively mate with criminals. If such assortative mating were demonstrated, then the higher rates of criminality in the children of schizophrenics could be due to either the genetic transmission of some characteristic of the criminal parent predisposing to criminality or to the child's learning of the criminal life from his criminal parent, or both.

The comparison of the fathers of the high-risk children with their matched controls provided little information because of the artificially high level of criminality among the control fathers. However, the experimental fathers proved to be considerably elevated in level of criminality in relation to Danish males of their age and generation.

In order to explore the possibility that their greater criminality was related to their social class level, a measure of the latter was obtained using Svalastoga's (1959) method (originally derived on a Danish population). On a scale from 1 (high) to 8 (low), the father's mean social class level was 5.8. Wolf and Høgh (1971) have completed a study of the frequency of criminality in Danish males as a function of social class, in which they also used the Svalastoga method. By linear interpolation from their results, we can estimate that at this level (5.8) of social class, 14.4% of the men are registered for having committed criminal offenses. This can be compared with 39.6% of the experimental fathers having been convicted of having committed at least one offense. Of the experimental fathers, 25.2% have committed serious offenses (see Table 2). It seems clear that the level of criminality among the experimental fathers is considerably above Danish men of their social level.

In comparison with men of the same age, generation, and social class, the experimental fathers evidence a higher level of criminality. Schizophrenic women and criminals may be said to assortatively mate with each other, supporting Kallmann's third explanation of the high level of criminality among the children of schizophrenics.

Criminality in children with schizophrenic mothers. The high-risk children evidenced higher levels of registration for criminality than did either the controls or corresponding sectors of the Danish population. This was true for both male and female high-risk children. A factor that may have played a role in this high level of criminality is the criminality in their parents.

Although factors relating to the method of selecting the control fathers made them inappropriate as a comparison group, their artificially high level of criminality is an advantage in comparisons between the high- and low-risk children. It has been demonstrated that criminality in a father will increase the probability of criminality in his sons on the basis of both genetic and environmental factors (see Chapter 7). Inasmuch as the levels of criminality of experimental and control fathers are almost equal (see Tables 2 and 3), any difference in the level of criminality between the high- and low-risk children cannot be ascribed to differences in the level of criminality of their fathers. On the other hand, the schizophrenic mothers did have a higher level of criminality than the control mothers. Although this higher level of criminality was statistically quite significant, the absolute level of registered criminality was quite low; only 14 of the experimental mothers were registered as serious criminals. In addition, (as mentioned above) these mothers' criminality began after they had been diagnosed as schizophrenic. In order to assess the influence of the criminality of the schizophrenic mothers on the level of criminality of the high-risk children, the data were reanalyzed, removing the children of these 14 mothers from the analysis. Of the 25 children of these 14 mothers only 4 were registered for serious criminality. When these 25 children are removed from Table 2, the percentage of experimental children who were registered for serious offenses is reduced from 6.4% to 5.1%.

The experimental children evidence more registered criminality than the control children or corresponding sectors of the Danish population. This cannot be ascribed directly to the criminality in their parents, nor can it be ascribed to institutional experience, because the experimental and control groups are equated for this variable (Table 1). In view of the matching of these two groups, we can tentatively ascribe their heightened level of criminality to their having a schizophrenic mother.

INTERACTION OF FATHERS' CRIMINALITY AND MOTHERS' SCHIZOPHRENIA

In Table 6 we see that the increase in criminality of the high-risk children occurs only in the case where the father is criminal. If the father is not criminal, the schizophrenia in the mother does not heighten the level of criminality in the children.

We dismissed Kallmann's first hypothesis because of Heston's compelling results. The third hypothesis (assortative mating) seems to be supported by our findings. The second hypothesis can be best evaluated in the light of the data presented in Table 6. If schizophrenia and criminality were associated genetically, we would expect more criminality in the high-risk children than in the low-risk children in those cases in which the father is not criminal. This was not observed. If the father is criminal, however, the high-risk children evidence heightened criminality. Whether this schizophrenia-criminality connection is evidence for a genetic association or represents an environmental effect is impossible to be determined from our data. Heston's results do not permit us to reject the genetic interpretation. The findings recall analogous results reported by Hutchings and Mednick (Chapter 7). In Denmark they studied criminality levels in biological and adoptive fathers of criminal male adoptees and controls. In a type of cross-fostering design they present a table giving the amount of criminality in adopted males who had been raised by either a criminal or noncriminal adoptive father and born to either a criminal or noncriminal biological father. If the biological father was not criminal, the environmental effect of a criminal adoptive father did not increase the criminality of the adoptive sons. If, however, the biological father was criminal, criminality in the adoptive father was associated with increased levels of criminality in the adoptive sons. This could be interpreted as suggesting that the environmental factors associated with a rearing agent's criminality were only effective in producing criminality in the male offspring in the case in which a genetic predisposition already existed. In the case of the data of the present study, perhaps the analogous environmental agent was the schizophrenia in the mother. As is mentioned above, it is also possible that the contribution of the schizophrenic mother was genetic.

IMPLICATIONS FOR HIGH-RISK RESEARCH

The results of this study suggest that work on populations at high-risk for schizophrenia should not ignore the influence of one parent's criminality on the assessment of results and clinical outcomes in these high-risk children. With respect to clinical outcome, both Kallmann (1938) and Elsasser (1952) have remarked on the fact that the offspring of the mating of a schizophrenic with a psychopath evidence no more schizophrenia than the offspring of the mating of a schizophrenic with a normal. This is true despite the great likelihood that life conditions will be more stressful for children with a psychopathic parent. One would expect more schizophrenia in the children with a double burden of psychopathology in the parents. It is almost as if the psychopathic parents transmit characteristics that nullify predisposing characteristics transmitted by the schizophrenic parents and in this way compensate for the extra stress in the environment.

Chapter 17

A prospective study of predictors of criminality: 3. Electrodermal response patterns

Janice Loeb

and

Sarnoff A. Mednick

In the period since Lykken (1957) published his now-classic investigation relating properties of psychophysiological responsiveness, autonomic conditioning, and instrumental avoidance learning to the diagnosis of psychopathy, there has been a burgeoning of similar studies. An excellent summary of this literature is provided in Chapter 12. The general hypothesis of this work is that reduced autonomic responsiveness and deficits in capacity for classical conditioning produce the "inability to learn from experience" attributed to the psychopath. However, in the light of Lykken's results and those of other investigators, it would appear that, in fact, the psychopath's failure to learn is related specifically to situations dependent upon conditioned responses to *noxious* reinforcers (e.g., shock and loud noise). The approach (positive reward) learning of apprehended criminals and psychopaths has been repeatedly noted to be no different from that of control subjects. Furthermore, as Hare and Quinn (1971) have pointed out, of the peripheral autonomic nervous system (ANS) measures sampled so far, the electrodermal response (EDR) has been the one giving consistent results.

In this chapter we report the electrodermal functioning of individuals who have engaged in asocial behavior that has been registered by the police. Our underlying hypothesis is that failure to conform to society's sanctions and conventions is correlated with, and perhaps partially caused by, lowered ANS responsiveness and reduced capacity for learning to inhibit behavior that elicits punishment. This last characteristic may be seen as a form of deficit in aptitude for avoidance learning. The purposes of this study were to establish (1) if electrodermal deviations found in criminals diagnosed as psychopaths are also present in individuals who commit relatively minor infractions of the law and (2) whether these electrodermal characteristics are present prior to society's detection and punishment of the antisocial behavior.

It should be recalled that the sample consists of both high- and low-risk subjects. In this initial paper the children with schizophrenic mothers are omitted from consideration. Only the control group of 104 is included. It was possible, with one exception, to select subjects tested *prior* to the occurrence of the delinquency used to assign them to the experimental group. The criterion for delinquency was the commitment of legal offenses leading to at least two court convictions. Individuals meeting this criterion were compared with controls with no record of illegal activity. As indicated below, the offenses in some of the cases were of a relatively minor nature.

The experimental measures under investigation were (1) electrodermal basal conductance, (2) electrodermal response amplitude to a noxious stimulus such as a loud noise, (3) the recovery rate of the electrodermal response, and (4) the extent of conditioning and speed of extinction of this response. The prediction of the direction of differences expected in our two groups was based partly on the results of previous studies with psychopaths and partly on an explanation of avoidance learning proposed by Mednick (see Chapter 1). The lowered basal conductance and response conductance levels and retarded EDR conditioning found earlier with psychopaths were also expected in our offender group.

Recovery rate and avoidance learning.   Much of this psychophysiological conditioning literature has as a background assumption that a critical deficit characteristic of the psychopath is poor avoidance instrumental learning (Lykken, 1957). Mednick (1970, 1974, 1975 and Chapter 1) has proposed an explanation of avoidance learning and of individual differences in avoidance learning. In this explanation Mednick points out that fast recovery from autonomic nervous system (ANS) imbalance could serve as an aptitude for fast avoidance learning. On the other hand, an individual with slow ANS recovery should be retarded in avoidance learning involving ANS functioning.

An individual with a deficit in avoidance learning may be difficult for a family to socialize. He will have great difficulty in learning to inhibit asocial responses, which the family attempts to discourage by use of threats and punishment. On occasions when he does inhibit aggressive or stealing behavior, because of the threat of punishment, his reinforcement (via decreasing fear) for this conforming act will be relatively small because of his very slow ANS recovery. The individual with normal aptitude for avoidance learning will experience substantial reinforcement (via rapid ANS recovery). This repeated reinforcement will tend to maintain the conforming response. In the case of the individual with slow recovery, conforming responses (motivated by fear of punishment) will not be sufficiently reinforced and will be poorly learned and weakly maintained. As a consequence of this chain of reasoning (see Chapter 1 for details) we predict slow ANS recovery for the offender group in this study.

PROCEDURE

Testing began at 8:00 a.m. with the psychophysiological measurement described below. This was followed by a full day of further assessment as described in Mednick and Schulsinger (1968), including the Wechsler Intelligence Scale for Children (WISC).

PSYCHOPHYSIOLOGY

Recording was carried out on an Offner-Beckman Type R dynograph. After the points of electrode placement had been washed and sponged with alcohol, the subject reclined on a hospital bed and was asked to relax. Respiration, heart rate, electrodermal activity, and electromyographic (EMG) parameters were recorded. The electrodermal electrodes consisted of 7-mm diameter zinc discs embedded in plastic cups. Small sponges saturated in zinc sulphate solution were inserted in the plastic cup as electrolyte medium. A special wheatstone skin resistance bridge was constructed for the project (Ax and Zacharopoulous, 1962). The bridge reversed the polarity of the 1.5-volt reference current every 1.2 seconds. When all transducers were attached, recording was started and was continuous until the conclusion of the generalization testing. At the beginning of the testing session the subject was permitted to relax for 15 minutes, and then the earphones were attached.

Approximately 30 seconds after the tape recorder was started, the subject heard instructions informing him of the procedure, and was followed by eight presentations of the CS (1000 Hz, 54-db tone). These eight presentations were included to desensitize S to the CS. Nine seconds after the final "desensitization trial," conditioning trials began. The UCS was an irritating noise of 96 db presented for 4½ seconds following ½ second after the onset of CS. There were 14 partial reinforcement trials (9 CS-UCS pairings and 5 interspersed test presentations of the CS alone). The intertrial interval varied from 14 to 77 seconds.

Following the final conditioning trial, there was an interval of 3 minutes, after which conditioning and stimulus generalization testing began. Generalization stimuli were tones of 1311 Hz (GS_1) and 1967 Hz (GS_2). The order of CS, GS_1, and GS_2 was counterbalanced.

The final conditioning and stimulus generalization-testing trial marked the end of psychophysiological testing, which took about 50 minutes. S was then disconnected from the apparatus.

RESULTS

Delinquency

Police reports on the Ss were checked in 1972 when the Ss[1] age range was from 20 to 29 years. Seven boys and no girls were found to fulfill the criterion for the delinquent group (D), that is, the commitment of legal infractions that had led to at least two convictions. One of the Ss had reached this criterion at the age of 18 years shortly before he was tested, but he had not been imprisoned and thus was retained in the sample because of its limited size. The remaining Ss had *no* recorded offenses prior to testing.

A description of the offenses of each S in Group D is listed in Table 1.

Table 2 contains information descriptive of the entire sample pool. As may also be seen in Table 2, the basic composition of Group D was quite different from that of the other controls, particularly in regard to age and sex. Therefore, a control group who had no record of legal offenses was selected from the Ss remaining in the sample pool. They were matched individual by individual for four variables in the following order: sex, age, social class (father's occupation level), and rearing in children's

Table 1

Description of Convictions in Seven Delinquent Ss (Group D)

Subject	Age Tested (1962)	Age First Conviction	Total Convictions to Date	Types of Offense	Types of Penalty
1A	16	18	3	Illegal possession of property and two traffic cases	Fines
61A	16	19	7	All burglary or theft	Youth prison, probation, social agency supervision and prison
90	17	21	2	Disturbing peace and burglary	Probation
93	20	26	2	One traffic case and creating disturbance in public transportation	Fines
95A	20	18	2	Failure to report to draft board; sex offense without violence	Agency supervision
99	18	21	3	Two violations of the civil defense code; traffic case	Jail; fine
100	19	19	3	Minor civil offense, and two traffic cases, one with alcohol involved	Jail, fines, and revocation of drivers license

Table 2

Characteristics of Subject Groups

	GROUPS		
Item	Total Control Sample	Delinquent	Nondelinquent
Total Number	104	7	7
Boys	60	7	7
Girls	44	0	0
Mean Age in 1962 (nearest year)	15.1	18.0	17.7
Mean Social Class[a]	2.3	2.3	2.7
Number Raised in Children's Homes	14	2	1

[a]The social class scale was adopted from Svalastoga (1959).

home (as opposed to rearing with a family). Because of the limited number of potential matches fulfilling the age and sex requirements, the other variables could not be matched with absolute precision. The background information of Group ND is also listed in Table 2. Although not specifically matched for intellectual level, the mean IQ of the two groups as measured by the WISC did not differ significantly. The mean full scale IQ of Group D was 102 and of Group ND was 107. No child in either group had been reported as having had psychiatric problems.

Electrodermal measures

In the following analyses the seven members of Group D and the seven members of Group ND are compared by t-test for matched samples. Because the direction of differences is predicted, one-tail tests are used.

Basal conductance levels

Measurements of basal levels of electrodermal activity, converted to skin conductance (SC) units (micromhos) were taken prior to each of the trials of the psychophysiological procedure. Although six of the seven Ss in Group D had lower initial SC levels ($\bar{X} = 4.21$ micromhos) than their Group ND matches ($\bar{X} = 6.5$ micromhos), these differences did not reach statistical significance. The mean of all basal SC levels throughout testing showed a more pronounced trend in the same direction; that is, six out of seven Ss in Group D had a lower Basal SC ($\overline{X} = 5.1$ micromhos) than did Group ND ($\overline{X} = 8.5$ micromhos), but again the differences failed to be statistically significant [t (6) = 1.82, $p > .05$].

Amplitude

The mean SC amplitudes for Groups D and ND for each block of three conditioning trials are presented in Table 3. An analysis of variance for repeated measures indicated that Group D was significantly less responsive than Group ND [F (1/12) = 15.11, $p < .005$]. The change in response amplitude over trials was also significant [F (2/24 = 6.07, $p < .01$]. However, the significant Groups x trials interaction [F (2/24) = 26.50, $p < .001$] as well as inspection of Table 3 indicated that the trials effect was due mainly to reduction in amplitude over trials in Group ND. A comparison of the first and last blocks of trials for each group confirmed that a significant reduction in amplitude had occurred

Table 3

**Electrodermal Responsiveness of
Delinquents and Nondelinquents**

Trial Block	MEAN CONDUCTANCE AMPLITUDE (µmhos)		PERCENT GROUP RESPONDING	
	Delinquent	Nondelinquent	Delinquent	Nondelinquent
Conditioning				
1−3	.21	1.67	86	100
4−6	.12	1.10	51	100
7−9	.16	.79	43	100
Tests for Conditioning				
1−5	.03	.33	29	57
Generalization and Extinction Trials				
1−3	0	.41	14	57
4−6	0	.11	0	29
7−9	0	.08	0	14

in Group ND, whereas the change in amplitude in Group D was not significant. It should be added that even in the first block of trials, the mean amplitude for Group D was extremely low.

In Table 3, the mean percentage of Ss responding with a measurable deflection to presentation of the UCS is also presented for blocks of three trials. In Group ND, every S gave at least one measurable response to the UCS within a block of three trials. In Group D, on the other hand, the percentage of Ss failing to respond in any measurable way to the UCS increased progressively over trials. The reduction in mean response between the first and last block of trials was statistically significant [t (6) = 2.95, $p < .01$]. Also significant was the difference in mean response of Groups D and ND during the third trial block [t (6) = 3.29, $p < .01$].

To summarize, Group ND responded to repeated presentations of the noxious UCS (loud noise) with continued measurable responses of decreasing amplitude. Group D, starting at a lower initial response level, did not substantially reduce the amplitude of their measurable responses, but showed a tendency over trials to stop responding completely.

Because the trend for Ss in Group D to give responses of zero amplitude was so marked and these zeros were, of course, included in the calculation of mean amplitudes, a second measure of mean response amplitude was calculated. These means were based on a denominator of total measurable responses only. This alternate method of calculation indicated that reduced amplitude in Group D was *not* solely due to the greater number of nonresponders. Even with only measurable responses were considered, Group D was responding at a significantly lower level of amplitude than Group ND.

Recovery rate. The rate of recovery of responses to the UCS was calculated using the following formula:

$$\frac{\frac{1}{2} \text{ response amplitude}}{\text{time to recover } \frac{1}{2} \text{ response amplitude}}$$

The unit of electrodermal measurement in this instance is that of skin resistance (ohms) and follows the convention adopted previously (Mednick, 1970). Using this formula, the mean recovery rate for Group D was 365 ohms/second, significantly slower than that of Group ND, which was 760 ohms/second [t (6) = 2.67, $p < .025$].

Test for conditioning and generalization. The mean response amplitude of Group D for the five trials which constituted the test for conditioning was .03 micromhos, as opposed to a mean of .33 micromhos in Group ND, a statistically significant difference [t (6) = 2.25, $p < .05$]. The reduced amount of conditioning in Group D was reflected even more convincingly in the difference in mean percentage of Ss responding in a measurable way during the five trials (Table 3). A comparison of mean number of responses in the two groups indicated significantly fewer responses for Group D [t (6) = 3.31, $p < .01$]. In view of recent methodological developments (Martin, 1964) it is likely that the "conditioning" results are confounded by orienting responses.

On the nine generalization trials, there was only one S who gave a (barely) measurable response in Group D. Group ND, on the other hand, included four Ss who gave at least two responses each. These data were not submitted to statistical analysis, but clearly show a continued trend of the findings on other measures: reduced amplitude and frequency of response in Group D. Recovery rates were not computed for this part of the procedure because so few responses occurred. In the absence of a response no measure of recovery is possible.

DISCUSSION

The electrodermal measures were obtained well before the subjects (except one) had been registered for any asocial behavior. The electrodermal measures, therefore, are unlikely to have been a *result* of events associated with registration for asocial acts. Because they predate the asocial acts, they fulfill one of the reasonable conditions for joining the host of possible factors that might have "caused" the asocial acts.

The nature of the asocial acts used to select the "offender" group was rather mild. Yet moderate and statistically reliable differences were observed in the electrodermal activity of the two groups. The mild offender group (examined before they had committed a registered offense) has the type of psychophysiological behavior reported by others to be common in already registered psychopaths and criminals.

The relationship of this psychophysiological pattern to poor avoidance conditioning (Lykken, 1957: Schmauk, 1970) suggests the role ANS functioning might play in the etiology of some criminal behavior. In Chapters 1 and 2 we have suggested how low ANS responsiveness, a slow rate of ANS recovery, and certain family circumstances may provide a poor aptitude for learning to avoid or inhibit asocial responses that are regularly followed by censure or punishment. There is no reason to repeat this theoretical formulation here. There have been some recent findings not disconfirming this hypothesized relationship between recovery and asocial behavior (see Chapters 1, 2, 12, and 13). The evidence from the present study adds additional support to this hypothesis. The fact that the psychophysiological differences predated the onset of asocial behavior in almost all these delinquent subjects makes it clear that they are not a result of the contact of the subjects with the legal process.

The results of this study must be viewed with great caution because of the very small number of subjects involved. However, the concordance of these data with the research results cited encourages giving them serious consideration.

Chapter 18

A prospective study of predictors of criminality: 4. School behavior

Lis Kirkegaard-Sørensen

and

Sarnoff A. Mednick

In this chapter we present information on how school teachers describe children who later evidenced registered criminality. In 1962 the school teacher who best knew each child was asked to complete a questionnaire concerning the child's school behavior. The questionnaire tapped a wide variety of forms of behavior. This chapter concerns itself with determining whether the answers to any of these questions and other school-related information distinguish those individuals who later evidenced registered criminality. This type of research has been attempted before. Robins (1970) found that children who later evidenced criminality distinguished themselves from other children by manifesting "rejection of the teachers' authority, school failure and discipline problems" (page 432). Ackerly (1933) also remarked on the poor school achievement of young criminals. Cline and Wangrow (1959) retrospectively compared 70 criminals' life histories with those of 70 controls matched for age, social class, intelligence, socioeconomic status, and race. Despite the fact that they were matched for intelligence, those who later became criminal were less involved in their school work and less positive towards school. Although 60% of the control group were characterized as being high in social conformity, only 20% of the criminals were so characterized.

Conger and Miller (1966) studied the school behavior of 184 boys who (before the age of 18 years) had committed offenses that resulted in their appearance before a Colorado juvenile court. These delinquents were matched with controls for age, social class, residence area, IQ, school background, and ethnic group. Quite early in their school careers the social behavior of the delinquents was relatively unacceptable to both their classmates and teachers; the teachers characterized them as being aggressive and unable to concentrate. In the middle school years the teachers reported that they had poor study habits and did poorly in their studies.

The above-mentioned studies are retrospective and perhaps suffer from the types of difficulties inherent in this method (Mednick and McNeil, 1968). Several studies have attempted prospectively to predict delinquency on the basis of teachers' statements. In the Cambridge-Somerville study (Powers and Witmer, 1951) teachers of 200 children were interviewed. The children were between 8 and 12 years of age, and the teacher had known them for at least half a year. On the basis of teachers' statements, one of the researchers predicted which of the 200 would become criminal. When the boys were between 17 and 22 years of age the predictions were tested by examining police records. The predictions regarding those who became criminal tended to be correct; however, there were many false positives. In the judgement of the teacher, children who later became serious criminals tended to fail in school; they had lower IQs, they played hookey, were restless, hyperactive, and negative. They were also described as irresponsible, shifting in mood, and very easily distracted and chattery.

Hathaway and Monachesi (1963) asked teachers to predict which 15-year-old children would become delinquents. They waited 4 years and found that teachers' judgements (heavily influenced by poor school ability and achievement) were significantly related to later criminal behavior on the part of the children.

West and Farrington (1973) examined 411 working-class London boys at 8-9 years of age and followed them through adolescence. One quarter of the group were convicted of having committed a delinquent act. One of the best predictors was the teachers' rating of the 8-9-year-old boys as troublesome, disciplinary problems.

Other prospective studies that have supported this picture of the predelinquent are Mulligan, Douglas, Hammond, and Tizard (1963); Reckless and Dinitz (1967), and Kvaraceus, (1969). All these studies have been completed in the United States and Great Britain.

The present study is also prospective, but it has certain distinctive features:

Age of sample. When the sample was originally examined in 1962, the subjects averaged 15.1 years of age and were between 10 and 20 years of age. At the time of the current study they averaged 28 years of age and ranged between 23 and 33 years of age. Thus, in comparison with most of the other prospective studies, we have followed the subjects for a longer time (13 years). Inasmuch as most criminal careers begin before an individual is 25 years of age (Hurwitz and Christiansen, 1971), it seems likely that we have identified most of those individuals in the sample who will be criminals. It is also true that by following these individuals to a higher age level, we make it possible to see forms of criminality that are not commonly observed in teenagers.

HYPOTHESES

In the light of the results of the studies cited, we hypothesized that the criminal group would have been characterized by their school teachers as being aggressive, evidencing disciplinary problems, being overactive, having poor study habits, and poor school achievement.

METHOD

Materials

School report. The school report consists of 27 questions covering a broad spectrum of school behavior relating to psychopathology. The teacher could check true or false or don't know for each item. The school grades in Danish (reading and writing), mathematics, geography and history, diligence, and neatness were all coded on a five-point scale in which 5 implied excellent, and 1 was very poor. This coding was completed with the close consultation of Danish teachers. The school reports were completed by the teacher who best knew the subject; 310 of the 311 forms were completed. Only the 14 items relevant to the hypotheses were examined.

Determination of criminality. Our analysis limits itself to registered criminality. Information we have concerning hidden criminality is not systematically gathered. For purposes of this study an individual is deemed to be criminal if he has one court conviction registered in the Danish Penal Register. The number of criminal females proved to be too small (four high-risk and one low-risk) for reliable analysis. Analyses are restricted to the males. Seven low-risk and thirty-two high-risk males had experienced at least one court conviction. The overwhelming majority of the subjects are registered for property crimes (thievery, fraud, receiving and selling stolen goods, etc.). Only three subjects (all from the high-risk group) were convicted of crimes involving violence. Seven were convicted of "special" law crimes; six of these seven received prison sentences. It is tempting to compare the frequency of delinquency in this sample with other studies, but differences in age level and definition discourage such superficial comparisons.

Reduction of sample.   The school reports were gathered in 1962. Eight of the males had already been in contact with the police before this date. Consequently, it is conceivable that in these cases the teachers' judgements could have been influenced by such information. These eight subjects (seven high-risk and one low-risk) were dropped from the sample. This left 25 high-risk and 6 low-risk males classified as criminal.

The social class and age of the groups are presented in Table 1A. Although none of the group differences are statistically significant, the social class of the criminals is noticeably lower than that of controls. Social class is a factor that might strongly influence a teacher's judgements of a child. Consequently, it was deemed important to equate the criminal and noncriminal groups for social class. Rather than statistically control for the social class differences (and perhaps risk making unwarranted assumptions), we decided to bring the criminal and noncriminal group social class averages into better agreement. In view of the fact that there was a disproportionately large number of higher social class individuals in the noncriminal group and that the noncriminal group was substantially larger than the criminal group, six high-social-class, high-risk and 20 high-social-class, low-risk noncriminals were dropped from the analysis. The resulting social class averages for the final groups are presented in Table 1B.

RESULTS

The results are presented in terms of the hypotheses of the study. After comparison of the results for the total group of criminals and

Table 1

Mean Social Class of Rearing and Age of Criminal and Noncriminal Groups at Time Teacher Completed School Report

	HIGH-RISK		LOW-RISK		TOTAL	
	Criminal	*Not Criminal*	*Criminal*	*Not Criminal*	*Criminal*	*Not Criminal*
A. Before matching for social class						
Age	13.6	15.2	15.0	15.2	13.8	15.2
Social Class	2.12	2.46	1.17	2.53	1.94	2.49
N	25	83	6	53	31	136
B. After matching for social class						
Age	13.6	15.3	15.0	15.3	13.8	15.3
Social Class	2.12	2.18	1.17	1.21	1.94	1.89
N	25	77	6	33	31	110

Table 2

Teachers' Rating of Behavior of Criminals and Noncriminals

| | PERCENT RATED TRUE BY TEACHERS | | | | | |
| | HIGH-RISK | | LOW-RISK | | TOTAL | |
	Criminal	Not Criminal	Criminal	Not Criminal	Criminal	Not Criminal
Aggression-related items						
1. Pupil is unusually violent and aggressive, creates conflicts	24	10	17	3	23	8[a]
2. Pupil is a disciplinary problem	32	7[b]	33	3	32	6[c]
3. Pupil is easily angered or irritated with little apparent reason	48	26	50	9[a]	48	20[b]
Activity level-related items						
4. Pupil is quiet and unengaged	38	45	83	32[a]	47	41
5. Pupil rarely takes initiative, waits passively for teacher	52	49	83	34	59	45
6. Pupil's behavior is marked by strong activity	17	12	0	3	14	9

Table 2 (Continued)

Teachers' Rating of Behavior of Criminals and Noncriminals

	PERCENT RATED TRUE BY TEACHERS					
	HIGH-RISK		LOW-RISK		TOTAL	
	Criminal	Not Criminal	Criminal	Not Criminal	Criminal	Not Criminal
7. Pupil's behavior is marked by normal activity	52	64	17	88[a]	45	71
8. Pupil's behavior is marked by passivity	30	24	83	9[c]	41	20[a]
Study habits-related items						
9. Pupil repeated a grade	19	12	0	7	16	10
10. Pupil examined by psychologist or psychiatrist	47	10[b]	0	0	37	6[b]
11. Pupil will, in the future, develop psychological-emotional problems requiring psychiatric treatment	29	23	67	3[a]	33	17
12. Pupil performs below his abilities	50	24[a]	50	21	50	23[b]
13. Pupil has attended special education class	37	29	40	10	38	22

Note: The items are translated and abbreviated from the original Danish questionnaire.
[a] p < .025.
[b] p < .005.
[c] p < .0005 (Fisher Exact Test based on frequencies).

noncriminals, differences between the high- and low-risk group results are then presented. Table 2 presents the percentage of affirmative responses of the teachers to each of the hypothesis-relevant questionnaire items as well as the Fisher Exact Test results for group comparisons. Because direction of differences is predicted, one-tail tests are used.

Aggression

Total group. Item 1 refers to behavior that is clearly identified as aggressive. Item 2 refers to disciplinary problems that in almost all cases have reference to aggressive school behavior. In the cases of both these items the criminal group was characterized by the teacher as more aggressive. The percentage of criminals described as disciplinary problems was over 5 times higher than that of noncriminals. Though not unequivocally related to aggression, in item 3 the teacher identified the children who become easily angered or irritated. The criminal group was described thusly by the teacher significantly more often than was the noncriminal group.

The hypothesis relating aggressive school behavior to later criminal behavior is well supported by these data. It is interesting that of the six criminals whose offenses involved violence, three were described as aggressive by the teacher. In the remainder of the sample, only 7.4% of the children are so described.

High- and low-risk groups. The pattern of differences for the criminals versus noncriminals is the same for the high- and low-risk groups. In both cases the criminals are described as evidencing more aggressive behavior.

Activity level—passivity

Total groups. The aggressivity hypothesis and findings might lead one to expect fewer individuals among the criminals who evidence passivity. The opposite is the case. Twice as many criminals as noncriminals were described as passive. We checked to see whether the aggressive (item 1) individuals were the same as the passive (item 8) individuals. There were very few children the teacher characterized as both passive and aggressive.

High- and low-risk groups. Inspection of the results for item 8 for the high- and low-risk groups indicates that the findings for the total groups are heavily dependent on the highly significant differences between the criminals and noncriminals in the low-risk group. Of the low-risk criminals, 83% (five out of six) were characterized as passive; only 9% of the noncriminal controls were so characterized. Although the direction of the differences is the same in the high-risk group, the difference is neither impressive nor significant. Items 4 and 5 support the finding of item 8. As opposed to the high-risk criminals, the low-risk criminals are described as relatively quiet and unengaged and passive in class.

Activity level—overactivity

Total groups.   Item 6 permitted the teacher to identify children marked by strong activity. Although the criminal group had more members so characterized, the difference was small and not statistically significant.

High- and low-risk groups.   Rating of strong activity was almost entirely restricted to the high-risk group. Criminal versus noncriminal differences were not significant.

Poor study habits and poor school achievement

Total groups.   Table 3 presents the groups' mean school performance in reading, written Danish, mathematics, geography and history, diligence, neatness, and a score that sums the child's teacher's ratings in all these subjects. As can be seen, the criminals evidenced a lower total performance score than the noncriminals. The scores of the criminals were especially poor in diligence and neatness. In Table 2 the data for item 9 indicate that more of the criminals tended to repeat a grade in school; this difference was not significant. More of the criminals attended special education classes (item 13) than did the noncriminals; this difference also was not significant. As can be seen in item 12 (Table 2) the teacher characterized the to-be criminals as performing below their ability level. Rather indirect evidence of the criminals' difficulty in performing well and adjusting to school is the fact that so many of them (37%) have been referred to a school psychologist or psychiatrist for examination (Item 10, Table 2).

High and low-risk groups.   It should first be pointed out that criminal-noncriminal differences in total performance score are significant and in the same direction (poorer for criminals) in both high- and

Table 3

Mean School Grades of Criminals and Noncriminals

	HIGH-RISK		LOW-RISK		TOTAL	
	Criminal	Not Criminal	Criminal	Not Criminal	Criminal	Not Criminal
Reading	2.67	2.89	2.67	3.06	2.67	2.94
Written Danish	2.67	2.69	1.83	3.00[b]	2.50	2.79
Mathematics	2.71	2.99	2.40	3.00	2.65	2.99
Geography and History	2.77	3.00	2.20	2.9[a]	2.67	2.99
Diligence	2.55	3.15[b]	1.83	3.12[b]	2.39	3.14[c]
Neatness	2.33	2.76	1.67	3.06[c]	2.20	2.85[b]
Sum	15.32	17.64[a]	12.20	17.97[a]	14.67	17.75[b]

Note: Grades can range between 5 (Excellent) and 1 (very poor).
[a] p < .025.
[b] p < .005.
[c] p < .0005 (one-tailed, t test).

low-risk groups. The difference is greater in the low-risk group. This is reflected in significantly poorer performance for the low-risk criminals for written Danish, geography and history, diligence and neatness. The criminal-noncriminal differences in the high-risk groups are relatively small and only reach significance in the case of diligence.

Almost all of the individuals who repeated a grade were in the high-risk group. Criminal-noncriminal differences were not significant. In both the high- and low-risk groups the criminals are said to perform more poorly than their abilities allow. This result is significant in the high-risk group but not in the low-risk group (Item 12, Table 2). The criminals in both the high- and low-risk groups tend to be placed in special education classes (Item 13, Table 2). While neither difference reaches significance, it is more marked in the low-risk group.

All the children examined by a school psychologist or school psychiatrist (Item 10) were from the high-risk group. This is not surprising in view of the expectancy for deviant behavior in these individuals (Mednick and McNeil, 1968; Heston, 1966). Among the high-risk children, those who later became criminal were significantly more likely to have been examined by a psychologist or psychiatrist. The same type of result is seen in the low-risk group where for two-thirds of those that become criminal, the teacher predicted that they would later develop severe psychological difficulties (Item 11, Table 2).

DISCUSSION

The results suggest that adolescents who later commit criminal acts are seen by their teachers either as overtly aggressive, disturbing, disciplinary problems, or as passive. They perform poorly in school and evidence little diligence.

There are several important factors which sharply limit the possibilities of generalizing from this sample to the wider criminal community. The mothers of the subjects of one of the subsamples are severely schizophrenic; the control sample is unusual in being composed of individuals with parents and grandparents, none of whom have ever been hospitalized for a mental illness. In the case of both subsamples the fathers have unusually high levels of criminality (see Chapter 16). In addition, the low-risk subsample has only seven criminals (one of whom had to be dropped because he began his criminal career before the teachers' judgements were made).

It is striking that, despite the peculiarities and limitations of these two subsamples, the differences between the criminals and noncriminals are very much like those which have been reported in the literature. They are significantly more aggressive and perform more poorly in school. In the West and Farrington (1973) study the teachers' rating relating to disciplinary problems and aggressiveness proved to be the best single predictor to later delinquency. In the present study these items proved to be the best predictor among the teachers' ratings. With respect to the finding on disciplinary problems and aggression it should be pointed out that the teachers only noted this behavior in 10% of the entire sample and that this was characteristic of only 23-32% of the children who later became criminals. The majority of the later criminals did not behave in this manner in school. It is again difficult to compare this frequency of aggressive school behavior with other studies because of differences in definitions of criminality and school aggression. Also in agreement with the results of other investigators (Ackerley, 1933; Conger and Miller, 1966; Hathaway and Monachesi, 1963; Robins, 1970; Powers and Witmer, 1951) is the consistently poor school performance of the later criminals. It is interesting that this is especially marked in the case of low-risk group criminals. It should also be mentioned in this connection that the low-risk criminals are especially described as overly passive, disinterested and unengaged by school activities. The high-risk criminals are not so described. Serious psychopathology of the mother seems to be a variable influencing the mode of expression of precriminal adolescent school behavior.

As mentioned, these conclusions must be considered tentative in view of the lack of a basis for generalization from these samples.

Chapter 19

A prospective study of predictors of criminality: 5. Intelligence

Lis Kirkegaard-Sørensen
and
Sarnoff A. Mednick

A recent longitudinal, prospective study by West and Farrington (1973) studied the performance of 411 boys on the Raven Progressive Matrices. They found that those who later became criminal were characterized by a lower IQ than those boys who did not become criminal. The authors conclude that intelligence is a meaningful predictive factor with respect to future delinquency. These results are supported by a number of studies of incarcerated criminals (Frost and Frost, 1962; Wiens et al., 1959; Hoghughi and Forrest, 1967). Like the West and Farrington study, the current project is a longitudinal, prospective investigation of the value of adolescent intelligence test scores for the prediction of later criminality.

From these previous investigations we hypothesized that our pre-criminals would be characterized by lower IQ than those who later did not commit criminal offenses.

Table 1

Social Class of Rearing and Age of Criminal and Noncriminal Groups at Time of WISC Testing

	HIGH-RISK		LOW-RISK		TOTAL	
	Criminal	Not Criminal	Criminal	Not Criminal	Criminal	Not Criminal
A. Before matching for social class and age						
Mean Age	13.6	15.2	15.0	15.2	13.8	15.2
Mean Social Class	2.12	2.46	1.17	2.53	1.94	2.44
N	25	83	6	53	31	136
B. After matching for social class and age						
Mean Age	13.6	13.3	15.0	15.3	13.8	14.1
Mean Social Class	2.12	2.58	1.17	1.21	1.94	2.05
N	25	55	6	33	31	88

METHOD

Materials

Intelligence testing. In 1962 all 311 children were tested with the WISC; in 1972, in a follow-up examination, the children were examined with four subtests from the WAIS (vocabulary, similarities, block designs, and object assembly). In both cases the tests were administered in accordance with the instructions of the Manuals.

Determination of criminality. The criminal subjects are all the same as those selected in Chapter 18.

Selection of controls. Norms do not exist for the Danish translation of the WISC; instead the United States norms are used in clinical practice. In view of the possibility of the inappropriateness of this practice (especially in the case of the verbal subtests) raw scores were used for the analysis of the WISC scores. Because of this, it was necessary to match the groups for age. The groups were also matched for social class, as explained in Chapter 18. These matchings are described in Table 1A and 1B.

In the follow-up examination we did not succeed in retesting all of the subjects (see Mednick, Schulsinger, and Schulsinger, 1975). As a consequence, in the high-risk group only 21 criminals and 47 noncriminals were tested with the WAIS. In the low-risk group these numbers were 5 and 29, respectively. Inasmuch as the direction of results was predicted, one-tail tests of significance were used throughout.

RESULTS

WISC scores

Total group. Table 2 presents the various subgroups. As can be seen, the noncriminals scored higher on all of the WISC subtests (except for Mazes) and on verbal, performance and total IQ. The results reached significance for the coding, [t (117) = 1.65. $p < .05$] and block design subtests [t (117) = 1.83, $p < .05$]. These IQs are based on United States

Table 2

Mean WISC Subtest Scores for Criminal and Noncriminal Groups

	HIGH-RISK		LOW-RISK		TOTAL	
	Criminal	Not Criminal	Criminal	Not Criminal	Criminal	Not Criminal
Verbal						
Information	16.9	17.3	14.8	19.0	16.5	17.9
Comprehension	12.2	13.4	13.0	15.1	12.4	14.0
Arithmetic	11.3	11.1	11.0	12.0	11.2	11.5
Similarities	13.6	14.1	13.3	14.5	13.5	14.2
Vocabulary	45.1	47.6	45.8	53.6	45.2	49.8
Digit Span	9.2	9.4	10.0	9.6	9.4	9.5
Performance						
Picture Completion	13.0	13.2	11.7	13.3	12.7	13.2
Picture Arrangement	28.5	28.8	27.8	31.0	28.4	29.6
Block Design	29.9	31.2	21.3	35.2	28.2	32.7
Object Assembly	24.4	24.3	23.0	26.8	24.1	25.2
Coding	40.3	42.7	42.5	49.3	40.7	45.1
Mazes	17.2	15.9	16.0	16.9	16.9	16.3
IQ Verbal	99.4	101.5	95.0	104.5	98.6	102.6
IQ Performance	99.9	98.6	88.5	102.0	97.7	99.9
Total IQ	94.6	100.2	91.3	103.7	98.0	101.5

norms and are presented for heuristic reasons (see the statement concerning the use of United States norms in this context in Chapter 2.)

High-risk group

The results for the high-risk group are somewhat puzzling. The differences between the criminal and noncriminal groups are extremely small and not statistically significant.

Low-risk group

The noncriminals outperformed the criminals on every subtest but digit span. The differences reached significance on the information subtest [t (37) = 1.90, $p < .05$], on the block design [t (37) = 3.05, $p < .0025$], on the object assembly [t (37) = 2.24, $p < .025$], on the performance IQ [t (37) = 2.95, $p < .005$] and total IQ [t (37) = 2.23, $p < .025$].

WAIS scores

Table 3 contains the mean WAIS scale scores for criminals and noncriminals. As can be seen, the noncriminals outperformed the criminals on every subtest. The differences reached significance on the block design [t (100) = 1.86, $p < .05$] on the performance [t (100) = 1.82, $p < .05$], and in total IQ [t (100) = 1.73, $p < .05$]. In the high-risk group there were no significant differences. In the low-risk group the vocabulary [t (32) = 3.09, $p < .022$] and block design [t (32) = 1.97, $p < .05$] subtests were significantly superior for the noncriminals; they also evidenced significantly higher total IQ [t (32) = 1.80, $p < .05$].

DISCUSSION

The results suggest that adolescents who later commit criminal acts have a lower tested intelligence than their more law-abiding peers. The results are in keeping with the previous research, which has shown lower IQs for criminals (Frost and Frost, 1962; Wiens et al., 1959; Hoghughi and Forrest, 1967), and lower IQs for children who later become delinquent (West and Farrington, 1973). The results for the low-

Table 3

Mean WAIS Scaled Score for Criminal and Noncriminal Groups

	HIGH-RISK		LOW-RISK		TOTAL	
	Criminal	Not Criminal	Criminal	Not Criminal	Criminal	Not Criminal
Verbal						
Similarities	12.1	12.5	11.0	12.6	11.9	12.5
Vocabulary	10.6	11.2	9.6	11.5	10.4	11.3
Performance						
Block Design	11.1	11.7	9.6	12.2	10.9	11.9
Object Assembly	10.7	11.4	10.4	11.7	10.7	11.5
IQ Verbal	108.6	111.5	102.2	112.0	107.4	111.7
IQ Performance	106.1	110.3	100.4	113.1	105.0	111.3
IQ Total	108.2	111.6	101.6	113.4	107.0	112.2

risk group certainly are in conformance with these previous findings.

In the high-risk group, the differences were small and not significant. This could be related to the mental illness in the high-risk group. As a consequence, we determined to try to remove the effects of mental illness from the high-risk group and see if the relationship of criminality with intelligence would change. During the course of the 1972 reassessment, the subjects were interviewed; a part of the interview consisted of the CAPPS (Endicott and Spitzer, 1972) which includes a rating of the degree of severity of mental disorder in the subject. These ratings run from zero to six, with six being extremely disturbed. (It is in group six that schizophrenics may be found.) We removed individuals with severity of illness ratings of five and six to see whether the criminal-noncriminal differences would then come to resemble those from the low-risk group more closely. There was no change in the results. We continued to peel layers of severity of mental illness out of the high-risk group, but this resulted in no change in the pattern of results.

In most studies, criminals score somewhat better in performance IQ than in verbal IQ. For both the high- and low-risk criminal groups, the Verbal IQ is the higher. When WAIS test scores for Danes are evaluated by United States norms, the mean score is not 100 but 107. This is explained by easier items being used in some of the verbal subtests of the translation (Hess, 1973). Thus, we would not expect an absolutely higher performance IQ for the criminals. However, what is worth noting is that for the *low-risk* criminals, the verbal subtest score is especially elevated over the performance. In the report on the school behavior of these same low-risk criminals (Chapter 18) we noted that the teacher described them as especially passive and lacking initiative. This may be related to their poor showing on the timed performance tests.

For children with mentally ill mothers, adolescent intelligence levels are unrelated to later criminality. It seems likely that factors related to personality and temperament may be more critical for these individuals. For the children with no mental illness in their family background, intelligence may make a modest contribution to the probability of their later evidencing criminal behavior. It is possible that the modest contribution of this variable to the etiology of criminality is in determining the rewards to a child for intellectual performance in the school system. This may provide generalized rewards for the child's conformance and law-abiding behavior. These rewards may tend to be less in those with lower intelligence levels.

References

Ackerly, S. Rebellion and its relation to delinquency and neurosis in sixty adolescents. *American Journal of Orthopsychiatry*, 1933, 3, 147–160.

Alexander, F. The neurotic character. *International Journal of Psychoanalysis*, 1930, 11, 292.

Amark, C. A study in alcoholism: Clinical, social-psychiatric and genetic investigations. *Acta Psychiatrica Neurologica Scandinavia*, Supplement 70, 1951.

American Psychiatric Association. *Diagnostic and statistical manual: Mental disorders*. Washington, D.C.: Author, 1968.

Andersen, E., Andersen, H., Hutchings, B., Peitersen, B., Rosen, J., Thamdrup, E., Wichmann, R., Nyholm, M. Højde og vægt hos danske skolebørn 1971-1972. *Ugeskrift for Læger*, 1974, 136, 2796–2802.

Arieti, S. Psychopathic personality: some views on its psychopathology and psychodynamics. *Comprehensive Psychiatry*, 1963, 4, 301–302.

Ax, A., and Zacharopolous, G. Psychophysiological data processing. In P. L. Frommer, (Ed.). *Fourth International Conference on Medical Electronics*. Washington: McGregor and Werver, 1961.

Bader-Bartfai, A., and Schalling, D. *Recovery times of skin conductance responses as related to some personality and physiological variables*. Psychological Institute, University of Stockholm, 1974.

Baker, D., Telfer, M. A., Richardson, C. E. and Clarck, G. R. Chromosome errors in men with antisocial behavior. Comparison of selected men with "Klinefelter's Syndrome" and XYY chromosome pattern. *Journal of the American Medical Association*, 1970, 214, 869–878.

Barr, M. D. and Bertram, E. G.: "A Morphological Distinction between Neurones of the Male and Female, and the Behavior of the Nuclear Satellite during Accelerated Nucleoprotein Synthesis." *Nature*, London 1949, 163, 676–677.

Bartlett, D. J., Hurley, W. P., Brand, C. R., Poole, E. W. Chromosomes of male patients in a security prison. *Nature*, 1968, 219, 351–354.

Baughman, F. A. Jr., and Mann, J. D. Ascertainment of seven YY males in a private neurology practice. *Journal of the American Medical Association*, 1972, 222, 446–448.

Berlit, B. Erblichkeitsuntersuchungen bei Psychopathen. *Zeitschrift für die gesamte Neurologie und Psychiatrie*, 1931, 134, 382.

Binswanger, L. *Alkoholismus, Neue Deutsche Klinik*. Berlin: Urban & Schwarzenberg, 1928, vol. 1.

Bishop, Y., Fienberg, S., Holland, P. *Discrete Multivariate Analysis.* Cambridge, Massachusetts: MIT Press, 1975.

Blank, L. The intellectual functioning of delinquents. *The Journal of Social Psychology*, 1958, 47, 9–14.

Bleuler, M. Psychotische Belastung von korperlich Kranken. *Zeitschrift für die gesamte Neurologie und Psychiatrie*, 1932, 142, 780.

Bohman, M. *Adopted children and their families.* Stockholm: Proprius, 1970.

Borgaonkar, D. S. and Shah, S. A. The XYY chromosome male—or syndrome? In A. G. Steinberg and A. G. Bearn (Eds.), *Progress in Medical Genetics*, Vol. 10. New York: Grune & Stratton, 1974.

Borganokar, D. S., Murdoch, J. L., McKusick, V. A. Borkowf, S. P., Money, J. W., and Robinson, B. W. The XYY Syndrome. *Lancet*, 1968, 2, 461–462.

Borgström, C. A. Eine serie von Kriminellen Zwillingen. *Archiv für Rassenbiologie*, 1939.

Borkovee, T. D. Autonomic reactivity to sensory stimulation in psychopathic, neurotic, and normal juvenile delinquents. *Journal of Consulting and Clinical Psychology*, 1970, 35, 217–222.

Boss, M. Zur Frage der erbbiologischen Bedeutung des Alkohols. *Monatsschrift für Psychiatrie und Neurologie*, 1929, 72, 264.

Boue, J., Boue, A., Lazar, P. Retrospective and prospective epidemiological studies of 1500 karyotyped spontaneous human abortions. *Teratology*, 1975, 12, 11–26.

Bowlby, J. *Maternal care and mental health.* Geneva: World Health Organization WHO Monogram Series, No. 2., 1951.

Bundy, R. S. and Fitzgerald, H. E. Stimulus specificity of electrodermal recovery time: an examination and reinterpretation of the evidence. *Psychophysiology*, 1975, 12, 406–411.

Brugger, C. Familienuntersuchungen bei Alkoholdeliranten. *Zeitschrift für die gesamte Neurologie und Psychiatrie*, 1934, 151, 740.

Burlingham, D. *Twins. A study of three pairs of identical twins.* London: Allen & Unwin, 1952.

Cairns, J. The cancer problem. *Scientific American*, 1975, 233, 64–78.

Carlsson G. Random-walk effects in behavioral data. *Behavioral Science*, 1972, 17, 64–78.

Carlsson, G. *Kriminalitetsnivå och belastningsfördelningar.* Swedish Council for Crime Prevention, 1975.

Carlsson G. The audiences of deterrence. In *General Deterrence.* Conference on current research and standpoints, June 2-4, 1975. Swedish Council for Crime Prevention, 1976.

Caspersson, T., Zech, L., and Johansson, C. Analysis of human metaphase chromosome set by aid of DNA-binding fluorescent agents. *Experimental Cell Research*, 1970, 62, 490–492.

Christiansen, K. O. Recidivism among collaborators. In M. Wolfgang (Ed.), *Crime and culture. Essays in honour of Thorsten Sellin.* New York: 1968.

Christiansen, K. O. and Pál, L. Det mandlige recidiv i Danmark; 1933-60. *Nordisk Tidsskrift for Kriminalvidenskab*, 1965, 29–45.

Christie, M. J. & Todd, J. L. Experimenter-subject-situational interactions. In. P. H. Venables and M. J. Christie (Eds.), *Research in psychophysiology.* London: Wiley, 1975.

Christie, N., Andenæs, J., and Skerbækk, S. A study of self-reported crime. *Scandinavian Studies in Criminology*, 1965, 1, 86–116.

Claridge, G. S. *Personality and arousal.* Oxford: Pergamon, 1967.

Clarke, A. D. B. Problems in assessing the later effects of early experience. In E. Miller (Ed.), *Foundations of child psychiatry.* Oxford: Pergamon, 1968.

Cleckley, H. *The mask of sanity.* St. Louis: Mosby, 1964.
Cline, V. B., and Wangrow, A. S. Life history correlates of delinquent and psychopathic behavior. *Journal of Clinical Psychology,* 1959, *15,* 266–270.
Cochran, W. G. The effectiveness of adjustment by subclassification in removing bias in observational studies. *Biometrics,* 1968, *24,* 295–313.
Conger, J. J. and Miller, W. C. *Personality, social class and delinquency.* New York: Wiley, 1966.
Court Brown, W. M. Males with an XYY sex chromosome complement. *Journal of Medical Genetics,* 1968, *5,* 341.
Craft, M. J. *Ten studies into psychopathic personality.* Bristol: John Wright, 1965.
Craft, M. *Psychopathic disorders.* Oxford: Pergamon, 1966.
Crandall, B. F., Carrel, R. E., Sparkes, R. S. Chromosome findings in 700 children referred to a psychiatric clinic. *Journal of Pediatrics,* 1972, *80,* 62–68.
Crowe, R. An adoptive study of psychopathy: preliminary results from arrest records and psychiatric hospital records. In R. Fieve, D. Rosenthal, and H. Brill (Eds.), *Genetic research in psychiatry.* Baltimore, Maryland: Johns Hopkins University Press, 1975.
Curran, D. and Mallinson, P. Psychopathic personality. *Journal of Mental Science,* 1944, *90,* 266.
Dahlberg, G. A new method in crime statistics applied to the population of Sweden. *Journal of Criminal Law and Criminology,* 1948, *39.*
Dahlberg, G. & Stenberg, S. *Alkoholismen som Samhallsproblem.* Stockholm: Oskar Eklunds, 1934.
Dalgaard, O. S. and Kringlen, E. A Norwegian twin study of criminality. *British Journal of Criminology.* In press.
Dalton, K. Menstruation and crime. *British Medical Journal,* 1961, *2,* 1752–1753.
Dalton, K. *The premenstrual syndrome.* Springfield, Ill.: Thomas, 1964.
Dawson, M. E. and Furedy, J. J. The role of awareness in human differential autonomic classical conditioning: the necessary-gate hypothesis. *Psychophysiology,* 1976, *13,* 50–53.
DeBault, L. E., Johnston, E., Loeffelholtz, P. Incidence of XYY and XXY individuals in a security hospital population. *Diseases of the Nervous System,* 1972, *33,* 590–593.
Dencker, S. J. Significance of environmental factors on development of some social and personality components. *Acta Psychiatrica Scandinavica 40: Supplement 180,* 1963, 317–321.
Depue, R. A. and Fowles, D. C. Electrodermal activity as an index of arousal in schizophrenics. *Psychological Bulletin,* 1973, *79,* 233–238.
Dummermuth, G. EEG-Untersuchungen beim jugendlichen Klinefelter-Syndrom. *Helvetia Paedriatrica Acta,* 1961, *16,* 702–710.
Dustman, R. E. and Beck, E. C. The visual evoked response in twins. *EEG clin. Neurophysiol.,* 1965, *19,* 570–575.
Edelberg, R. The information content of the recovery limb of the electrodermal response. *Psychophysiology,* 1970, *6,* 527–539.
Edelberg, R. Electrodermal recovery rate, goal-orientation, and aversion. *Psychophysiology,* 1972, *9,* 512–528.
Ekstrøm, R. B., French, J. W., Harman, H. H. Technical Report No. 8, Office of Naval Research Contract N 00014-71-C-0017, HR 150 329 (1975).
Elsasser, G. *Die Nachkommen geisteskranker Elternpaare.* Stuttgart: Thieme, 1952.
Endicott, J. and Spitzer, R. Current and past psychopathology scales (CAPPS). *Archives of General Psychiatry,* November 1972, *27.*
Exner, F. Kriminalbiologie in Ihren Grunzügen. Hamburg: Hanseatische Verlagsanstalt, 1939.
Eysenck, H. J. (Ed.), *Experiments with drugs.* Oxford: Pergamon, 1963.

Falek, A., Craddick, R., and Collum, J. An attempt to identify prisoners with an XYY chromosome complement by psychiatric and psychological means. *Journal of Nervous and Mental Disease,* 1970, *150,* 165–170.

Fenton, G. W., Tennent, T. G., Comish, K. A., and Rattray, N. The EEG and sex chromosome abnormalities. *British Journal of Psychiatry,* 1971, *119,* 185–190.

Ferri, E. *Sociologia Criminale,* third edition. Torino: 1892.

Fields, J. G. The performance-verbal IQ discrepancy in a group of sociopaths. *Journal of Clinical Psychology,* 1960, *16,* 321–322.

Forssman, H., and Hambert, G. Chromosomes and antisocial behavior. *Lancet,* 1966, *2,* 282.

Forssman, H., and Hambert G. Chromosomes and antisocial behavior. *Excepta Criminologica,* 1967, *7,* 113–117.

Fox, R. and Lippert, W. Spontaneous GSR and anxiety level in sociopathic delinquents. *Journal of Consulting Psychology,* 1963, *27,* 368.

Fremming, K. H. *Sygdomsrisikoen for Sindslidlser og andre sjaelelige Abnormtilstande i den danske Gennemsnitsbefolkning.* Copenhagen: Ejnar Munksgaard, 1947.

Frost, B. P. and Frost, R. The pattern of WISC scores in a group of juvenile sociopaths. *Journal of Clinical Psychology,* 1962, *18,* 354–355.

Gale, A. Can EEG studies make a contribution to the experimental investigation of psychopathy? In R. D. Hare and D. Schalling (Eds.), *Current research in psychopathy.* London: Wiley, in press.

Gibson, H. B., and West, D. J. Social and intellectual handicap as precursors of early delinquency. *British Journal of Criminology,* 1970, *10,* 21–32.

Glueck, S., and Glueck, E. *Unraveling juvenile delinquency.* New York: Commonwealth Fund, 1950.

Goldstein, I. B. The relationship of muscle tension and autonomic activity to psychiatric disorders. *Psychosomatic Medicine,* 1965, *27,* 39–52.

Goodman, R. M., Smith, W. S., and Migeon, C. J. Sex chromosome abnormalities. *Nature,* 1967, *216,* 942–943.

Goodwin, D. W. Is alcoholism hereditary? A review and critique. *Archives of General Psychiatry,* December 1971, *25,* 545–549.

Goodwin, D. W., Schulsinger, F., Hermansen, L., Guze, S. B. and Winokur, G. Alcohol problems in adoptees raised apart from alcoholic biological parents. *Archives of General Psychiatry,* February 1973, *28,* 238–243.

Goodwin, D. W., Schulsinger, F., Møller, N., Hermansen, L., Winokur, G. and Guze, S. B. Drinking problems in adopted and nonadopted sons of alcoholics. *Archives of General Psychiatry,* 1974, *31,* 164–169.

Gottesman, I. and Shields, J. *Schizophrenia and genetics—a twin study vantage point.* New York: Academic Press, 1972.

Graham, F. K. Habituation and dishabituation of responses innervated by the autonomic nervous system. In H. V. S. Peeke and M. J. Herz (Eds.), *Habituation,* Vol. 1. *Behavioral studies.* New York: Academic Press, 1973.

Greenacre, P. Conscience in the psychopath. *American Journal of Orthopsychiatry,* 1945, *15,* 495.

Gregory, I. Family data concerning the hypothesis of hereditary predisposition toward alcoholism. *Journal of Mental Science,* 1960, *106,* 1068.

Gruzelier, J. H. The investigation of possible limbic dysfunction in schizophrenia by psychophysiological methods. Unpublished Ph.D. thesis, University of London, 1973.

Gruzelier, J. H. and Venables, P. H. Skin conductance orienting activity in a heterogeneous sample of schizophrenics. *The Journal of Nervous and Mental Disease,* 1972, *155,* 277–287.

Guze, S., Wolfgram, E., McKinney, J. Psychiatric illness in the families of convicted criminals: A study of 519 first degree relatives. *Diseases of the Nervous System*, 1967, *28*, 651–659.

Hambert, G., and Sison Frey, T. The electroencephalogram in the Klinefelter syndrome. *Acta Psychiatrica Scandinavia*, 1964, *40*, 28–36.

Hare, R. D. Temporal gradient of fear arousal in psychopaths. *Journal of Abnormal Psychology*, 1965, *70*, 442–445.

Hare, R. D. Psychopathy, autonomic functioning, and the orienting response, *Journal of Abnormal Psychology*. Monograph supplement, 1968, *73*, 1–24.

Hare, R. D. Autonomic activity and conditioning in psychopaths. Paper presented at the *Annual Meeting of the Society for Psychophysiological Research*, New Orleans, 1970. (a)

Hare, R. D. *Psychopathy: theory and research*. New York: Wiley, 1970. (b)

Hare, R. D. Psychopathy and sensitivity to adrenaline. *Journal of Abnormal Psychology*, 1972, *79*, 138–147.

Hare, R. D. Psychopathy. In P. H. Venables and M. J. Christie (Eds.), *Research in psychophysiology*. London: Wiley, 1975. (a)

Hare, R. D. Talk presented at NATO meeting on Psychopathic Behavior, September, 1975. (b)

Hare, R. D. and Craigen, D. Psychopathy and physiological activity in a mixed-motive game situation. *Psychophysiology*, 1974, *11*, 197–206.

Hare, R. D. and Quinn, M. J. Psychopathy and autonomic conditioning. *Journal of Abnormal Psychology*, 1971, *77*, 223–235.

Harvald, B. and Hauge, M. *Genetics and the epidemiology of chronic diseases*. Washington, D.C.: U.S. Public Health Services, 1965.

Hathaway, S. R., and Monachesi, E. D. *Adolescent personality and behavior*. Minneapolis: Jones Press, 1963.

Hayashi, S. A study of juvenile delinquency by twin method. *Acta Criminologiae et Medicinae Legalis Japanica*, 1963, *29*, 153–172.

Hebb, D. O. *A textbook of psychology*. Philadelphia: Saunders Co., 1958.

Henderson, D. K. *Psychopathic states*. New York: Norton, 1939.

Hess, G. *WAIS anvendt på 698 50-årige*. Copenhagen: Akademisk Forlag, 1973.

Heston, L. L. Psychiatric disorders in foster-home reared children of schizophrenic mothers. *British Journal of Psychiatry*, 1966, *112*, 819–825.

Hill, D. EEG in episodic psychiatric and psychopathic behavior. *Electroencephalography and Clinical Neurophysiology*, 1952, *4*, 419–642.

Hill, D. The EEG in psychiatry. In D. Hill and G. Parr (Eds.), *Electroencephalography*. New York: Macmillan, 1963.

Hirschhorn, K. *Histocompatibility testing*. National Academy of Science, National Research Council, 1965, 177–178.

Hirschi, T. *Causes of delinquency*. Berkeley: Univ. of California Press, 1969.

Hook, E. B. Behavioral implications of the human XYY genotype. *Science*, 1973, *179*, 139–150.

Hook, E. B. and Kim, D. S. Height and antisocial behavior in XY and XYY boys. *Science*, 1971, *172*, 284–286.

Hume, W. I. Physiological measures in twins. In G. S. Claridge, *Personality Differences and Biological Variations. A Study of Twins*. Oxford: Pergamon, 1973. Pp. 87–114.

Hurwitz, S., and Christiansen, K. O. *Kriminologi*. Copenhagen: Gyldendal, 1971.

Husén, T. *Psychological twin research. I. A. methodological study*. Uppsala: Stockholm studies in educational psychology, 1959.

Hutchings, B. *Genetic and environmental factors in psychopathology and criminality*. M. Phil. Thesis, University of London: 1972.

Hutchings, B., and Mednick, S. A. Registered criminality in adoptive and biological parents of registered male criminal adoptees. In S. A. Mednick, et al., (Eds.), *Genetics, environment, and psychopathology.* Amsterdam: North Holland/American Elsevier, 1974.

Hutchings, B. and Mednick, S. A. Registered criminality in the adoptee and biological parents of registered male criminal adoptees. In R. R. Fieve, D. Rosenthal, and H. Brill (Eds.), *Genetic research in psychiatry.* Baltimore: Johns Hopkins University Press, 1975.

Inghe, G. Mental abnormalities among criminals. *Acta Psychiatrica et Neurologica,* 1941, *16,* 421–458.

Jacobs, P. A., Price, W. H., Richmond, S., Ratcliff, R. A. W. Chromosome surveys in penal institutions and approved schools. *Journal of Medical Genetics,* 1971, *8,* 49–58.

Jarvik, L. F., Klodin, V., Matsuyama, S. S. Human aggression and the extra Y chromosome: Fact or fantasy? *American Psychologist,* 1973, *28,* 674–682.

Jonsson, B. *Delinquent boys, their parents and grandparents.* Copenhagen: Munksgaard, 1967.

Jost, H. and Sontag, L. W. The genetic factor in autonomic nervous system function. Psychosom. Med., 1944, *6,* 308–310.

Juel-Nielsen, N. *Individual and environment. A psychiatric-psychological investigation of twins reared apart.* Copenhagen: Munksgaard, 1965.

Kahn, E. *Psychopathic personalities.* New Haven: Yale University Press, 1931.

Kallmann, F. J. *The genetics of schizophrenia.* New York: J. J. Augustin, 1938.

Karpman, B. The myth of the psychopathic personality. *American Journal of Psychiatry,* 1947, *104,* 523.

Kelly, S., Almy, R., and Barnard, M. Another XYY phenotype. *Nature,* 1967, *215,* 405.

Kety, S. S., Rosenthal, D., Wender, P. H., and Schulsinger, F. The types and prevalence of mental illness in the biological and adoptive families of adopted schizophrenics. In D. Rosenthal & S. S. Kety (Eds.), *The transmission of schizophrenia.* Oxford: Pergamon, 1968.

Kimmel, H. D. Inhibition of the unconditioned response in classical conditioning. *Psychological Review,* 1966, *73,* 232–240.

Kirkegaard-Sørensen, L., and Mednick, S. A. Registered criminality in families with children at high risk for schizophrenia. *Journal of Abnormal Psychology,* 1975, *84,* 197–204.

Klorman, R., Wiesenfeld, A. R. and Austin, M. L. Autonomic responses to affective visual stimuli. *Psychophysiology,* 1975, *12,* 553–560.

Koch, J. L. A. *Die psychopathische Minderwertigkeiten.* Ravensburg: Maier, 1891.

Kraepelin, E. *Psychiatrie.* (8th ed.) Vol. 2. Leipzig: J. A. Barth, 1910.

Kraepelin, E. *Psychiatrie.* (8th ed.) Vol. 4. Leipzig: J. A. Barth, 1915.

Kranz, H. Discordant soziales Verhalten eineüger Zwillinge. *Monatschrift für Kriminalpsychologie und Strafrechtsreform,* 1935, *26,* 511–516.

Kranz, H. *Lebensschicksale kriminellen Zwillinge.* Berlin: Julius Springer, 1936.

Kretschmer, E. Cited in Schneider, 1934.

Kringlen, E. Heredity and environment in the functional psychoses: an epidemiological-clinical twin study. London: William Heinemann Medical Books, 1967.

Kroon, H. M. Die Erblichkeit der Trunksucht in der Familie X. *Genetica,* 1924, *6,* 391.

Kvaraceus, W. C. Forecasting delinquency: a three-year experiment. *Exceptional Children,* 1969, *27,* 429–35.

Lacey, J. I. and Lacey, B. C. The relationship of resting autonomic activity to motor impulsivity. In *The brain and human behavior*. Proceedings of the Association for Research in Nervous and Mental Disease. Baltimore: Williams & Wilkins, 1958.

Lacey, J. I., Kagan, J., Lacey, B. C. and Moss, H. A. The visceral level: situational determinants and behavioral correlates of autonomic response patterns. In P. H. Knapp (Ed.), *Expression of the emotions in man*. New York: International Universities, 1963.

Lader, M. H. and Wing, L. *Physiological Measures, Sedative Drugs, and Morbid Anxiety*. Oxford: Oxford Univ. Press, 1966.

Landau, R., Harth, P., Othnay, N. and Sharfhertz, L. The influence of psychotic parents on their children's development. *American Journal of Psychiatry*, 1972, *124*, 38–43.

Lange, J. *Verbrechen als Schisksal*. Leipzig: Georg Thieme, 1929. English edition, London: Unwin Brothers, 1931.

Lederberg, J.: "The Genetics of Human Nature." Social Research, 1973,40, 375–407.

Leff, J. P., and Scott, P. D. XYY and intelligence. *Lancet*, 1968, 1, 645.

Legras, A. M. *Psychese en Criminaliteit bij Twellingen*. Utrecht: Kemink en Zoon N.V. 1932. A summary in German can be found in Psychosen und Kriminalität bei Zwillingen. *Zeitschrift für die gesamte Neurologie und Psychiatrie*, 1933, 198–228.

Lindsley, D. B. A longitudinal study of the occipital alpha rhythm in normal children: frequency and amplitude standards. *Journal of Genetic Psychology*, 1939, 55, 197–213.

Lippert, W. W. and Senter, R. J. Electrodermal responses in the sociopath. *Psychonomic Science*, 1966, *4*, 25–26.

Lockhart, R. A. Interrelations between amplitude, latency, rise time, and the Edelberg recovery measure of the galvanic skin response. *Psychophysiology*, 1972, *9*, 437–442.

Loeb, L. and Mednick, S. A. Asocial behavior and electrodermal response patterns. To appear in K. O. Christiansen & S. A. Mednick (Eds.), *Biological and Social Bases of Asocial Behavior*. London: Wiley.

Luxenburger, H. Demographische und psychiatrische Untersuchungen in der engeren biologischen Familie von Paralytikerehegatten. *Zeitschrift für die gesamte Neurologie und Psychiatrie*, 1928, *112*, 331.

Luxenburger, H. *Psychiatrische-neurologische Zwillingspathologie*. Munich: Psychiatrische Erblehre, 1938.

Lykken, D. T. A study of anxiety in the sociopathic personality. *Journal of Abnormal and Social Psychology*, 1957, 55, 6–10.

Lykken, D. T. and Venables, P. H. Direct measurement of skin conductance: a proposal for standardization. *Psychophysiology*, 1971, 8, 656–672.

Lykken, D. T., Rose, R., Luther, B. and Maley, M. Correcting psychophysiological measures for individual differences in range. *Psychological Bulletin*, 1966, 66, 481–484.

McClintock, F. H., and Avison, N. H. *Crime in England and Wales*. London: Heinemann, 1968.

McCord, W. and McCord, J. *The psychopath: an essay on the criminal mind*. New York: Van Nostrand, 1964.

Maltzman, I. Individual differences in "attention": the orienting reflex. In R. M. Gagné (Ed.), *Learning and individual differences*. Columbus, Ohio: Charles E. Merrill, 1967.

Maltzman, I. and Raskin, D. C. Effects of individual differences in the orienting reflex on conditioning and complex processes. *Journal of Experimental Research in Personality*, 1965, *1*, 1–15.

Matousek, M. and Petersen, I. In P. Kellaway and I. Petersen (Eds.), *Automation in clinical electroencephalography*. New York: Raven Press, 1973.

Mednick, S. A. Breakdown in individuals at high risk for schizophrenia: possible predispositional perinatal factors. *Mental Hygiene*, 1970, *54*, 50–63.

Mednick, S. A. Electrodermal recovery and psychopathology. In S. A. Mednick, F. Schulsinger, J. Higgins & B. Bell (Eds.), *Genetics, environment and psychopathology*, Oxford: North-Holland, 1974.

Mednick, S. A. Autonomic nervous system recovery and psychopathology. *Scandinavian Journal of behavior therapy*, 1975, *4*, 55–68.

Mednick, S. A., and McNeil, T. F. Current methodology in research on the etiology of schizophrenia. *Psychological Bulletin*, 1968, *70*, 681–693.

Mednick, S. A. and Schulsinger, F. A pre-schizophrenic sample. *Acta Psychiatrica Scandinavica*, 1964, *40*, 135–139.

Mednick, S. A., and Schulsinger, F. Some premorbid characteristics related to breakdown in children with schizophrenic mothers. *Journal of Psychiatric Research*, 1968, *6*, 267–291.

Mednick, S. A. and Schulsinger, F. Studies of children at high risk for schizophrenia. In S. R. Dean (Ed.) *Schizophrenia: The First Ten Dean Award Lectures*. New York: MSS Information, 1973.

Mednick, S. A., Schulsinger, H., and Schulsinger, F. Schizophrenia in children with schizophrenic mothers. In A. Davids (Ed.) *Childhood, personality and psychopathology: Current topics*. Volume 2, New York: Wiley, 1975.

Mednick, S. A., Schulsinger, F., Higgins, J., and Bell, B. *Genetics, environment and psychopathology*. Amsterdam: North Holland/Elsevier, 1974.

Moorhead, P. S., Nowell, P. C., Mellman, W. J., Battips, D. M., and Hungerford, D. A. *Experimental Cellular Research*, 1960, *20*, 163.

Mowrer, O. H. *Learning theory and behavior*. New York: Wiley, 1960.

Mulligan, G., Douglas, J. W. B., Hammond, W. A., and Tizard, J. Delinquency and symptoms of maladjustment. *Proceedings of the Royal Society of Medicine*, 1963, *56*, 1083–6.

Newkirk, P. R. Psychopathic traits are inheritable. *Diseases of the Nervous System*, 1957, *18*, 52.

Newman, H. H. Freeman, F. N., Holzinger, K. J. *Twins, study of heredity and environment*. Chicago: University of Chicago Press, 1937.

Nielsen, J. Prevalence and a 2 years incidence of chromosome abnormalities among all males in a forensic psychiatric clinic. *British Journal of Psychiatry*, 1971, *119*, 503–512.

Nielsen, J. and Christensen, A. L. Thirty-five males with double Y chromosome. *Psychological Medicine*, 1974, *4*, 28–37.

Nielsen, J., Christensen, K. R., Friedrich, U., Zeuthen, E., and Østergaard, O. Childhood of males with XYY syndrome. *Journal of Autism and Childhood Schizophrenia*, 1973, *3*, 5–26.

Nielsen, J., Stürup, G., Tsuboi, T., & Romano, D. Prevalence of the XYY syndrome in an institution for psychologically abnormal criminals. *Acta Psychiatrica Scandinavica*, 1969, *45*, 383.

Noël, B., Dupont, J. P., Revil, D., Dussuyer, I., Quack, B. The XYY syndrome: Reality or myth? *Clinical Genetics*, 1974, *5*, 387–394.

Nudelman, A. E., et. al. A glossary of sociological terms. *Footnotes*, 1975, *3*, 2.

Owen, D. R. The 47,XYY male: a review. *Psychological Bulletin*, 1972, *78*, 209–233.

Owen, D. R. In preparation.

Partridge, G. E. Current conceptions of psychopathic personality. *American Journal of Psychiatry*, 1930, *10*, 53.

Pasqualini, R. Q., Vidal, G., and Bur, G. E. Psychopathology of Klinefelter's syndrome. *Lancet*, 1957, 2, 164–167.

Pearson, P. L., and Bobrow, M. J. J. Fluorescent staining of the Y chromosome in meiotic stages of the human male. *Journal of Reproduction and Fertility*, 1970, *22*, 177–179.

Persson, T. An XYY man and his relatives. *Journal of Mental Deficiency Research*, 1967, *11*, 239–245.

Peterson, D. R., Quay, H. C. and Tiffany, T. L. Personality factors related to juvenile delinquency. *Child Development*, 1961, *32*, 355–372.

Philip, J., Lundsteen, C., Owen, D., and Hirschhorn, K. The frequency of chromosome aberrations in tall men: with special regard to 47,XYY and 47,XXY. *American Journal of Human Genetics*. In press.

Pinel, P. *Abhandlung über Geistesverirrungen oder Manie*. Wien: Carl Schaumburg, 1801.

Pinneau, S. R. The infantile disorders of hospitalism and anaclitic depression. *Psychological Bulletin*, 1955, *52*, 429.

Pohlisch, K. Soziale und personliche Bedingungen des chronischen Alcoholismus. In *Sammlung psychiatrischer und neurologischer Einzeldarstellungen*. Leipzig, Germany: G. Thieme Verlag, 1933.

Poole, E., Beauchamp, M., Booth, I., and Storm, M. XYY and XXY inmates of a security prison: EEG findings. *Electroencephalography and Clinical Neurophysiology*, 1970, *29*, 326.

Popham, R. E., deLint, J. E. E., Schmidt, W. *Inheritance of drinking behavior. Alkoholpolitik*, 1967, *3*.

Powers, E., and Witmer, H. *An experiment in the prevention of delinquency. The Cambridge-Somerville youth study*. New York: Columbia University Press, 1951.

Pribram, K. H. and McGuinness, D.: "Arousal, activation and effort in the control of attention." Psychological Review, 82, 2, 1975. 75, 116–49.

Price, Bronson: "Primary biases in twin studies. A review of prenatal and natal difference-producing factors in monozygotic pairs." American Journal of Human Genetics, 1950, 2, 293–352.

Price, W. H. and Whatmore, P. B. Criminal behavior and the XYY male. *Nature*, 1969, *213*, 815.

Pritchard, J. D. *Treatise on insanity*. London: Sherwood, Gilbert & Piper, 1835.

Quay, H. C. Personality dimensions in delinquent males as inferred from the factor analysis of behavior rating. *Journal of Research in Crime and Delinquency*, 1964, *1*, 35–37.

Quay, H. C. Psychopathic personality as pathological stimulation seeking. *American Journal of Psychiatry*, 1965, *122*, 180–183.

Rachman, S. Galvanic skin response in identical twins. *Psychol. Rep.*, 1960, *6*, 298.

Rasch, G. *Probablistic models for some intelligence and attainment tests*. Copenhagen: Danish Institute for Educational Research, 1960.

Reckless, W. C., and Dinitz, S. Pioneering with self-concept as a vulnerability factor in delinquency. *Journal of Criminal Law, Criminology and Police Science*, 1967, *58*, 515–23.

Reiter, H. Auswirkung von Anlage und Milieu, untersucht an Adoptierren uneheliche Goebrenen. *Klinische Wochenschrift*, 1930, 2358.

Richards, B. W. and Stewart, A., Sylvester, P. E., et al.: Cytogenetic survey of

225 patients diagnosed clinically as mongols." Journal of Mental Deficiency Research, 65, 245–59.

Riedel, H. Zur empirischen Erbprognose der Psychopathie. Zeitschrift für die gesamte Neurologie und Psychiatrie, 1937, 159, 648.

Rimmer, J., Chambers, D. S. Alcoholism: Methodological considerations in the study of family illness. American Journal of Orthopsychiatry, 1969, 39, 760–768.

Robins, L. N. Deviant children grown up. Baltimore: William and Wilkins, 1966.

Robins, L. N. The adult development of the antisocial child. Seminars in Psychiatry, 1970, 2, 420–434.

Roe, A., and Burks, B. Adult adjustment of foster chldren of alcoholic and psychotic parentage and the influence of the foster home. Memoirs of the Section on Alcohol Studies, Yale University No. 3, Quarterly Journal of Studies on Alcohol, New Haven, 1945.

Rosanoff, A. J. Handy, L. M. and Rosanoff, F. A.: "Criminality and Delinquency in Twins." Journal of Criminal Law and Criminology, 1934, 24, 923–934.

Rosenthal, D. A. A program of research on heredity in schizophrenia. Behavioral Science, 1971, 16, 191–201.

Rosenthal, D. Genetic theory and abnormal behavior. New York: McGraw-Hill, 1970.

Rosenthal, R. Experimenter effects in behavioral research. New York: Appleton-Century-Crofts, 1966.

Rybakow, T. Alkoholismus and Erblichkeit. Monatsschrift für Psychiatrie und Neurologie, Supplement 20, 221, 1906.

Scarr, Sandra: "Environmental Bias in Twin Studies." Eugenics Quarterly, 15, 1, 1968, 34–40.

Schalling D. Psychopathic behavior: personality and neuropsychology. In R. D. Hare & D. Schalling (Eds.), Current research in psychopathy. London: Wiley, in press.

Schalling, D., Lidberg, L., Levander, S. E. and Dahlin, Y. Spontaneous autonomic activity as related to psychopathy. Biological Psychology, 1973, 1, 83–97.

Schmauk, F. J. Punishment, arousal, and avoidance learning in sociopaths. Journal of Abnormal Psychology, 1970, 76, 325–335.

Schneider, K. Die psychopathischen Persönlichkeiten. Leipzig: Thieme, 1934.

Schulsinger, F. Psychopathy, heredity, and environment. International Journal of Mental Health, 1972, 1, 190–206.

Schulsinger, F., Mednick, S. A., Venables, P. H., Raman, A. C., and Bell, B. The early detection and prevention of mental illness: The Mauritius Project. A preliminary report. Neuropsychobiology, 1975, 1, 166–179.

Schwesinger G. The effect of differential parent-child relations on identical twin resemblance in personality. Acta Geneticae Medicae et Gemellologiae, 1952.

Seabright, M. A rapid banding technique for human chromosomes. Lancet, 1971, 2, 971–972.

Sellin T. Culture, conflict and crime. A report of the subcommittee on delinquency of the committee on personality and culture. New York: 1938.

Sergeant, J. Intercorrelations between skin conductance measures. Unpublished report, Psykologisk Institut, Copenhagen, 1974.

Shah, S. A. National Institute of Mental Health Center for Studies of Crime and Delinquency. Report on the XYY chromosomal abnormality. (Public Health Service Publication No. 2103) (1970).

Shah, S. and Roth, L. Biological and psychophysiological factors in criminality. In D. Glaser (Ed.), Handbook of criminology. Chicago: Rand McNally, 1974.

Shaw, L., and Sichel, H. S. *Accident proneness*. Oxford: Pergamon Press, 1971.

Shields, J. *Monozygotic twins brought up apart and brought up together*. London: 1962.

Siddle, D. A. T. and Heron, P. A. Stimulus omission and recovery of the electrodermal and digital vasoconstrictive components of the orienting response. *Biological Psychology*, 1975, *3*, 277–293.

Siddle, D. A. T., Nicol, A. R. and Foggitt, R. H. Habituation and over-extinction of the GSR component of the orienting response in anti-social adolescents. *British Journal of Social and Clinical Psychology*, 1973, *12*, 303–308.

Siddle, D. A. T., Mednick, S. A., Nicol, A. R. and Foggitt, R. H. Skin conductance recovery in anti-social adolescents. *British Journal of Social and Clinical Psychology*, 1976, *15*, 425–428.

Sjogren, T. Genetic-statistical and psychiatric investigations of a west Swedish population. *Acta Psychiatrica et Neurologica*, Supplement *52*, 1948.

Slater, E. The incidence of mental disorder. *Annals of Eugenics*, 1935, *6*, 172.

Slater, E., and Cowie, V. *The genetics of mental disorders*. London: Oxford University Press, 1971.

Sokolov, E. N. *Perception and the conditioned reflex*. Oxford: Pergamon, 1963.

Sokolov, E. N. Orienting reflex as information regulator. In A. Leontiev, A. Luria, and A. Smirnov (Eds.), *Psychological research in the U.S.S.R.* Vol. 1, Moscow: Progress Publishers, 1966.

Spiegelman, M. *Introduction to demography*. Rev. ed. Cambridge, Mass.: Harvard Univ. Press, 1968.

Spinks, J. A. and Siddle, D. A. T. Effects of stimulus information and stimulus duration on amplitude and habituation of the electrodermal orienting response. *Biological Psychology*, in press.

Spitz, R. A. Hospitalism. *Psychoanalytic Studies of the Child*, 1945, *1*, 53.

State of California, Department of Institutions. The etiology of child behavior difficulties, juvenile delinquency and adult criminality with special reference to their occurrence in twins. *Psychiatric Monographs*, 1941.

Stein, K. B., Gough, H. G. and Sarbin, T. R. The dimensionality of the CPI socialization scale and an empirically derived typology among delinquent and non-delinquent boys. *Multi-variate Behavioral Research*, 1966, *1*, 197–208.

Street, D. R. K., and Watson, R. A. In D. J. West (Ed.), *Criminological Implications of chromosome abnormalities*. Cambridge: Cambridge University Press, 1969.

Stumpfl, F. *Erbanlage und Verbrechen. Charakterologische und Psychiatrische Sippenuntersuchungen*. Berlin: Julius Springer, 1936. (a)

Stumpfl, F. *Die Ursprunge des Verbrechens. Dargestellt am Lebenslauf von Zwillingen*. Leipzig: Georg Thieme, 1936. (b)

Sugmati. Psychiatric studies of the criminal by the twin method. *Twin Studies 1. Japanese Society for Promotion of Scientific Research*, 1954, *137*.

Sutker, P. B. Vicarious conditioning and sociopathy. *Journal of Abnormal Psychology*, 1970, *76*, 380–386.

Svalastoga, K. *Prestige, class and mobility*. Copenhagen: Gyldendal, 1959.

Swedish Council for Crime Prevention. *Swedish studies on juvenile delinquency*, 1976.

Tienari, P. *Psychiatric illnesses in identical twins*. Copenhagen: Munksgaard, 1963.

Trasler, G. Criminal behavior. In H. J. Eysenck, (Ed.) *Handbook of Abnormal Psychology*. London: Putnam, 1972.

Trasler, G. The relations between psychopathy and persistent criminality—methodological and theoretical issues. In R. D. Hare and D. Schalling (Eds.), *Current research in psychopathy*. London: Wiley, in press.

Vandenberg, S. G., Clark, P. J. and Samuels, I. Psychophysiological reactions of twins: hereditary factors in galvanic skin resistance, heart beat, and breathing rates. *Eugen. Quart.*, 1965, *12*, 7–10.

Vanggaard, T. Neurose og psykopati. *Nordisk Psykiatrisk Tidskrift*, 1968, *22*, 277 (in Danish).

Vedel-Petersen, J. Psychosocial environment, adaptation and development in school children. In L. Levi (Ed.), *Society, Stress and Disease*, Vol. 2. London: Oxford University Press, 1975.

Venables, P. H. Psychophysiological research in schizophrenia. Paper presented at symposium on Applications of Psychophysiology to Clinical Psychology. Iowa, 1973. (a)

Venables, P. H. Input regulation and psychopathology. In M. Hammer, K. Salzinger and S. Sutton (Eds.), *Psychopathology: contributions from the social, behavioral, and biological sciences*. New York: Wiley, 1973 (b).

Venables, P. H. The recovery limb of the skin conductance response in "high-risk" research. In S. A. Mednick, F. Schulsinger, J. Higgins & B. Bell (Eds.), *Genetics, environment and psychopathology*. Oxford: North-Holland, 1974.

Venables, P. H. and Christie, M. J. Mechanisms, instrumentation, recording, and quantification. In W. F. Prokasy and D. C. Raskin (Eds.), *Electrodermal activity in psychological research*. New York: Academic, 1973.

Vianna, A. M., Frota-Pessoa, O., Lion, M. F., Decourt, L. Searching for XYY males through electrocardiograms. *Journal of Medical Genetics*, 1972, *9*, 165–167.

Volavka, J., and Matousek, M. The relation of pre- and perinatal pathology to the adult EEG. *Electroencephalography and Clinical Neurophysiology*, 1969, *27*, 667.

von Bracken, H.: "Mutual Intimacy in Twins: Types of Social Structure in Pairs of Identical and Fraternal Twins." Character and Personality, 1933, *2*, 293–309.

Walker, N. *Crime and punishment*. Edinburgh: Edinburgh Univ. Press, 1965.

Wender, P. H., Rosenthal, D., Kety, S. S., Schulsinger, F., and Welner, J. Social class and psychopathology in adoptees. Archives of General Psychiatry, 1973, *28*, 318–325.

West, D. J., and Farrington, D. P. *Who becomes delinquent?* Heinemann: London, 1973.

Wiens, A. N., Matarazzo, J. D. and Gaver, K. D. Performance and verbal IQ in a group of sociopaths. Journal of Clinical Psychology, 1959, *15*, 191–193.

Winokur, G., Clayton, P. J. Family history studies: IV. Comparison of male and female alcoholics. *Quarterly Journal of Studies on Alcohol*, 1968, *29*, 885–891.

Winokur, G., Reich, T., Rimmer, J., et al. Alcoholism: III, Diagnosis and familial psychiatric illness in 259 alcoholic probands. *Archives of General Psychiatry*, 1970, *23*, 104–111.

Witkin, H. A., Mednick, S. A., Schulsinger, F., Bakkestrøm, E., Christiansen, K. O., Goodenough, D. R. Hirschhorn, K., Lundsteen, C., Owen, D. R., Philip, J. and Rubin, D. B. Criminality, aggression and intelligence among XYY and XXY men, 1976. In press.

Wolf, P. and Høgh, E. Kriminalitet i velfærds samfundet. Cited in Hurwitz, S. and Christiansen, K. O. *Kriminologi*, Volume II. Copenhagen: Cyldental, 1971.

Wolfgang, M. E., Figlio, R. M., and Sellin, T. *Delinquency in a birth cohort*. Chicago: Univ. of Chicago Press, 1972.

Yoshimasu, S. Psychopatie und Kriminalität. Die Bedeutung der Erbanlage für die Entstehung von Verbrechen im Lichte der Zwillingforschung. *Acta Criminologiae et Medicinae Legalis Japanica*, 1941.

Yoshimasu, S. Crime and heredity, studies on criminal twins. *Japanese Journal on Race Hygiene*, 1947.

Yoshimasu, S. The criminological significance of the family in the light of the studies of criminal twins. *Acta Criminologiae et Medicinae Legalis Japanica*, 1961, *27*.

Yoshimasu, S. Criminal life curves of monozygotic twin-pairs. *Acta Criminologiae et Medicinae Legalis Japanica*, 1965.

Young, J. P. R. and Fenton, G. W. The measurement of autonomic balance in children: method and normative data. *Psychosom. Med.*, 1971, *5*, 241–253.

Zazzo, R. *La métode des jumeaux*. Paris: Presses Universitaires de France, 1960 (a).

Zazzo, R. *Les jumeaux. Le couple et al personne*. Paris: Presses Universitaires de France, 1960 (b).

Zeuthen, S. and Nielsen, J. Prevalence of chromosome abnormalities among males examined for military service. *Clinical Genetics*, 1973, *4*, 422–428.

Zubin, J. Classification of the behavior disorders. *Annual Review of Psychology*, 1967, *18*, 373–407.

Zuppinger, K., Engel, E., Forbes, A. P., Mantooth, L., and Claffey, J. Klinefelter's syndrome, a clinical and cytogenic study in twenty-four cases. *Acta Endocrinologica*, 1967, *Supplement 113*, 27–33.

Zvolský, P. Jirák, R. and Drábková, H. Psychophysiological reactions in twins. *Activ. Nerv. Sup.*, 1973, *15*, 57–59.

Name Index

Comish, K. A. 189, 196, 197
Conger, J. J. 256, 266
Court Brown, W. M. 113
Craddick, R. 197
Craft, M. J. 111, 199
Craigen, D. 202, 203, 205
Crandall, B. F. 167
Crowe, R. 127
Curran, D. 111

Dahlberg, G. 107, 144, 145
Dahlin, Y. 201, 202, 203, 204, 207
Dalgaard, O. S. 45, 64, 72, 77, 78, 79,
    80, 81, 82, 91
Dawson, M. E. 208
DeBault, L. E. 167
Decourt, L. 167
Dencker, S. J. 93
Dengerink, H. A. 204
Dinitz, S. 256
Douglas, J. W. B. 6
Douglas, J. W. E. 256
Drábková, H. 218
Dummermuth, G. 197
Dupont, J. P. 168, 183
Dussuyer, I. 168, 183
Dustman, R. E. 217

Edelberg, R. 205, 208, 211, 214, 216
Ekstrøm, R. B. 184
Elsasser, G. 243
Endicott, J. 15, 273
Engel, E. 197
Erlenmeyer-Kimling, L. 109
Exner, F. 60
Eysenck, H. J. 204

Falek, A. 197
Farrington, D. P. 21, 256, 266, 267, 271
Fenton, G. W. 189, 196, 197, 217
Ferri, E. 74
Fields, J. G. 10
Fienberg, S. 179
Figlio, R. M. 1, 6, 28, 39
Fitzgerald, H. E. 211
Foggitt, R. H. 4, 201, 202, 203, 205,
    206, 213, 214

Forbes, A. P. 197
Forssman, H. 166, 197
Fox, R. 201, 203, 210
Freeman, F. N. 82, 84, 88
Fremming, K. H. 144
French, J. W. 184
Frey, S. T. 193, 196, 197
Friedrich, U. 197
Frost, B. P. 10, 267, 271
Frost, R. 10, 267, 271
Frota-Pessoa, O. 167
Furedy, J. J. 208

Gale, A. 207, 210
Gaver, K. D. 267, 271
Gibson, H. B. 37
Glueck, E. 39, 55
Glueck, S. 39, 55
Goldstein, I. B. 201, 205
Goodenough, D. R. 189, 190
Goodman, R. M. 166
Goodwin, D. W. 143, 157, 159
Gottesman, I. I. 5, 18, 52, 93, 95, 108,
    109, 217, 140
Gough, H. G. 202
Graham, F. K. 211
Greenacre, P. 112
Gregory, I. 144
Gruzelier, J. H. 209
Guze, S. B. 143, 145

Hambert, G. 193, 196, 197
Hammond, W. A. 256
Handy, L. M. 45, 51, 54, 55, 72, 80, 81
Hare, R. 2, 6, 127, 200, 202, 203, 204,
    205, 206, 207, 208, 209, 245
Harman, H. H. 184
Harth, P. 230, 240
Harvald, B. 89, 90, 91
Hathaway, S. R. 256, 266
Hauge, M. 89, 90, 91
Hayashi, S. 75
Hebb, D. O. 157
Henderson, D. K. 111
Hermansen, L. 143
Heron, P. A. 211
Hess, G. 15

292 Name Index

Subject Index